ENCOUNTERS & REFLECTIONS

Seth Benardete, 1957. Courtesy Jacqueline Gourevitch

ENCOUNTERS & REFLECTIONS

Conversations with Seth Benardete

WITH ROBERT BERMAN, RONNA BURGER, AND MICHAEL DAVIS

EDITED BY RONNA BURGER

THE UNIVERSITY OF CHICAGO PRESS
CHICAGO AND LONDON

SETH BENARDETE (1930–2001) was professor of classics at New York University. He was the author or translator of many books, most recently *The Argument of the Action, Plato's "Laws,"* and *Plato's "Symposium,"* all published by the University of Chicago Press.
ROBERT BERMAN teaches philosophy at Xavier University in New Orleans. He has written on Hegel, ethics, and philosophy of law.
RONNA BURGER is professor of philosophy at Tulane University. She has published books on Plato's *Phaedrus* and *Phaedo* and is currently at work on a book on Aristotle's *Ethics*.
MICHAEL DAVIS is professor of philosophy at Sarah Lawrence College. He is the author of books on Aristotle's *Poetics,* Aristotle's *Politics,* and most recently, Rousseau's *Reveries.*

The University of Chicago Press, Chicago 60637
The University of Chicago Press, Ltd., London
© 2002 by The University of Chicago
All rights reserved. Published 2002
Printed in the United States of America

ISBN (cloth): 0-226-04278-2

Library of Congress Cataloging-in-Publication Data

Benardete, Seth.
    Encounters and reflections : conversations with Seth Benardete : with
    Robert Berman, Ronna Burger, and Michael Davis / Seth Benardete ; edited
    by Ronna Burger.
        p.   cm.
    Includes bibliographical references and index.
    ISBN 0-226-04278-2 (alk. paper)
    1. Benardete, Seth—Interviews. 2. Classicists—United States—
Interviews. 3. Classical philology—Study and teaching (Higher)
4. Philosophy, Ancient—Study and teaching (Higher) 5. Philosophy
teachers—United States—Interviews. 6. College teachers—United
States—Interviews.   I. Burger, Ronna, 1947– . II. Title.
PA85.B43A3   2002
880.9—dc21

                                                    2002008276

Contents

Preface

It's hard—you extraordinary being!—without the use of paradigms to indicate adequately any of the bigger things, for it's probable that each of us knows everything as if in a dream and then again is ignorant of everything as it is in waking.

—Plato's *Statesman* 277d, translated by Seth Benardete

The roots of this project can be traced to the early 1970s, when a small group of us would drift out of Seth Benardete's evening class on Plato or Aristotle at the New School for Social Research and settle in a few blocks away, upstairs at the Cedar Tavern. The venue later shifted to Homer's Diner, where we sat in a booth under a portrait of Homer and nobody bothered us for hours. Conversations started out with questions about the text we were studying, and ranged over politics and history, classical scholarship and contemporary physics, Greek and Roman writers, Judaism and Christianity, the British and the Germans, circling back to Plato from Homer or Hegel or Heidegger.

The stream of talk was always punctuated by Benardete's jewel-like vignettes of fascinating characters who belonged to a world of scholars that was disappearing and looked as if it could be forgotten. Much smaller than the academic world as we know it, it was made up mostly of Europeans, many of whom ended up, through all the turns of history, teaching a generation of American students after the war. Upon entering the University of Chicago in the early 1950s, Benardete found himself a fellow student with Allan Bloom, Stanley Rosen, George Steiner, and Severn Darden, among others. He came into contact with visitors like Martin Buber, Arnold Toynbee, and T. S. Eliot, and was taught by professors including David Grene and Peter von Blanckenhagen; but it was above all his encounter at Chicago with Leo Strauss that proved decisive for his philosophic development. After pursuing his studies abroad, in Athens, Rome, and Florence on a series of fellowships, Benardete went on to his first teaching position at St. John's, and from there to the Junior Fellows Program at Harvard. In the course of these years he was not only honing his philological skills and deepening his understanding of ancient thought, but also developing an appreciation of human nature as it revealed itself through the variety of individuals he encountered—eccentric, devoted, and complex in their own special ways. It was not enough, of course, to have had the good fortune to be at certain interesting places in interesting times; Benardete brought to those opportunities a sharp eye and a concrete memory. But the stories he recounts are, most importantly, the product of a philosophic mind: they illustrate, more specifically, his own understanding of philosophy as the concrete encounter of thought with the unexpected.

Conversations with Benardete over the years recreated a world that enriched the books we were studying; our own students would stand at a further degree of remove. A record of such conversations, I began to think, might provide some access to that world: it would be a way, as Socrates puts it in the *Phaedrus,* to store up a treasure of reminders for ourselves against forgetfulness, and for others who follow the same path. With that aim in mind, and tape recorder in hand, three of us—Robert Berman, Michael Davis, and I—met with Benardete in his office for several hours on six occasions in 1992 and '93. We began by asking him about the teachers and scholars he met up with in the various institutions through which he passed. In the course of his recollections, questions began to emerge about what one can be taught by another and what it means to learn by experience. Benardete was struck, more than once, by how long a time it seems to take until one really understands what one was somehow aware of long before: we have to come to know in a waking state what we knew as if in a dream. Looking back on his dissertation on Homer, his book on Herodotus, his early essays on Greek tragedy and the Platonic dialogues, after forty years of repeatedly returning to the study of these works, Benardete recounted a series of errors he thought he had made, in which he now began to discern more clearly a common form. As we explored its character and significance, the recurrent themes of Benardete's work—*eros* and punishment, the beautiful and the just, the city, the soul, and the gods—came up in the flow of conversation and spilled over into discussions about natural science, poetry, religion, and their relation to philosophy.

The pages that follow represent the conversations we shared, recorded, and later transcribed. The transcriptions were edited with the aim of omitting repetitions and making the discussions coherent while sacrificing as little as possible of the spontaneity of the original occasions. Although the sequence of our conversations followed more or less the order presented here, we did not initially conceive of it as a whole divided into two parts. The title of the volume, *Encounters and Reflections,* is meant to apply to those two parts, as they exhibit the structure Benardete liked to call an "indeterminate dyad"—a pair whose members are not independent units that can simply be counted up as two, but rather, parts of a whole, each of which in some way contains the other in itself. While part 1 consists of Benardete's reflections on his formative encounters with people and places, the theme that runs through part 2 concerns the nature of reflection as it arises in the encounter with a work of poetry or philosophy. The duality of each part in itself and of both together is encapsulated in the formula for Greek tragedy, *pathei mathos*—learning by experience: there is an analogy, our discussions suggested, between the process of acquiring insight from what one undergoes in life, in particular from the mistakes one makes, and the process of interpreting a text, insofar as it involves the uncovering of one's erroneous starting point, followed by the deeper recognition of the necessity of that starting point. Plato provides a paradigm in Socrates' description of his "second sailing"—the discovery of his own path through recognition of the mistaken one he initially shared with his predecessors. This way of proceeding is vividly exemplified, as these conversations confirm, by the activity of philosophic interpretation as Benardete practiced it.

However serious its aim to capture something of Benardete's unique voice, this project was at its inception and throughout a playful one. It takes on a different tone now: just at the time we received the news that this book was approved for publication, Benardete became ill. He had read an earlier version of the manuscript; but when he died, on 14 November 2001, the last draft was sitting on his desk waiting to be examined. We hope our own editorial judgments coincide closely enough with those he would have made, but of course we cannot be sure.

In the course of editing these conversations, and seeing a kind of whole emerge, we thought of one theme in particular that seemed to be conspicuously absent, or at least insufficiently highlighted, which we hoped to take up in one more conversation. The question of what the law is, and what its role is in making human beings human, is central to Benardete's interpretations of Greek tragedy, and he had long thought about it in connection with the Hebrew bible; he taught various courses on ancient law, and especially enjoyed reading David Daube on Greek, Roman, and biblical law; his last book was a masterly reading of Plato's *Laws,* a long and complex work, and we thought about how helpful it would be to speak with him more casually about its fundamental intention as he understood it. But the one further discussion we planned was not to be. To begin to try to reconstruct some of the directions it might have taken is to be reminded of the irreplaceable character of conversation with Benardete, with all the leaps and turns of thought that brought such startling insights, although, or because, they were so unpredictable.

Benardete liked the image of thinking as a process of walking in sand, leaving footprints only for a moment, to be covered over again as one proceeds on a trackless way forward. He came as close as anyone could to being able and willing always to start afresh, and seemed to be much more excited about the unknown way ahead than about leaving any monuments behind. But in his absence, it is some comfort, however small, to have preserved these faint traces of his footsteps.

ACKNOWLEDGMENTS

We are grateful to Jane Benardete for reading the manuscript and offering helpful suggestions and advice. For the wonderful photographs they sent (not all of which we were able to use), we want to thank the Benardete family, Victor and Jacqueline Gourevitch, Sam Kutler, and Michael Platt. We appreciate assistance with the notes offered by a number of individuals, in particular, Laurence Berns, Larissa Bonfante, Amy Kealiher, Mary Nichols, Stanley Rosen, Martin Sitte, and Stuart Warner. The final draft of the manuscript owes much to the intelligent and careful editorial work done by Claudia Rex. This is a project that falls outside the usual categories; for his initial interest in it and continued support, we are indebted to John Tryneski.

Prologue

Seth: My father used to tell us stories of Nasreddin Hoja, this half wise man and half fool. My brother and I had a favorite, which we constantly had him tell us, once a year at least.

Nasreddin Hoja had become quite famous, but he always traveled in a very meager way. He came to this village on Friday, and before going to the mosque to pray, naturally he went to the bath. Once they took a look at him, the servants plunged him into the coldest water and gave him the roughest towel and dismissed him. But like all Turkish servants they closed their eyes and opened their hands when they were about to be paid. So Nasreddin put a coin in their palms and then proceeded to the mosque. He was half way to the mosque when they opened their eyes and saw there was a gold coin there. They told everyone. "Here was this man, we treated him like dirt, and he gave us a gold coin." So a week later Nasreddin came back to the same bath, on Friday before going to the mosque, and there were flute girls and teas and ices and perfumes, and they were all lined up, and they treated him exquisitely, like royalty itself. Afterward they all lined up and closed their eyes, and put out their hands. So Nasreddin put the coins in their hands and he proceeded to the mosque. The first servant opened his hand and there was a penny. They were very shocked. They ran after him and said, "Master, master, there surely has been a mistake." Nasreddin said, "What mistake?" "Well, last week we treated you like a beggar and you gave us a gold coin, and this week we treated you like a king and you gave us as penny." And Nasreddin said, "Oh, the penny was for last week and the gold coin is for this week."

Another great story my father used to tell about Nasreddin is more skeptical.

> Nasreddin was coming to this town, and everybody in the town, knowing about him, asked him if would speak at the mosque on Friday. He said, "No, no, I have errands elsewhere, I can't stay." But they said, "We'll put you up at the richest man's house for a week." And Nasreddin said, "Okay, I'll reconsider." So Friday came around and everybody was expecting him to speak. He gets up and he says, "Mohammedans, women, and children. Do you know what I'm going to say today?" They say, "No." So he says, "Well, if you don't understand, I'm not going to speak." And he leaves. Well, they're very disturbed and they insist that he stay another week at the richest man's house. And he says, "Alright." The next week he gets up and asks the same question, and everybody says, "Yes." So he says, "Well, if you already know there's no point in talking." Now they really want to hear what he has to say, so they make up a plan. When he asks the question in the third week, he hears some people saying "Yes" and other people saying "No." And he says, "Well, those who know tell those who don't know. Goodbye." Now they think they really have to hear what he has to say. So he stays a fourth week at the richest man's house in the town. Friday comes around and he asks his usual question, and there's silence. He repeats the question and there's still silence. So he shouts "Mohammedans, women, and children, do you know what I'm going to say today?" Still silence. Finally he says, "It seems that my old eyes deceive me and there's no one here."

I thought my father made these stories up. He did have an invention of his own, Hajiosman, who had other adventures, about a man who gives up his immortality, and then is resurrected and so forth—a kind of Prometheus character. But Nasreddin, I discovered many years later, is a well-known figure throughout Turkey and Persia. When I went to Istanbul, I was sitting in the office of one of my uncles and picked up the Turkish-English trade magazine and there, each week, was a Nasreddin Hoja story.

Part One

ENCOUNTERS

Seth Benardete and Elliott Carter, Rome, 1953. Courtesy Jane Benardete

Chapter 1

THE UNIVERSITY OF CHICAGO
1948–52, 1954–55

COMING TO THE COLLEGE

Michael: Maybe we should start by asking how you ended up going to Chicago.

Seth: I was in high school at Brooklyn Tech, and my mother remembered that she knew someone from Chicago whom she had met at Dartmouth during the summer when we were on our vacation. His name was Donald Lamb, and he was a pupil of McKeon.[1] She wrote to him and he said maybe they would consider me if I were to apply. So that's how I applied. When I met him, he was in fact a lamb.

Ronna: He was in the classics department?

Seth: No, Lamb was in philosophy—spent his entire life on Kant—but he was a worshipper of McKeon.

Ronna: Which there were a lot of, weren't there?

Seth: Well, there was Gewirth,[2] who was much higher up. I think Lamb only taught in the college and very rarely was given a graduate course.

Robert: Did you know what you wanted to study at Chicago?

Seth: My intention when I left Brooklyn Tech was to go into mathematics.

Ronna: But you had already studied Greek, right? Did they have Greek in the high school?

---

1. Richard McKeon (1900–1985), professor in the department of philosophy at the University of Chicago from 1925 to 1973, conceived and chaired the interdisciplinary program of the Committee on Analysis of Ideas and Methods.

2. Alan Gewirth (1912–), a professor in the department of philosophy whose field is moral philosophy.

Seth: No, I went to Brooklyn College to take it.

Ronna: How did you first get interested in it?

Seth: My father said, "You should study Greek."

Robert: But he didn't say why? Did Jose study Greek?[3]

Seth: No.

Robert: Did he have something that he was assigned to do, as an analogue to Greek?

Seth: No, he was into poetry, and then philosophy.

Ronna: Did you immediately take to Greek?

Seth: Yes, but I didn't think I was going to stick with it.

Robert: Was the professor a classicist?

Seth: The professor turned out to be Vera Lachmann, whom I later met here.[4] But I didn't ask her if she had been my professor years before.

EARLIER YEARS

BROOKLYN TECH

Ronna: Do you have any memories of Brooklyn Tech? Was it a boys' school?

Seth: It was a boys' school, very well organized. There were thousands of students, and it was totally disciplined.

Robert: What about the class structure of the student population? Was it homogeneous?

Seth: It ranged from lower to upper class. But there were only about two or three in our class who were very wealthy. They were much more poised than everybody else. It was very noticeable.

Ronna: Was it admission by testing?

Seth: Yes.

Ronna: And it was meant to foster math and science in particular?

Seth: Yes. It was very old-fashioned though. There were four years of mechanical drawing, two years of freehand drawing, four years of shop, two years of lathe work.

Michael: So that's where the diagrams in your books come from!

Robert: Were you exposed to anything like philosophy?

Seth: No . . . Well, I do remember reading Marx, and also Toynbee.

---

3. Jose Benardete, Seth's older brother, professor of philosophy at Syracuse University. His work is primarily in metaphysics and philosophy of mathematics.

4. Vera Lachmann (1904–85), who emigrated to the United States in 1939, was a poet and teacher of classical languages at Brooklyn College and later at New York University.

BROOKLYN COLLEGE

Ronna: Your father was a Spanish professor, wasn't he?[5]

Seth: Yes, at Brooklyn College.

Robert: And your mother? What was her name?

Seth: Doris. She taught in the English department.

Ronna: Was your mother's father a professor?

Seth: He was a businessman, from Austria, I think. My parents were caught up in the activities of the Rapp-Coudert Committee, which was organized to root out communists in the city colleges.

Ronna: What year was that?

Seth: It must have been 1938 or '39, something like that.

Robert: You were about eight years old?

Seth: Yes. There was a man in the English Department who had testified that a number of people were communists and, since he needed two witnesses, that my mother knew they were. They delivered a subpoena at midnight, and it was very frightening. Now, of course, one is used to this kind of thing, but then you don't expect anything like this. Well, my mother immediately went to the Teachers' Union, and they offered her a lawyer to plead the case.

Robert: Did she know the fellow?

Seth: Yes, I'll tell you about that, there's an amazing twist to the story. They knew that my father was vehemently anticommunist, and used to denounce these people in the lunchroom of Brooklyn College. So they subpoenaed him separately to appear at a meeting in downtown Brooklyn at the same time as my mother, without telling them. Then they treated my father with great respect and totally ignored my mother, because they assumed that, being a Turk, he would tolerate the fact that his wife was being despised. He was so angry at this that the whole strategy backfired.

Michael: And what happened to your mother?

Seth: They decided they would bring it to trial and accuse her of perjury. She very wisely went to the number-one law firm in Brooklyn, which had the most connections. The first thing they asked her was, "What do you know about this man who made the accusation?" My mother told them, "You know, when he was a student, my father took him in off the street. And while he was living in our house he seduced a girl." The lawyers said, "Leave it to

---

5. Mair Jose Benardete, born in the Dardanelles, Turkey, in 1895. He was professor of Spanish and Sephardic Studies at Brooklyn College and director of the Sephardic Studies Section of Columbia University's Hispanic Institute.

us." It never came to court. They must have said "You bring her to court and we'll destroy him."

Michael: The good ole' days, when you could destroy people with something like that.

Seth: Isn't that amazing? Then years later, during the time of the House Committee on Un-American Activities, my uncle was subpoenaed. He was a dentist in Brooklyn. By that time he was living on Long Island and had a very good practice, and they were going to destroy him. So he was in an absolute panic, and my mother said, "Go to this law firm." It never became public at all.

NEW ENGLAND SUMMERS

Robert: You said your mother met Donald Lamb in Dartmouth when you were on vacation. Did you go there regularly?

Seth: We used to go to Hannover in the summer. My mother and father were given cubicles in the library. A college student would take care of my brother and me. One of them was named George Klein. He later became a psychologist. One summer Roosevelt came to town. Everybody in town gathered in front of the hotel opposite the Baker Library at Dartmouth to see this beautiful black car, with the top down, and Roosevelt with a cigarette in the middle. A servant came out with a glass of milk, and he drank it. Everyone in town was watching. And George said to us, "Well I bet this is the biggest crowd that Hannover's ever seen." And an old woman said, "Young man, you should have been here when Cal Coolidge came." It's a really Republican town.

Robert: Has anyone else actually seen a president?

Seth: I saw Eisenhower in Paris. I was there with [Allan] Bloom, who immediately noticed his vanity, the way he lapped up the crowd, and expanded with its enthusiasm.

Ronna: So did you go to Hannover every summer?

Seth: For a while we went in the summer to Vermont. We rented a house owned by a family named Rousseau. The husband ran a farm, with his two huge sons, one named Francis, and the other, I don't remember. The mother ran a boarding house, where people came every summer. There was a daughter, Missy, who did all the work, from morning to night. She was thin as a rail and smoked all the time. Then there was a brother named Lucien, who was a butler in a very fancy house in the town nearby. Lucien would come back and tell his mother how to behave. There was another daughter, whose name was Lucy, who used to be our cook during the summer. She baked the most perfect apple pie. No one had ever tasted pies like this. Every day we had apple pie. And she would beam as everyone praised her. One day, one of my uncles was there. After taking a slice of pie, he put a piece of cheese on it. And my father said, "You can't put cheese on this pie," and walked out. He wouldn't be in the same room.

Ronna: Such desecration.

Seth: Yes. My father had a friend named Arce, José Maria Arce, who was a professor of Spanish at Dartmouth. He was from Costa Rica. He had been given an inheritance of about ten thousand dollars one year when he was visiting in Italy. In Milan he wooed a woman who was sought after at the same time by the future head of Fiat. The woman was so impressed by the ten thousand dollars he spent on her that she married him, and regretted it for the rest of her life, since that was all the money he ever had. He had a daughter with this woman. And he never gave them any money to live on; he spent all the money he had on himself. He had extraordinarily expensive habits. One year it would be cameras. So he bought the most expensive cameras, with all the equipment for them. Then he would have another enthusiasm, say wood-working. So the first thing he would do is buy the most expensive wood from South America and plan to replace all the handles on his chisels with this very expensive wood, which he ended up only doing to one of them. Anyway, one summer we were not only going to have Lucy, but also a maid and her husband, who would be the chauffeur. And there were three college students who were going to be with us.

Michael: Students of your parents?

Seth: Either of my mother or my father. One was named Goldberg, whom my father immediately named Montoro, which is Spanish for "gold mountain." He loved it, so he was always called "Montoro." One was a man named Bogart, I think, who later became a television director. The third was dismissed during the summer, I don't know why. Well, the day before we were planning to go to Vermont, Arce called at our house in Brooklyn and asked if he could stay over. My father wasn't there. When he came home late that night, he went into the bathroom and there was this case of extraordinarily expensive toiletries, with gold-backed brushes and so forth. My father looked at it and said, "My God, this is what the chauffeur is coming with? What are we going to do?" This was all before the war. One summer we had a student named Janofski, who was a fantastic photographer. I don't know what happened to him. Anyway, Missy fell in love with him. Everybody discussed it, that this was doomed.

Robert: How would you typically spend time with these students?

Seth: They would chop wood, I think.

Robert: You mean for a stove?

Seth: Yes.

Michael: What would you and Jose do?

Seth: Oh, we played croquet, and walked in the woods, and visited farms and so forth. I remember going up the road where someone was remodeling a house. I made friends with the carpenter and stayed there all summer, watching him work. I think my brother wrote poetry. There was really nothing to do.

Michael: You have a portrait in your house that must come from this time.

Seth: Right, that was 1942. That was done by a man named Esteban Vicente, a Spanish refugee who came over in 1936 and had no money.[6] So my parents decided that I should be painted. When they told me, I immediately went into the bathroom to see why he wanted to paint my face. This is the problem of the image! He was to come every week, before Sunday lunch. He later became very famous as an abstract painter. He's still alive, he must be ninety years old.

Ronna: So this was an early work, realism.

Michael: He moved from the real Benardete to abstract.

Ronna: Did the summers in Vermont go on well into your childhood, or later?

Seth: I think they ended in '44. They were extraordinarily long summers, geared to the college schedule. So we had to get out of school early and came back late, which was always protested by the school. But everything was so completely different then. Such a time warp.

DONALD LAMB AND A PAPER ON *DON QUIXOTE*

Michael: Did you end up actually studying with Donald Lamb when you got to Chicago?

Seth: Well, you could write an honors paper in the college, and Lamb agreed to be my adviser. At the end of the year I gave him a paper on *Don Quixote.*

Ronna: Do you remember why you chose that?

Seth: I came back after one term and talked to my father, and he said, "Why don't you write on *Don Quixote?*"

Robert: This was your first year?

Seth: My first year.

Ronna: You had declared a major?

---

6. Esteban Vicente (1904–2001) was an abstract/expressionist painter.

Seth: At Chicago there was no major. There was just the college, which only lasted a year. You took all these exams that allowed you to be placed out of the college.

Ronna: So you got the equivalent of a B.A. degree in that first year?

Seth: Well, it was not equivalent to a B.A. degree anywhere else. Of course, I didn't go anywhere else with it.

Michael: So you submitted the *Don Quixote* paper to Lamb?

Seth: And he said, "Oh this can't be submitted, you know this can't be submitted." So I said "yes," but I never asked why it was nixed.

Robert: Do you remember what the thesis was?

Seth: It was all about how he was very careful not to test reality after it proved that he was wrong. I remember this thing about Manbrino's helmet.

Robert: What's that?

Seth: He made a helmet out of cardboard, which he then brought out in the backyard and took a sword to it, and immediately it smashed. So he then made another one, but didn't test it. He knew.

Ronna: That was the solution?

Seth: Right. The solution was never to test anything.

Ronna: So you went through the book and found all these instances . . .

Seth: About how he had carefully avoided reality. Anyway, Lamb said, "You know it won't do. It is interesting," he said, "but you know it won't do." I never asked him why it wouldn't do. He was so certain. I was so very shy, I suppose.

Robert: This strange thing he said never got clarified. Did that require doing something else?

Seth: No, it's just that I didn't get a degree with honors.

THE COMMITTEE ON SOCIAL THOUGHT

Michael: How did you get onto the Committee after being in the College?

Seth: It was through Blanckenhagen.[7] He gave a lecture in the spring that first year. I met him on the walkway of the university and stopped to ask a question about his lecture. We had a long talk, and he said, "Why don't you come and join the Committee?"

Robert: Just like that?

---

7. Peter Heinrich von Blanckenhagen (1909–90). After receiving his doctorate in Munich in 1936 and teaching at Marburg and Hamburg, he came to Chicago as a visiting professor in 1947 and became a member of the Committee on Social Thought in 1949. He joined the faculty of the Institute of Fine Arts at New York University in 1959 and was largely responsible for building its program in ancient studies. He lectured on Greek, Hellenistic, and Roman art, and had a particular interest in Pompeian painting. His last, posthumous article was on Plato's *Symposium*.

Seth: Just like that.

Michael: What did you think you were going to do when you started on the Committee? You didn't just do it because Blanckenhagen said, come along.

Seth: Death!

Ronna: Was that going to be your theme?

Seth: Yes.

Michael: Is it true that you always wore black?

Seth: I think that's the only thing I had. There was a guy named Oxman, a student on the Committee, who was working on the medieval, Nicholas Oresme—the theory of money, the origin of calculus, and everything else. Anyway, the Committee was on the fifth floor of the social sciences building, and what happened was, he was introduced to me as he was stepping into the hall from the elevator while I was getting in. He asked me what my subject was, and as the doors closed he heard the word "Death."

Ronna: It came to you on the spur of the moment?

Seth: Right, that this was the way to summarize it. I had no idea that years later it would turn out to be true that that's what I had been doing. It was orchestrated from that point by some higher power.

FELLOW STUDENTS

SEVERN DARDEN, GEORGE STEINER, STANLEY ROSEN

Michael: What did you do your first year in the Committee?

Seth: I didn't attend the four courses I was assigned, I remember that.

Ronna: You mean you skipped class?

Seth: I skipped class entirely.

Robert: What did you do instead?

Seth: I read, all sorts of things.

Ronna: Do you remember what?

Seth: Zoroastrianism in the ninth-century texts, Cyrus Bailey, Toynbee—I read all of Toynbee.

Ronna: Any principle of selection?

Seth: No, just things that I came across in the library.

Michael: Were there other people you talked with?

Seth: I had a roommate whose name was Conboy, who came from Nebraska. He was the son of a sergeant and he had two loves. One was Thoreau. He spent his entire first year, while I was writing on *Don Quixote*, translating a treatise on Thoreau by Georges Duhamel into English. That was his project. Then he also loved Wagner.

Ronna: What a combination!

Seth: And he looked like Ichabod Crane: you know, very tall, stooped. He became the butt of many of Severn's jokes.

Robert: Did you already know Severn?[8]

Seth: I'll tell you how I met him. We arrived on the first day at the dormitory. I was talking to Conboy just outside the door to our room. Then Severn, who had a room at the other end of the corridor, came and said to me, "Do you know where we're supposed to go?" I said "No." So he said, "Well let's go together." That's how we met.

Michael: So your first conversation was a joke.

Ronna: You were both sixteen at the time?

Seth: No, eighteen. He had come from the Putney School in Vermont, an experimental school. But he was from New Orleans. His father had just become district attorney there, the first district attorney who said he would treat any black man the same way he would treat any white man. No one had ever said that before. So he got some kind of medal from the NAACP.

Ronna: Did Severn write an honors thesis?

Seth: No, he didn't.

Ronna: Did he ever go to class?

Seth: Yes, he did go to class, that's where some of his best routines came from. Rosen, who also lived on the same corridor, right next to Severn, picked up some of those routines.[9]

Robert: How did he do that?

Seth: One episode involved George Steiner.[10] Steiner lived across the quad. He had been there more than one year and was graduating that year. He was also a student of Donald Lamb, for whom he did write an appropriate thesis.

Michael: Not on *Don Quixote.*

Seth: No. Well, Severn once went to a class and reported back that someone had said to the teacher, "I was wondering perhaps whether there is not another possibility in addition to the two you have so speciously posited."

8. Severn Darden (1930–95) was a charter member of The Compass Theater, the improvisational group that would later evolve into the Second City Comedy Troop. He was known for his monologues filled with allusions to Freud or Kant or Heraclitus, which displayed his unique comic mind. He later worked in films as a character actor, writer, or director. Mike Nichols, at a memorial, said he would cheer himself up when depressed by recalling a line from Severn's lecture on zoology: "Of motion, the oyster has but a dim racial memory."

9. Stanley Rosen (1930–) has played an important role educating students in philosophy, currently at Boston University, and previously at Pennsylvania State University. He has lectured in colleges around the United States, as well as in Italy, France, Germany, Spain, England, and elsewhere. His wide-ranging work includes books on Plato, Hegel, Nietzsche, Heidegger, metaphysics, contemporary philosophy, and social and political thought.

10. George Steiner (1929–), extraordinary fellow of Churchill College, Cambridge, is an internationally renowned scholar of Western culture, language, and intellectual history.

Rosen was in seventh heaven. He loved this line. There was a college radio station, which had discussions of books, one of which was to be on *Flowering Judas,* and Steiner was going to appear on the program. Severn was told by Rosen to apply to become a member of this radio program, and he, Rosen, would supply all the lines he had to speak during the discussion. So, he got on it. We all tuned in, at 7:30. For the first twenty minutes, Severn didn't say anything. George Steiner was dominating it entirely. Then suddenly, a pause, and Severn says, "I am wondering, perhaps, whether there is not possibly a third alternative to the two which you have so speciously posited. I am referring of course to the Cathedral of the Fields and William Morris of the neo-Hegelian movement . . ." It had absolutely nothing to do with anything. And it was all for the following lines, for George Steiner to say, which he in fact did say, "I know nothing about Neo-Hegelianism, but—" At this point, the moderator said, "Surely Mr. Darden is joking." And Severn said, "Certainly not." And it was exactly the end of the program.[11]

Seth: Severn had a knack of finding locked doors open. They would always be open for him. He somehow found out there was a way of getting into Rockefeller Chapel. So he used to go in at midnight, dressed in his cloak, and play the organ. One night he pulled out all the stops. The whole place shook. And it awakened the guard sleeping in the basement, who came with a flashlight, looked at the organ, saw this guy in a cloak, and began this wild pursuit. Severn didn't know what to do, so he flung himself across the altar, and shouted, "Sanctuary!" The man dropped the flashlight, and he escaped.
Ronna: No eyewitnesses?
Seth: No, but this is a story that he told immediately.
Ronna: So it has the stamp of truth.

11. Stanley Rosen reports: I wrote out a monologue for Darden to memorize and deliver at 7:22 P.M., just a few minutes or so before the end of the program. As agreed, Darden launched the monologue which began, "I am wondering, perhaps, if there is not possibly a third alternative to the two which you have so speciously posited. I refer, of course, to the lily, the cathedral of the fields . . ." and so on. This was one of my best scholarly works, unfortunately never published. The participants in the radio show grew progressively more flustered, and people coughed anxiously. Then Severn came to the punch line, which included the expression "neo-Hegelian diureticism." Chairs were overturned, and bodies fell to the floor, George Steiner's determined voice could be heard cutting across the chaos: "I know very little about neo-Hegelian diureticism, but . . ."
Rosen adds: Seth, Severn, Bob Charles, and I were inseparable companions every evening after dinner, when we would drive around in Severn's 1933 Rolls Royce and commit various pranks. Seth was not available during the day, since he was studying Greek. Once we went to the Art Institute and sat on camp stools while Severn delivered a lecture about some painting of a nude woman, filled with unintelligible gibberish, which was avidly watched by a group of genteel ladies from the North Shore. All this took place in '48–'49. After our one year in the College, Seth joined the Committee and I went off to the New School for a semester, but returned to study with Leo Strauss.

Seth: He repeated this trick in the girls' shower in the spring term. He apparently sneaked in late at night, when everyone was asleep. There he was when they came traipsing in, in the morning, holding onto the curtain rail, saying "Is this the way to Clark Street?"

Robert: Did he get in trouble?

Seth: I don't recall. That same spring, Severn and I were walking to a party. He was wearing his cloak, and at the corner we met Allan Bloom,[12] who had heard about Severn, and said with great disdain to him, "Is it worth the candle?" Severn immediately pulled out a candle and lit it and Bloom was absolutely blown away.

Michael: What did Severn look like?

Seth: Well, he said he looked exactly like Charles Laughton. He had a very bad skin disease, which vanished many years later, some terrible form of eczema. They thought it was psychosomatic, and he was constantly going to psychiatrists. He had all these fantastic stories about his analysts, he'd become so inquisitive about where they hung their clothes.

Ronna: He was always collecting material.

Michael: Did Bloom come at the same time you did?

Seth: No, he had come younger, when he was sixteen, when you were supposed to, then you had two or three years.

Michael: When did you first meet him?

Seth: That was the first time I met him, on the way to the party. Then I got to know him when we became students in the Committee the next year.

Michael: That's when you became known as the "gold dust twins"? What was the origin of that?

Seth: There used to be a soap that had two black figures on it, called Gold Dust soap powder. We were in a tutorial together and somehow got that designation.

Ronna: Did Severn go on to the Committee?

Seth: No, no, no. I don't think he ever graduated. He went to Bard College, where he pulled all sorts of pranks. One Christmas they knew that the president was away from the college. So he got a whole group of people to build a huge cross, because the president's house was on a hill, with a very steep slope going up to it, so until the last minute you wouldn't see anything, but all of a sudden there it would be. So they built this huge cross, and put Severn, with a little thing around his waist, on this cross. When the presi-

12. Allan Bloom (1930–92) was an influential teacher at the University of Chicago (1979–92) and before that at Cornell (1963–70) and Toronto (1970–79). His books include translations of Plato's *Republic* and of Rousseau's *Emile*, studies of Shakespeare and Rousseau, and the 1987 best-seller, *The Closing of the American Mind*.

dent of the college went up the hill, he would see him crucified. Severn was
expelled.

Ronna: For that episode?

Seth: Yes. As he was being expelled, he said to the president, "You know, I
was about to write you a check."

Ronna: After that, he gave up on academic goals?

Seth: He decided to become an actor.

Michael: Was he very wealthy?

Seth: He had an income of about $3,000 a year, which was a lot of money
in those days. But it didn't look as though it was going to go up for many
years. It kept him in shirts, because he would never go to the laundry. You
went into his room and opened his closet door, there were white shirts from
the bottom up to the top, and he would say, "Oh, I'm out of shirts" and he
would immediately go to Brooks Brothers and buy five more shirts. And they
would go into his closet.

Ronna: You kept up contact with him for quite a long time.

Seth: Oh yes. He bought a Rolls Royce in the spring for $800. It was a 1929
Rolls Royce, which at the time it disappeared in a hurricane in Louisiana
years later was worth a quarter of a million. Anyway we drove from Chicago
to Gloucester, Massachusetts, in this Rolls Royce, and in every state we were
stopped by the police.

Ronna: As a stolen vehicle?

Seth: Yes, but what they really wanted to know was how many miles a gal-
lon it got. Such an enormous thing, you know, and these two kids were in it.

Ronna: Why was that your destination?

Seth: He was going to an acting school. On the way we stopped off at a place
in Connecticut, late at night, because a friend who had gone to Putney was
there. We were introduced to him in the evening and then immediately
shown to our beds. In the morning, all over the house, there were these loud
speakers blaring out *South Pacific.* So I said to Severn, "Can't this junk be
turned off?" And he said, "Sure, of course," and turned it off. We had break-
fast with this guy, and then we got into the Rolls Royce and proceeded on our
way. An hour after we had left, I said, "Whose house was that?" And he said,
"Mary Martin's house."

Michael: Wasn't there a story about Severn putting you in a movie?

Seth: Yes, he put Blanckenhagen in one movie and me in another. One
Saturday afternoon Blanckenhagen was in Paris and he had nothing to do
so he went into a theater. What he saw—he recognized one of the characters—was Severn, playing an abortionist. On the operating table was a

woman, and Severn, as abortionist, was talking to his fellow abortionist, having a vehement discussion about Roman art. The other guy said, "Well Blanckenhagen says that this is the case." And Severn said, "Blanckenhagen is an ass." He was completely shocked. There he was in the middle of Paris.

Michael: What's the movie with you in it?

Seth: Many years later, when I was already here at NYU, Martha Nussbaum became a Danforth fellow, which was a four-year graduate fellowship.[13] So it must have been in her senior year. She had already married a fellow student. Anyway, she arranged that I come to this conference, outside a nuclear defense plant in the middle of the wastelands of Illinois, where all the Danforth fellows went. And who was the main speaker? Hilary Putnam,[14] who at that time, it seems, was a Maoist, and was selling newspapers in the middle of the lobby of the hotel where the conference was being held, surrounded by these right-wing Danforth fellows. Anyway, Mrs. Nussbaum asked me—she was on the entertainment committee—what movie to show. I said I knew that Severn had made a movie called *Virgin President,* though I had never seen it, but maybe she should get that. And she did. So there were three hundred Danforth fellows watching *The Virgin President.* It begins with Severn as movie maker telling the story of the United States and how it became the little country it was at this time, in the future. It starts out showing a forest: "This was once Washington, D.C." Then it goes into the story. Severn is both the president of the United States and also the son of the president, who is kept as the successor in the basement of the White House. His father, namely Severn, is killed by the bad guys, and Severn is elevated to be president, which is now an inherited job. He has been kept in this basement since he was a child, so naturally he has innocent clothes on. He's wearing a little sailor suit, that's how you first see him. Anyway, he fails to save the country from the evil guys, and it's blown up by a nuclear bomb. Then it goes back to Severn as a movie maker and he says, "Now you've heard the story of the United States. Next week we will discuss the rise of Equador with Seth Benardete." And that's the end. This movie was not well appreciated.

Ronna: Wasn't there a record in which you play a part?

Seth: No, that's Jose on the record. It's "The Lecture on the Universe," by

13. Martha Nussbaum, professor of law and ethics at the University of Chicago, taught previously at Harvard, Brown, and Oxford. She is the author of books on Aristotle, Greek tragedy and philosophy, and social justice.

14. Hilary Putnam (1926–) taught at Northwestern, Princeton, and MIT before joining the philosophy department at Harvard. He works in philosophy of mind, language, and logic.

Professor Wandervogelweiter. It begins with, "Why am I talking about the universe? Well, because there isn't anything else." Then he presents his criticism of Jose's book. "There is this book by Jose Benardete on Heraclitus, who says that time is a river, flowing endlessly through the universe. Heraclitus doesn't say that. He says, 'Time is *like* a river, flowing endlessly through the universe.' See there, Benardete!" So that's his moment of fame.

Ronna: Isn't there something about you on the jacket?

Seth: Oh yes, the story about the Rockefeller Chapel is told, and so forth.

Ronna: Where do you come into it?

Seth: I think there's a description of me on the jacket by the man who wrote it, a friend of ours, which said "either a medieval scholar or an expert on foot fetishism." That's the description of me.

RICHARD RORTY

Robert: Did you have any contact in Chicago with Rorty?[15] Was he on the Committee?

Seth: I knew Rorty. He was in the philosophy department. He must have entered the same year that Bloom had, at sixteen, I think. He seemed to have an extraordinary case of Weltschmerz, from a very early age. But it wasn't clear there was any basis for it. It looks consistent with his later thinking.

Ronna: How is that?

Seth: When he came to philosophy, it provided the proof of his despair. He now had an argument for his psychological state, which he then expresses in the book. It's an amazing match, it seems to me.

Robert: The denial that knowledge represents beings, so knowledge is not a mirror?

Seth: That it's a matter of metaphors, right? There's really nothing to know, that's the point.

Robert: I see. Was Rorty a good student?

Seth: He must have been a very good student. He had a very self-deprecating manner about everything. He was always apologetic. His dissertation was on Aristotle's notion of potentiality, it was six hundred pages long; actuality would have been very short.

---

15. Richard Rorty (1931–), professor of comparative literature and philosophy at Stanford, taught previously at the University of Virginia and at Princeton. His distinctive form of pragmatism developed out of a critical analysis of traditional problems of epistemology and metaphysics, in works like the widely read *Philosophy and the Mirror of Nature* (1979).

RICHARD KENNINGTON

Michael: Do you remember how you met Kennington?[16]

Seth: I think Bloom introduced us.

Michael: That must have been in '55, or something like that?

Seth: It was slightly later, I think.

Michael: You don't remember what the situation was?

Seth: No, but I remember hitting it off right away.

Ronna: Was this in Chicago?

Michael: I know Kennington was a student at the New School and then came to Chicago afterwards.

Ronna: To study with Strauss?[17]

Seth: Yes, right. He didn't finish his dissertation until many years later, when I was already at the New School. So I was on the committee. That was the most extraordinary examination. It was Cairns and Jonas and Gurwitsch and myself, we were the examining committee.[18] Each one had a question. I think Jonas began. And Kennington responded, "Well this question has three large parts and each part has three large subsections. Let me go through it." Then he talked for, I don't know, forty minutes describing the structure of the first question. No one had ever heard anything like this.

Ronna: How old was he at the time?

Michael: I think he was about fifty. When I went to Penn State he didn't have his degree yet.

Robert: Was this a well-known trait of his, to give lectures that way?

Seth: I had never heard him talk that way.

Michael: Of your contemporaries, it seems to me the one whom you've

16. Richard Kennington (1921–99), a major interpreter of early modern philosophy, taught in the philosophy department at Pennsylvania State University from 1960 to 1974 and at The Catholic University of America from 1975 to 1995.

17. Leo Strauss (1899–1973) was the Robert Maynard Hutchins Distinguished Service Professor in Political Science at Chicago and, at the time of his death, the Scott Buchanan Distinguished Scholar in residence at St. John's. With an eye in particular on the question of the character of philosophy and its relation to the political community, which made him attentive to the connection between a philosopher's thought and his mode of writing, he produced a body of work that includes studies of Machiavelli, Hobbes, and Spinoza, Nietzsche and Heidegger, Thucydides and Aristophanes, Xenophon and Plato, Alfarabi and Maimonides. These studies exhibit his critical examination of the underlying roots of modern philosophy and his distinctive rediscovery of Platonic political philosophy.

18. Dorion Cairns (1901–73), a Husserl scholar, taught in the philosophy department of the New School from 1954 to 1969. Hans Jonas (1903–93) emigrated from Germany to England in 1933, then to Palestine in 1935, and finally joined the New School philosophy department in 1955. His work ranged from studies of gnosticism to the philosophy of biology, in particular, issues concerning the relation of ethics and technology. Aron Gurwitsch (1901–73), a phenomenologist and scholar of modern philosophy, taught in the philosophy department of the New School from 1959 to 1971.

admitted learning something from was Kennington. You talked to him regularly, didn't you?

Seth: Oh yes, or I wrote to him. The thing that impressed me about him was, he was always very profound, very deep, both, I think, psychologically and in terms of thought. He would go very far into whatever you were discussing, so that it was hard to catch up and connect it with what you had to say. I remember giving talks at Catholic when Kennington would ask a question, and it was hard to connect his question with the level at which I was talking. It always seemed to me to be so much deeper than anything I was doing that I couldn't catch up. That was the impression he gave. Isn't that true?

Michael: Well, as a graduate student, you would go to dinner at his house and ask a straightforward question and receive an answer that seemed to somehow lay out the whole world. You didn't recognize it as an answer to your question, but you did recognize it as an answer to something. And it was much better than your question. Do you remember a specific case where you thought Kennington extended what you said but you couldn't follow it?

Seth: I remember sending him my notes on Aristotle's triple account of the principle of noncontradiction.

Ronna: In *Metaphysics Gamma*?

Seth: Yes. He wrote back with some acute questions about how the three formulations were related to one another, but I was not able to do anything with it.

Michael: Did he talk to you about what he was studying?

Seth: Yes, about Descartes in the beginning. The first thing I read of his was on Descartes' dream. I reread it the other day; it's an amazing piece, so convincing.

Ronna: That's quite early?

Seth: Nineteen sixty-one, I think. It must be the first thing he wrote. I had told him about the indeterminate dyad. Then he wrote the review of *Natural Right and History* in which he discovered that it has that structure.[19] That was extraordinary.

Ronna: How did Kennington show that?

Seth: In various ways, like noting how Strauss used "idea" in a very curious

---

19. Kennington's article is "Decartes' 'Olympica,'" *Social Research* 28 (1961). His "Review of Strauss's *Natural Right and History*," *Metaphysics* 35 (1981), is reprinted in *Leo Strauss's Thought: Towards a Critical Engagement*, edited by Alan Udoff (Boulder: Lynne Rienner Publishers), 227–52.

manner. There are these refined distinctions between the Plato section and the Aristotle section about natural right. He discussed the way terms are used in the wrong chapter: it's always in the subsequent chapter that the idea of something comes up, as opposed to the chapter where it seems relevant.

Robert: When you wrote to him about the indeterminate dyad, were you referring to the *Philebus*?

Seth: I think I had already generalized it. I may have been talking about the *Republic*. I claimed that it was in fact *the* principle, not knowing anything about it!

Michael: Do you remember what other people thought of Kennington?

Seth: I do know what Bloom thought of him, but I don't know whether it's from the time Kennington came to Cornell or before. It was a big regret in Bloom's life that, of the people he admired, he could never really be a friend of Kennington's. There was something standing in the way.

Robert: Did you speculate about what it was, or did he?

Seth: He put it down to Kennington's vanity. But you could easily turn that around and be closer to the mark.

Ronna: But Bloom admired him or respected Kennington?

Seth: Yes, right, but he always talked about his dark Protestant soul.

ALLAN BLOOM

Michael: What was Bloom like when you first met him?

Seth: He was supersensitive to people's defects. He had antennae out, he knew exactly . . .

Robert: People's weak spots?

Seth: Oh yes, it was extraordinary.

Ronna: You continued talking to Bloom often over the years, didn't you?

Seth: Pretty often. But he was often distracted. He got impatient if you could not say what you wanted to say in more than half a sentence.

Robert: The pressure of the sound bite.

Seth: I remember the last time he came. He was about to write the book and he asked me what I thought the *Phaedrus* was about. I summed it up in a sentence, and it didn't make any impression.

Ronna: Do you remember what the sentence was?

Seth: Something about the second speech turning into the third speech, and how this was connected to the double character of the human being. I managed to get it into one sentence, but it wasn't something he wanted to hear.

Michael: He must have had something in mind.

Seth: That was very characteristic of him. The thing he objected to about what I did is that it didn't come to a point. It was all about very complicated matters. That was his criticism of the *Sophist,* all the problems that are raised in the first two pages before the dialogue gets started. What he wanted was the bottom line—which of these possibilities was the right one. It's obviously connected to his concern with edification, which seemed to become more and more dominant.

Michael: I can see how it would have been very hard for you to talk with him about what you were working on, but did you ever talk about what he was working on, say when he was doing the *Republic* in the sixties?

Seth: He would withdraw then.

Ronna: But you looked at the translation?

Seth: He sent things to me.

Ronna: He probably couldn't have written the books he wrote unless what you're saying were true.

Seth: It's interesting. It seems to me there's a connection between the interest in edification and the accusation of nihilism against him, or the Straussian branch that he represents, by Jaffa,[20] say.

Ronna: Is this the golden apple, that there's no possibility of philosophy?

Michael: I think the accusation is that there's no possibility of morality.

Seth: Right.

Michael: There's a superficial defense of morality but, underneath it all, the celebration of philosophy amounts to an attack on morality. Bloom has two strands that are hard to put together: on the one hand, edification, on the other hand, philosophy. The model seems to be Plato's *Apology,* somehow pretending that they're the same thing, which takes you some distance but not all the way.

Seth: So Bloom really reproduced in his life a certain reading of the *Ethics.*

Ronna: Addressing the gentlemen?

Seth: Which is odd, because there aren't any gentlemen around to address.

Michael: I think he knew that.

Ronna: Maybe he believed he was creating the gentlemen.

Seth: I think that is what he thought he was doing.

Ronna: Did he think he was doing what Strauss was doing?

Seth: That never came up. I do remember him saying, toward the end of

---

20. Harry Jaffa, professor emeritus of government at Claremont McKenna College and the Claremont Graduate School, is the author of books on Aristotle and Aquinas, the American Revolution, and Lincoln.

his life, "Oh, I now realize you always knew this. But I've just come to recognize how central the question *'Quid sit deus?'* is."

Seth: A year before Bloom died, he and Rosen were together at a conference in Salt Lake City, Utah. They had gone to a restaurant after one of the meetings. It was early spring and the snow had not completely melted yet. On the side of the road, as they passed by in the car, were three deer grazing from the patches of grass in the midst of the snow. They stopped the car. Bloom was absolutely enchanted and he asked, "Do you think they'll attack if I get out and approach them?" And Rosen said, "I don't think they've read *The Closing of the American Mind.*"[21]

PROFESSORS

BENEDICT SENECA EINARSON

Ronna: Did you study with anyone in those first years on the Committee who impressed you?
Seth: Well, there was Einarson, the great Einarson, in the classics department.[22]
Michael: Why do you call him "the great" Einarson?
Seth: He looked like the Michelin tire ad, do you remember?, the man made of tires. He had this very funny shape—totally rotund, as though he were blown up out of a balloon—a round head, with no hair, large glasses that were totally circular. He looked exactly like the Michelin tire man.
Ronna: What was his field?
Seth: His field was Greek, and he knew more than anybody else. Absolutely amazing knowledge. But everything he said was punctuated by a laugh. He was a student of Paul Shorey, and became a junior fellow on the recom-

---

21. At the end of the conference, Rosen recalls, he told Bloom, "I'll come to visit you in Chicago." Bloom replied, "I'll get you a senior citizens' pass and we'll ride the Chicago bus system all day and talk."

22. Benedict Seneca Einarson, professor in the department of classics at the University of Chicago and translator of Theophrastus and Plutarch.

Laurence Berns, now a tutor at St. John's College in Annapolis, recalls attending Einarson's classes at Chicago. His favorite occupation seemed to be to find strange and rare Greek forms, then go to learned German, Dutch, or French specialized commentaries on them, which he translated in class. Finally the coup: "Ho, ho, ho, he forgot the exceptions," which then followed. A rare form came up at one point in a course on Xenophon's *Anabasis:* "Ho, ho, ho, I learned Hawaian over the weekend, and they have a form just like this." In one class the word *hegoumai* came up, and Berns remarked that, though clearly it had to be translated as "I think" or "I believe," in this case the speaker was also suggesting the other meaning of the word, "I lead." Einarson broke into a low chuckle and said, "Ho, ho, ho, you have to watch out for that sort of thing. I once had a student named Benardete, and he used to make remarks like that."

mendation of Quine.[23] Quine was in the first batch of junior fellows, and he said to the senior fellows, "Now here's an interesting guy." So Einarson became a junior fellow. Einarson had his three years at Harvard and then was asked to teach. And the story goes—this was the story I heard, I have no idea if it's true—that the student evaluation of the teachers came out the next year and Einarson, who had given a course on elementary Greek, got the worst evaluation that any teacher ever got. Apparently he went bonkers and ended up in a loony bin in Western Massachusetts for two years. When he came out he couldn't stop laughing.

Ronna: The laughing cure.

Seth: Someone said he had a very rare disease called "gelotophilia." It's so rare it's not in the dictionary; so rare that no one has ever heard of it. He couldn't stop laughing. What happened was, from that moment—this is the etiology of it—Einarson had finally worked out a universe in which it turned out that in fact everything was funny. So he got it right, you see. It worked perfectly.

Ronna: Did he ever write anything?

Seth: He did the text and the translation of Theophrastus, "On the Causes of Plants," and he did almost all the emendations in Festugière's edition of Hermes Trismegistus. He was highly respected, in this very odd way.

Ronna: Did you learn anything from him?

Seth: He was very reluctant to teach anything, because he despised everybody for not knowing anything. So he had about a dozen things to say, which he would always trot out.

Robert: Always punctuated with a laugh.

Seth: Always. And he never allowed anybody to pause. If you wanted to translate, you had to translate at lightning speed, otherwise he would interrupt if you stopped. He would say, "yes," and then he would go on, absolutely flawlessly. So if you wanted to get through, you had to learn how to do it very rapidly. I remember one day I was coming down the steps of the library of the classics department, which used to be on the second and third floor of one of the buildings. Einarson was coming up the steps at the same time, carrying in two columns in his hands a pile of books. Each one was ten books high, and he was laughing his head off as he carried the books up the steps. When he got to the top I said, "Why are you laughing so hard?" And he said,

23. Paul Shorey (1857–1934), head of the Classics department at the University of Chicago until 1927, was a Plato scholar and editor-in-chief of *Classical Philology* from 1906 to 1934. Willard Van Orman Quine (1908–2000) was professor of philosophy at Harvard from 1936 to 1978 and made important contributions to logic and philosophy of language.

"Well, this is a complete set of Hazlitt which I just bought, but then I discovered that I already had a complete set."

Ronna: He didn't offer them to you?

Seth: No, he gave them to Bruère.[24] Bruère had a very high giggle. So when the two of them got together it was absolute chaos. Did I tell you the Bloom story about Einarson? Bloom once came in to talk to Einarson and sat down on a chair. When the conversation was finished, he got up, and as he got up his pants ripped from the top to bottom. He looked back at the chair and there were these huge spikes sticking out of it, going up the chair. And Einarson was laughing his head off saying, "That was old Professor Shorey's chair."

DAVID GRENE

Michael: Were there other teachers you admired on the Committee?

Seth: Well, Grene was interesting.[25] He was devoted to death, as a topic of his being.

Ronna: Did you take the theme from him?

Seth: No, I don't think so, because in his case it was the fact that he had already had all the peak experiences, and could only look forward to death.

Ronna: How old was he?

Seth: He was much the youngest of the teachers. And he has still survived, you see.

Ronna: The practice of dying.

Seth: Right. He once gave a very funny seminar with an English professor on Anthony and Cleopatra, which was all about the idea that this was the peak and the last experience for Anthony, and "I'm Anthony"; but no one knew who Cleopatra was. It couldn't be Mrs. Grene.

Ronna: Wasn't there more than one?

Seth: This was Marjorie Grene. They lived on a farm outside Chicago. Grene used to come to class in the winter with his muddy boots. I remember one time Mrs. Grene came to his class with her muddy boots. They were both wearing their farm clothes. So from the rear they looked like the Bobsy Twins, of a much larger size, going down into the classroom.

24. Richard Bruère, a Latinist who taught in the classics department of the University of Chicago until 1973, was a long-time editor of *Classical Philology*.

25. David Grene, professor emeritus in the Committee on Social Thought. His work includes studies of Greek political theory, ancient and modern drama, and translations of Hesiod, Herodotus, and Greek tragedies. He was the co-editor of *The Complete Greek Tragedies* (Chicago: University of Chicago Press).

Ronna: What did David Grene look like? Is he Irish?

Seth: He's Anglo-Irish. He had a very red face, red hair, very clipped speech. He used to like to gaze out the window in his office. There was a man named Edwin McClellan—who should therefore be a Scott, but is in fact Japanese—who came to the Committee to study British constitutional history, or something like that, until he learned he should really study Japanese. Grene was the secretary of the Committee, and McClellan came to introduce himself. He knocked on the door, and when he opened it, Grene was standing at the window staring outside. They had this very clipped British conversation, with Grene never looking at him. All of a sudden, Grene turns around, and sees this little Japanese man standing there.

Ronna: Do you know how Grene ended up on the Committee?

Seth: Oh yes, he ended up on the Committee after a big quarrel with someone in the classics department. Actually, he always quarreled. But he became a favorite of Hutchins,[26] and that's how he was saved. He had come from Harvard, where he had an instructorship, and Hutchins found him and put him in the classics department. Then he was going to be fired because of this quarrel. That's when they put him on the Committee. That's the story I heard, I don't really know whether it's true.

Ronna: What did you study with Grene?

Seth: Oh, we read the *Aeneid,* and some Euripides, or maybe it was Aeschylus.

Ronna: So you found him kind of interesting, but it wasn't very significant for you?

Seth: It wasn't really interesting in terms of thought.

Ronna: Just his character?

Seth: Right. One year Grene got a Fulbright, and he wanted somebody to run the farm. Bloom volunteered. It turned out to be the worst winter Chicago ever had. There were all these sheep on the farm. Grene was the only farmer in this whole area who did not use a tractor, but horses, to plow the land and to ride. So Bloom went out there with a group of students who were going to stay, but as soon as it got cold everybody else left, and Bloom was left all alone. The farmers around were very helpful. They helped him take care of the land and so forth. But there were certain things on the farm that changed. Bloom once found a dead rat under a bed and took it out. And there was a little piece of greasy curtain over the stove in the kitchen that he threw out. Also, the kitchen was so dirty, he decided to paint it. In the barn, there

26. Robert Maynard Hutchins (1899–1977), president of the University of Chicago from 1929 to 1951 and chairman of the Board of Editors of *Encyclopaedia Britannica* from 1943 to 1974.

was a pair of trousers so thick with grime, they stood up by themselves. So he threw those out. In the spring, the Grenes came back. Mrs. Grene looked at the kitchen and said, "I knew it would be different, but not this different!" He thought she was going to say, "And where's the dead rat?" Grene went into the barn and said, "Where are my trousers?" He was furious. Bloom came back with his eyes absolutely wild with rage and said, "They didn't even bring me a present." But they were later reconciled.

Ronna: Bloom and Grene?

Seth: Yes.

PETER HEINRICH VON BLANCKENHAGEN

Robert: Did you ever take a course with Blanckenhagen?

Seth: I think once, on ancient painting, beginning with Egyptian painting.

Ronna: But you conversed with him a lot?

Seth: Yes. He gave a series of lectures in the next year. No, no, it was Otto Georg von Simpson who lectured, an expert on Byzantine painting.[27] He was a descendant of Felix Mendelssohn, who had got titled and married a genuine Austrian princess, who was extremely nice and not snobbish at all, whereas Simpson was very snobbish. So Simpson gave three lectures on medieval art. Then at the end of the third one there were questions. The first question was by Blanckenhagen: "After you have considered the iconology, the naïveté, the charm, the symbolism of medieval art, what can one say? That it is fundamentally perverse." Simpson blew his top and said, "This is exactly the kind of remark which an eighteenth-century philosophe would make." "So much the better," said Blanckenhagen. At this point, a student said, "Professor Blanckenhagen, I don't quite understand what you mean by saying medieval art is morally perverse." "Morally perverse?," said Blanckenhagen, "I didn't say 'morally perverse.' Of moral perversity, I know nothing."

Michael: Blanckenhagen's expertise was Greek things?

Seth: Actually his expertise was Flavian art originally, and architecture. Then he expanded.

Robert: All his training was in Germany?

Seth: Yes, right. Blanckenhagen told me a funny story about his first visit to Rome, in the 1930s. He was walking down the street and a little boy came up behind him and pulled on his coat and said, "Una ragazza, signore?" The boy pulled again and said, "Una donna? Un ragazzo?" Finally he said in

---

27. Born in Berlin in 1912, Simpson was professor of art history at the University of Chicago, and is best known for his book on the Gothic cathedral.

desparation, "Che cosa vuole?" and he turned around, "Il papa?!" Really shocked, Blanckenhagen moved on. Suddenly the boy pulls on him again and says, "Un cardinale, signore?"

Ronna: One last offer. Where did Blanckenhagen come from?

Seth: From Riga. I remember him saying that the real experience he had of archaeology was after he had been in Rome and looked at monuments, when he went back to Riga, to the family estate. They had left in 1917 or '18. The first strange thing was that the peasants came out and kissed the hem of his garment.

Robert: When would this have been, do you know?

Seth: In the '30s, I think. So he went into the house, which had been totally destroyed. It was this archaeological ruin. He would pick up a piece of green marble and say, "That came from my mother's bedroom," and so forth. He said it was very strange to go over one's past now that he had been trained.

Robert: To look at these shards.

Seth: Right, and see that this was his life.

Ronna: So it was during the revolution that the estate had been taken away?

Seth: Yes. On this estate there were two dogs. One of them was extraordinarily stupid and ran after birds that were flying overhead; the other dog would just look on. One spring, when it was beginning to thaw, the stupid dog went out onto the ice of the pond and fell in. The other dog got down on his belly and crawled all the way to the other dog, pulled it out, dragged it back to land, and then walked off.

Ronna: Types in the animal kingdom. So what exactly was the background of the family?

Seth: It was a German-speaking family with this three-language distinction—Russian of the officials, Latvian of the peasants, and German of the rulers—who were all classically trained and read Thucydides at night before they went to bed. His mother seems to have been Scotch-English.

Ronna: Did he speak English without an accent?

Seth: No, he had an accent. He learned English in this country.

Robert: After they fled Riga where did they settle?

Seth: They settled in Germany, but I don't know exactly where.

Robert: Do you know how old he was at the time?

Seth: He must have been pretty young. He once told a story that happened when he was in Riga. He was old enough for his mother to allow him to come to an afternoon tea she was holding for the ladies. There was one woman at the tea whom he found extraordinarily beautiful. He couldn't take his eyes off her. After the tea, when his mother asked him what he had thought, he said, "Who was that beautiful woman?" And his mother said,

"You mean countess so-and-so?" "No, no, not that one. The other one." His mother said, "Oh that one. But she's so stupid." Anyway, he told this story to Strauss, who said, "Why, of course." Well, this woman made such a powerful impression on him that, when he became old enough, a few years later, to have his own stone on which the crest of the family would be put, he chose the stone of her husband. Amethyst.

Michael: Your story is about Blanckenhagen really understanding archaeology by going back to his own things: did it work at all the other way around?

Seth: I didn't see that. I used to think David Grene was the only person I knew whose character was really formed by the books he admired—of Joyce, Yeats, D. H. Lawrence. If you knew those books, then you knew David Grene. Somehow he was constituted by them. Then it occurred to me that it's also true of Blanckenhagen. He was constituted on the one hand by Proust, on the other, by Goethe's account of Winckelmann.

Robert: That fits with his story of himself as a young boy.

Seth: Right. I was thinking of Proust's description in "Sodom and Gomorrah" of a homosexual society, based on Baron Charlus. When you read it, if you knew Blanckenhagen, it looks like a perfect match.

Ronna: The aristocratic element is important?

Seth: Yes, and being discreet. Then I read this passage from Goethe about Winckelmann, which is identical to Blanckenhagen:

> Since the ancients, as we claim, were truly complete personalities in harmony with themselves and the world, they also had to experience the full scope of human relationships. They did not want to deny themselves the delight that results from the bond between people of similar temperament. Even in this respect there is a remarkable difference between ancient and modern times. The relationship to women, which in our time has become so tender and spiritual, scarcely rose above the level of physical need. The relationship of parent and child seems to have been somewhat more loving. But friendship among men was for them the only genuine relationship. . . . We react with astonishment when, with regard to two young men, we hear of passionate fulfillment of love's desire, the bliss of being inseparable, lifelong devotion, or the need to follow the other into death. . . . Winckelmann felt born for friendship of that kind. . . .
>
> Granted that a latter-day Greek in his intense need for friendship actually creates the objects of his affections, he would still gain only a one-sided, an emotional benefit from it and little from the external world, unless there emerged a different, yet related and similar need and a satisfactory object

for this need. We are referring to the need for physical beauty and the incarnation of beauty itself. For the ultimate goal of evolving nature is the
beautiful human being. . . . To be sure, nature only rarely succeeds in producing him because there are numerous obstacles to her plans, and even
her omnipotence cannot linger long with perfection and lend permanence
to the beauty she produces. We are justified in saying that a beautiful human being is beautiful only for one brief moment. At this point, art en-
ters. . . . Those who saw the *Olympian Jupiter* were seized by such feelings,
as we can gather from ancient descriptions, reports and testimony. A god
had become man in order to make man into a god. They saw supreme
majesty and were inspired by supreme beauty. . . . Winckelmann, by nature, was receptive to such beauty.[28]

It's so strange, that's Blanckenhagen. This is the way he understood himself.
Ronna: Both the passion and the art?
Seth: Yes, yes. And the notion of the eternal moment being preserved by
the work of art.
Ronna: But there's a tension between the two, isn't there?
Seth: Yes, they're completely at odds.
Ronna: It's interesting, he had this appreciation of the beauty of that woman.
Seth: Well, first, it's prepubescent. And the other thing, it's nonproductive,
and therefore lends itself to this transformation into art.
Michael: You have to read the story he told you through the eyes of some-
one who's already read Proust, going back to his past and so on, even the
story about the woman.
Seth: That's what was so extraordinary. By the way, he was not unique in
this regard. Many years later I met the widow of Ernst Robert Curtius, in
Geneva.[29] It turned out that he was the person who told the Germans about
Proust, in 1922 or something like that. He had married this woman, this was
a *marriage blanc.* They lived in Germany throughout the war. It was not so
unusual. Blanckenhagen himself was married.
Robert: But you think Blanckenhagen fits the two sides in the description
of Winckelmann? On the one hand, you have his devotion to this way of life
of the friend, who's ennobled by giving of himself, and on the other hand
there's his devotion to art.

28. Johann Wolfgang von Goethe, "Winckelmann and His Age" [1805], translated by Ellen von
Nardroff and Ernest H. von Nardroff, in *Goethe, Essays on Art and Literature,* vol. 3 of *Goethe's Collected
Works,* edited by John Gearey (New York: Suhrkamp, 1986), 102–4. Johann Joachim Winckelmann
(1717–68), who wrote on Greek painting and sculpture, is regarded as the father of modern archaeology.
29. Ernst Robert Curtius (1814–96), archaeologist and professor at the University of Berlin, was
author of a five-volume history of Greece.

Seth: But notice that, even in Goethe's own understanding of it, it's extraordinarily idealized. It's not about antiquity any more; it has to do with something you can't even get in contact with, which necessarily you'll fall short of. The perfect friend, the perfect work of art.

Ronna: Why do you say it's not about antiquity?

Seth: It's as if you failed to remember that the statues were colored. So it's this very Northern, pale, marble whiteness that you're really celebrating. It's much more ethereal. It's as if you took the literature as being the reality.

Michael: It's like saying the polis of literature is the polis.

Ronna: Do you think there is something particularly German about this?

Seth: I would think so.

Michael: You prefaced the story with the remark about David Grene, that he too was formed by certain books. What struck me was that both of them apparently were formed by books that didn't have anything to do with what they devoted their lives to. So that somehow there was Thucydides, for Grene, and then these three, what was it, Yeats?

Robert: Joyce and Lawrence.

Michael: And in the case of Blanckenhagen, it's Proust and Winckelmann. Winckelmann is easier, of course, because there's a connection. They're formed by books, but not the books to which their work was dedicated.

Seth: It's odd. But maybe it's not so uncommon. Cherniss was an interesting case.[30] He was a scholar of Plato and Aristotle; but he had an extraordinary hatred of Aristotle and devotion to Plato that totally dominated his scholarship. So there it was disastrous. This is much better, because it's separate.

Ronna: Now it's reminding me of what Daube said about himself and Scholem:[31] he couldn't have studied Jewish mysticism as Scholem did, because he had a temperament that would mesh with it and therefore, the implication was, prevent objectivity. He had to study law, he had such a passionate personality.

Seth: Blanckenhagen had a friend whom I met once, Count Colorado, who lived in Canada and came from a Czechoslovakian family that had not been very nice to Mozart. The family was very proud of the fact that it had a nine-

---

30. Harold Cherniss (1904–87) taught in the classics departments of Johns Hopkins, Berkeley, and Princeton, and was a member of Institute for Advanced Study. The primary subject of his scholarship is Aristotle's criticism of the Pre-Socratics, Plato, and the Academy.

31. David Daube (1909–90), distinguished scholar of Roman and Biblical law, New Testament, and Rabbinic Judaism, was a fellow at All Souls College, Oxford from 1955 to 1970 and Regius Professor of Civil Law before moving to Berkeley where he taught in the School of Law until 1993. Gershom Scholem (1897–1982), who became a professor at the Hebrew University after moving to Palestine in the 1920s, was the leading scholar of Jewish mysticism in the twentieth century.

hundred-year male line, no females for nine hundred years, and Colorado was proud of the fact that he was going to be the last. When I met him, it was in London, with Blanckenhagen, near the British Museum. Colorado had in tow an extraordinarily beautiful young man, with long delicate eyelashes, just like a movie star, beautifully dressed, beautiful manners, and dumb. It turned out that Colorado picked these people off the street, educated them, married them off, never slept with them, because that would give them power over him, but carried on this very funny . . .

Ronna: Pygmalian role?

Seth: Right. It was very different from Blanckenhagen.

Ronna: But they were friends for a long time?

Seth: Oh yes. There's a funny story about them in Prague or somewhere. Colorado's aunt was coming, and they were supposed to get her a hotel room. It turned out that this was the number-one brothel in Prague.

Ronna: And they didn't know?

Seth: They had no idea. Actually, something like that happened to me once, when I was traveling around Italy. I came to Padua, and I didn't know where to stay. So I found a place in the telephone book, and it said "pensione." I had my map and I marched over to it. I noticed something odd. It was about 11:00 in the morning, and there were men leaning against the wall at various points, not saying anything, so I rang the bell, but there wasn't any answer. I kept on ringing the bell. Finally a waiter across the street asked me what I wanted and he said, "Oh, this is the brothel. They're all waiting for it to open at 1:00."

Seth: Blanckenhagen was once traveling by ship and met on board a black steward, who became his lover. This black steward then married a German girl on one of his voyages. She became the housemaid of the Gourevitch family when they lived in Philadelphia.[32] Then the marriage with the German girl broke up, and the steward disappeared. Years later, when Blanckenhagen got very old, he couldn't get around his apartment. One day he got a phone call from this man, who was in Africa. He said, "I just dreamt of you last night. And I'm coming home, to take care of you." In the meantime, this man had retired, gone into Africa, come to a little village, where he gave the village the money that he had accumulated to set up telephone lines, water supply, and so forth. He was sitting there as king, and he had this dream. So the next day he left Africa for New York. He moved in with Blanckenhagen

32. Victor Gourevitch, professor emeritus of philosophy at Wesleyan University, is known for his work as a translator and interpreter of Rousseau.

and took care of him, to such an extent that he became a pest. Blancken-hagen wanted to get rid of him, but didn't know how. It was like being held prisoner. One of the things Blanckenhagen told this man was that he wanted to die at home. He did not want to go to the hospital. At one point he collapsed and the man sent him to the hospital, where he woke up. All Blanckenhagen's friends came around the bed, and he began to complain about the fact that he had been sent to the hospital. The man overheard him, and left that day. Blanckenhagen never saw him again. And he died at home. This is really a thirty-year episode.

Robert: How long a time was it since he came from Africa to the day he left?

Seth: Less than a year, I think.

Robert: When did Blanckenhagen die?

Seth: Five years ago maybe.

Ronna: He taught in the Institute of Fine Arts [at NYU], didn't he?

Seth: Yes, right.

Ronna: Did he have disciples of any sort?

Seth: Well, that was the sad thing at the memorial service for him at the IFA—how little anyone talked about him as a scholar. People at the Institute are into the swing of the social life of New York, which Blanckenhagen wanted to appear to conform to. So that's the account they gave of him, a perfect dinner companion for wealthy art lovers.

Ronna: He didn't want to be understood as being outside?

Seth: He used to tell me he read *Time* magazine every week, so he had a better understanding of America than I did; I wasn't in touch with the pulse. He was eager to be accepted by people who did not have the same capacity as he did, like those who were at the top of the American archaeological profession, who were unimaginative, or imaginative in a very professional way, not like him at all. So he took delight in the fact that they gave him a medal for his achievements. He wouldn't publish his lectures on the Parthenon because they wouldn't pass muster with the professionals. He had all the beliefs of these people in New York about the fascism of the country. He absorbed them, and was railing about it for the last twenty years of his life.

Michael: He didn't have that before he came?

Seth: I think he was always very liberal, actually. So America seemed like a wonderful country.

Michael: Did Blanckenhagen ever talk about his hunchback?

Seth: Not very much. But he was conscious of conditions that made him behave differently from people around him. He was always very forgiving of communists, because they had not had the experience of communism that he had had.

Ronna: American communists?

Seth: This was particularly in connection with [Anthony] Blunt. Blancken-hagen said he and Isaiah Berlin agreed about this, that Berlin was saved from this taint by experience, otherwise, the implication was, he would be one too. So, the hunchback, I think, was very important for that. He couldn't be a Nazi.

Ronna: Why do you say that?

Seth: Somehow he was saved by his experiences from a mistake of this kind. For instance, Ernst Buschor, his teacher, became a Nazi, according to Blanckenhagen, because Hitler was an extremely uncanny judge of people's weak points. Hitler met him at a party in Munich and knew that Buschor above all loved his own writing style. So he came up to him and said, "I love the way your write."

Michael: Isn't there a Stalin story like that, about a poet?

Seth: Oh, that's different though, the story about [Osip] Mandelstam and the telephone call?

Michael: What was it?

Seth: Mandelstam was arrested. Pasternak got a telephone call on Sunday morning. A voice says, "This is Stalin." Pasternak hung up, because he thought it was someone making a joke. Then the phone rang again. "This is Stalin. Tell me what you think about Mandelstam." And Pasternak apparently gave him a literary account of Mandelstam's poetry. At that point Stalin said, "If I had been a friend of his, I could have done better." Pasternak thought that meant Mandelstam would be exterminated. But he was released. Exterminated later. This is the Jesuitical cruelty of Stalin.

LEO STRAUSS

Michael: Can you tell us about how you first met Leo Strauss?

Seth: It was through Petry, his adopted son, who was a student in the Committee at the time.[33] Petry invited us over to his house—I think it must have been in the spring of my first year—and we met Mr. and Mrs. Strauss over tea at the kitchen table.

Robert: But nothing like a reputation preceded your meeting with him?

Seth: No.

Robert: Where had Strauss been exactly before the appointment to Chicago?

Seth: Well, originally he was on a fellowship in Cambridge, sponsored by

---

33. Thomas Petry Strauss is the son of Miriam Strauss and Walter Petry.

Barker.[34] Strauss said he had realized England is very different from Germany from the moment in which the customs official had to blow his nose and said "Excuse me," and he realized that no German official would ever apologize. Anyway, it took him some time to get used to English ways, like when they said "Maybe," it meant "Necessarily so." He didn't have it perfectly down. So when Barker had to tell him there was no money for the following year, which meant Strauss would have to try to go to America, being an Englishman, Barker couldn't tell him outright. They had this terrible misunderstanding until Barker was forced to say, "You have to go to America." He got red in the face and very embarrassed.

Robert: Strauss had to have it told straight.

Seth: Right. The consequence was that it was arranged for Strauss to give a lecture at a meeting of the American Historical Association in Philadelphia. The first thing he did was go to an insurance company and say, "I am traveling the high seas and I have this very valuable manuscript. Can you suggest how I can protect it?" And they said, "We recommend that you wrap it in oil skins." So he got this huge piece of oil skin and wrapped his manuscript in it. Then went to the tailor and said, "I am traveling on the high seas. I need a seaworthy suit." And being a British tailor, of course he took it absolutely straight, and said, "I will make you a suit out of the cloth used by the British navy." So they dressed him in a navy blue suit when he came to the Queen Mary, to travel the high seas, with his oilskin manuscript under his arms.

Robert: To the new world.

Seth: So he came and gave the lecture. But he had never lectured in his entire life.

Ronna: How old was he?

Robert: Thirty-nine or forty years old?

Seth: Yes. So he had written this very long paper and after he had been speaking for about fifty minutes, people began to yawn. He had about fifteen pages to go. More people began to yawn, and he decided he'd better cut it short. So he left out the last fourteen pages and just put in the concluding paragraph, and everybody in the audience thought he was crazy, because apparently they were following it very closely!

Robert: The yawning meant nothing.

Seth: No.

Ronna: There was a gap in the argument.

34. Ernest Barker (1874–1960), professor of political science at Cambridge wrote on Greek political theory.

Seth: Right. Anyway, the consequence of his learning English ways was this. McKeon interviewed him for Chicago and said, "Maybe there will be a job for you at Chicago." Well Strauss immediately went back to England and said, "I have a job at Chicago," because he knew that for the English, "Maybe" meant "Certainly." But in American English it meant, "No."

Michael: Wasn't there a story about Strauss in England, about a Hobbes manuscript?

Seth: Oh yes, that's a fantastic story, another one from the horse's mouth. One of the great puzzles in Hobbes scholarship had been that he had written so late—what happened before? Strauss had gone to England and had access to the Duke of Devonshire's library where the Hobbes papers were. He found a manuscript in Hobbes' handwriting that could be dated before anything published. On the basis of this, he had submitted a proposal to Cambridge for a whole new edition of Hobbes' works, with this as the first piece. One of the syndics of the Press had suggested, just by happenstance, that they should look up some of the words in this manuscript in the OED. And lo and behold, they were in a printed book, which was written under a pseudonym that Hobbes had used. So they wrote a nice letter saying, we have discovered that this in fact has been published, and we'll have to reconsider the edition. Strauss jumped to the conclusion that he was going to be arrested by Scotland Yard for attempting to defraud the university press. And he immediately left the house, with his wife, so they couldn't find him for hours.

Ronna: I remember your once saying that you were struck by his experience as a refugee, the sense of insecurity that brought.

Seth: Yes.

Michael: I know it doesn't explain anything, but maybe being suspicious, intellectually, is a virtue that allowed him to see everything he saw. But what you're describing wouldn't be surprising, especially given his life—what he had to run away from.

Robert: Do you know where Strauss went when he left England?

Seth: He went to Bard, I think, as his first job. He met a classicist there who impressed him.

Robert: How did he make the connection to Bard?

Seth: That I don't know.

Robert: Wasn't Bard where Hannah Arendt's husband was?

Ronna: Hans Blücher?

Robert: But he didn't know him?

Seth: No.

Robert: There may have been other émigrés at Bard. He went from there to the New School?

Seth: Right.

Robert: Do you know anything about how that move was made?

Seth: All I know is Strauss's detective story. This story is guaranteed because it came out of his mouth, you know. Strauss had been at the New School for several years before he got the position at Chicago through Hutchins. They had a dinner for him, to celebrate his departure. Strauss said, "I completely lost my head when I had to get up and make a speech. Instead of making a speech I told a detective story based on all the characters at the New School." There was a member of the faculty who was a great ladies' man, another who was a great ascetic, and there was a secretary who was extremely vulgar. So he made up a detective story on the spot, using these characters. One day in the men's bathroom, the womanizer was discovered murdered. The body was discovered at a certain hour early in the morning by the vulgar secretary, who went to the men's bathroom to use it because it was so convenient, but, being embarrassed, didn't tell the police that she had found the body two hours before it was discovered. But the vulgar woman was also the detective and realized that there was no motive for the murder except the fact that someone was offended by the man's womanizing, who must have been the ascetic. The vulgar secretary figured out that if you're ascetic like that, you must have a diary. So there's an epic struggle as she goes up the fire escape into the man's apartment, into his bedroom, and finds the diary. Strauss made up this complicated story on the spot and told it to the whole faculty, and everybody knew who all these people were.

Ronna: Fabulous.

Seth: When he heard about the appointment to Chicago, the first thing he did was to stop a taxi in New York and ask how much to go to Chicago.

Ronna: He never looked at a map?

Seth: He had no idea. One spring day in Chicago, Blanckenhagen knocked at Strauss's door. In the past, Strauss had always come to open it, but this time he didn't open it and said, "You'll have to come in on your own." When he came in, Strauss said, "I can't get up to greet you," as he sat at his desk with both his hands on a pile of papers. So Blanckenhagen asked, "Why are you in this funny position?" And Strauss said, "Because of the fan. The fan is blowing, and if I take my hands away, the papers will blow away." So Blanckenhagen went over to the switch that turned the fan off. And Strauss turned to him and said, "You are a mechanical genius."

Ronna: Didn't you once tell us that Strauss didn't know how to boil water?
Seth: No, that was Wach, in the sociology of religion.[35]

Robert: You said you first met Strauss through his adopted son?
Seth: Right, Petry.
Ronna: It was his mother who married Strauss?
Seth: Yes. His mother had been married to a painter named Petry, who died in an accident. She met him on Capri while she was standing with her girl-friend under a tree. Petry saw her and immediately fell in love with her. He went over and said, "You must be my wife." So they went back to Berlin, and came into the study of her banker husband and she said, "Unless you give me a divorce, we will kill ourselves on the spot." This was the romantic Mrs. Strauss, who married Mr. Strauss; it sounds so extraordinary.
Michael: So Strauss was her third husband?
Seth: Strauss was her third husband.
Robert: This was before the Machtergreifung, before Hitler?
Seth: Yes.
Robert: He granted her the divorce?
Seth: Immediately.
Ronna: He didn't want a suicide on his hands.
Seth: That was the story.
Ronna: What about Jenny Strauss Clay?
Seth: She is the daughter of Strauss's sister, Bettina, and the great Arabic scholar, Paul Kraus.[36] Both of the parents died, and that's how Jenny came to live with the Strausses. When I came to NYU in the 1960s, I heard about Kraus from the chairman of the department [Frank Peters]. He was an Arabic-Greek scholar, did Aristotle in the tradition, and an ex-Jesuit—he ceased to be a Jesuit the day before he was to be ordained. Anyway, he told me he had gone to Cairo, and met many people who knew Paul Kraus, who was still very famous, because he was absolutely top-notch as an editor, and knew more medieval Arabic than anyone else. He was the one who edited the Farabi manuscript.
Ronna: What's that?

35. Joachim Wach (1898–1955), professor at the Divinity School of the University of Chicago.
36. Jenny Strauss Clay is professor of classics at the University of Virginia and the author of books on Homer's *Odyssey* and the Homeric Hymns. Paul Kraus (1904–44), an orientalist educated in Prague, Berlin, and Paris, took a position in 1937 teaching textual criticism and semitic languages in Cairo, where he was living at the time of his death. See Joel Kraemer's biographical sketch, "The Death of an Orientalist: Paul Kraus from Prague to Cairo," in *The Jewish Discovery of Islam*, ed. Martin S. Kramer (Tel Aviv: Moshe Dayan Center, distributed by Syracuse University Press, 1999).

Seth: You know, *The Philosophy of Plato and Aristotle* and the commentary on the *Laws*.[37]

Ronna: They were not known before that?

Seth: No, they were edited by him.

Robert: When was the discovery made, do you know?

Seth: Must have been in the early '30s.

Robert: So when he was still in Germany?

Seth: Yes, on one of his travels, in Istanbul. He found it in the library.

Ronna: And realized what it was?

Seth: Yes, and showed it to Strauss, of course. They were so excited, they were going to have an Alfarabi conference in Istanbul in 1939, with the stamp of the Turkish government. That was going to be the celebration of his seven-hundreth anniversary or something. But the war put an end to that.

Ronna: It was really a small world, wasn't it?

Seth: Yes it was.

Michael: After you met Strauss, did you start going to his classes right away?

Seth: I think that was in the following spring. Oxman reported to all of us that he had just come back from the first lecture of this guy Strauss on the *Republic,* and he had never heard anything like it. He was so enthusiastic that we all went. I don't remember the details, but Strauss was talking about the beginning of book I of the *Republic,* and listed on the board seven items that occurred in a row, and circled the fourth one, this was the crucial one. No one had ever heard that you could do this with a text.

Ronna: Examine the details?

Seth: That you could take the details and in fact make something of it that linked up with a larger argument that was perfectly intelligible. It was a re-markable ability of attaching the pixel to the whole in a perfectly natural way. I realize how extraordinary it was when I think about Klein.[38] He always saw pixels, but the consequence was that the whole would vanish. You couldn't re-construct the argument and see what it was as a whole, because this little bit

37. *Alfarabi: The Political Writings,* "Philosophy of Plato and Aristotle," translated and with an in-troduction by Muhsin Mahdi (rev. ed., Ithaca, NY: Cornell University Press, 2001), and Plato's "Laws," trans. Muhsin Mahdi, in *Alfarabi: The Political Writings, "Political Regime" and Other Texts,* edited and with an introduction by Charles E. Butterworth (Cornell University Press, forthcoming).

38. Jacob Klein (1899–1978), who taught at St. John's from 1937 until his death and was dean from 1949 to 1958, played a central role in shaping the great books curriculum of the college. His scholarly work includes his important study of Greek mathematical thought (see chap. 3, n. 3) and commentaries on Plato's *Meno* and on the trilogy *Theaetetus, Sophist,* and *Statesman.* The broad range of his interests is evident in the collection *Jacob Klein: Lectures and Essays,* edited by Robert B. Williams and Elliott Zuckerman (Annapolis, MD: St. John's College Press, 1985).

took over the entire argument and you didn't need anything else. And whatever the thesis was that Klein had established, it was not so obviously connected with either the first impression of the argument of the dialogue or with a deeper interpretation of that argument. So, it was extraordinarily ingenious, but not natural, the way Strauss's interpretations always seemed to be. What Strauss was doing, when I think about it now, was really like ancient teleology, like Galen. I mean, "Why is this here? It's here because of this."

Ronna: You could see the function of the parts as they fit into the whole?

Seth: Exactly

Michael: So what you've called burst-like and filament-like arguments, Strauss put together, but what Klein did in bursts didn't correspond to the filaments.

Seth: This became clear to me when I was at St. John's. Klein had gotten interested again in thinking—I don't know why it happened, but he suddenly got reinvigorated, maybe because of Nietzsche. We read the *Philebus* together, Klein and four other tutors. The whole thing was based on the *apeiron* [the unlimited], which the beginning and the end of the dialogue displayed. But that insight he never could develop in the argument. So the conclusion he once stated, while we were reading it, was "It's spurious."

Ronna: Because he didn't see the connection?

Seth: I don't think he was serious about it. But it was revealing; precisely because he was not able to work out all these fantastic details and make the connections, he wanted to reject the dialogue.

Robert: So after going to hear Strauss, you were all impressed. What did you go on to study with him?

Seth: I went to see him and asked if he would do a tutorial with me.

Robert: That's the second time you took the initiative. You had been bold in going up to Blanckenhagen.

Seth: Right, I was very rash. I was put on the alert from Donald Lamb. I think it was Gourevitch who gave me the idea. Gourevitch had asked him to read something, Hegel, I think.

Michael: Was this after you had been in class for a while?

Seth: Right.

Michael: So what did Strauss say?

Seth: He said yes, and then we read the *Theages*, that was the first thing. Or maybe it was the *Euthyphro*, I don't remember.

Ronna: In Greek?

Seth: Yes.

Ronna: Didn't you write your master's thesis on the *Theages*?

Seth: Right, but I don't remember if it was the first thing I studied with Strauss.

Ronna: Was the thesis a result of doing the tutorial with him?

Seth: Yes, it was because of that. What I remember was Strauss laughing.

Ronna: When he read it?

Seth: When the M.A. thesis was completed, I had to present it in a public lecture. That was a Committee requirement. The room was set up in such a way that Strauss was behind me while I was reading this thing, I think the first half of it. And he was laughing his head off. I didn't know it was he who was laughing. No one else was laughing. Only he thought it was very, very funny—which it was meant to be. And he said the next day, "I didn't know you were such a funny fellow."

Michael: What was it like to read something with him?

Seth: It was done in this very regular way. I would read a page, or half a page, and he would talk about what was peculiar, or what the argument was.

Ronna: He did most of the talking?

Seth: I would ask questions. I was learning the kinds of things to look for, you know, why was this there, and so forth. And he was very good at making up hypotheses that he would then discard, and develop others as it went on.

Michael: Had Strauss published yet?

Robert: The Hobbes book was surely out.

Seth: Yes, but I don't think *Natural Right and History* was published yet.

Robert: Some of the essays must have been done.

Seth: The Xenophon essay was out.

Michael: Did you read these things?

Seth: We read the *Hiero;* his commentary must have come out pretty much at that time. But I wonder if anybody really understood what he was doing, though they got the main point. I think that several of Strauss's essays or lectures came out of these tutorials, one on the *Euthyphro,* one on Thucydides.

Ronna: Did he read that with you?

Seth: Yes. We read the *Minos*—maybe that was the first thing we read—and he wrote on it.[39] So he got an insight into the whole from studying it, which I never got until I read the essay.

---

39. *The Political Philosophy of Hobbes: Its Basis and Its Genesis,* translated by Elsa Sinclair (Chicago: University of Chicago Press, 1952); *Natural Right and History* (Chicago: University of Chicago Press, 1953); Strauss's study of Xenophon's *Hiero,* first published in 1948, is reprinted in *On Tyranny,* edited by Victor Gourevitch and Michael S. Roth (New York: Free Press, 1991); "On the *Euthypron*" and "Thucydides: The Meaning of Political History," in *The Rebirth of Classical Political Radicalism: Essays and Lectures by Leo Strauss,* selected and edited by Thomas Pangle (Chicago: University of Chicago Press, 1989); "On the *Minos,*" in *The Roots of Political Philosophy: Ten Forgotten Socratic Dialogues,* edited by Thomas Pangle (Ithaca, NY: Cornell University Press, 1987).

Michael: That means, as you were going along, you must have been extraordinarily impressed by the way the details came out.

Seth: By his ability to turn these burst-like insights into whole arguments, or at least give the sketch of a whole argument. So whatever peculiarity he had discovered, you could understand what it was pointing to. But curiously enough, he never got bogged down in details. Once he showed me the notebook he had written on Xenophon, and he had lists of every "He said," in the *Memorabilia* and for every other Xenophontic Socratic dialogue, he had listed all these incredible things, you know. He never explained what it meant, why he did it.

Ronna: Did you ever discuss hermeneutic principles?

Seth: Heidegger became very important, and we had lots of discussions of his hermeneutic principles and how it looked as though, in a very extraordinary way, the refutation of the hermeneutics refuted the philosophy simultaneously. He thought that was very surprising, as opposed to Nietzsche.

Ronna: Whose insights would be independent—

Seth: Of whether he was right about what Plato was saying. But we talked about that much later. I think the really extraordinary experience happened when I had heard a lecture course on Machiavelli and a second lecture course on the *Republic,* not the first one, which I don't remember at all. Then the Machiavelli book was written while I was abroad, and he wrote me all these letters about what he had discovered, and it came out in the book, which was entirely different from that set of lectures.

Ronna: So he was open.

Seth: Completely open. And the same thing happened with the *Republic.* He knew about *thumos* [spiritedness], from Alfarabi, this passage about the way of Socrates and the way of Thrasymachus which Plato combined. But he had not understood at all the centrality of *techne,* which came in *The City and Man.*[40] That was completely absent from the lectures on the *Republic.* Then they turned out to link up. But only in retrospect would you realize that.

Robert: Did he ever say anything to you about why he had failed to see this?

Seth: I think he was too much under the spell of the original insight, from Alfarabi. So he had to work through it again.

Ronna: It seems as if reading many different authors must have played an interesting role in how Strauss understood any one thing, like rereading the *Republic* after having understood Machiavelli.

Seth: But he never mixed things up. Everything looked extraordinarily . . .

Robert: Discrete?

40. Leo Strauss, *The City and Man* (Chicago: University of Chicago Press, 1964).

Seth: It must not have been the case in his thinking, but that was the way it was presented.

Ronna: Does that mean the overarching theses he developed, say about ancients and moderns, were secondary to working through each text?

Seth: He obviously had a set of markers, from different texts he had not studied, passages he knew were very important.

Ronna: Before he knew the book?

Seth: Or whether he ever knew the book. So his awareness of the passage about *physis* [nature] in the *Odyssey* (10.303), that was not dependent on an interpretation of the work as a whole.

Ronna: He just knew.

Seth: That this was really decisive. It stikes me now that it's really like Socrates, isn't it?, in his autobiography in the *Phaedo* (97b–e). Socrates figures out what must have been in Anaxagoras's book without ever opening it up. I think Strauss had this ability, just given some hint, to fill it in rapidly.

Ronna: That means he must have known the fundamental problems.

Seth: Well, you have this very funny spiral, in which he began with Jewish things, and kept on spinning back to antiquity. So, everybody always felt that the framework he had was much larger than anything that we had; we felt we didn't really understand what he was saying.

Ronna: Did he ever say anything like, "When you're reading this book, try to understand the author as he understood himself." Things like that?

Seth: I do remember that, after having imbibed this doctrine, I told Blanckenhagen that if Shakespeare had wanted to, he could have written dialogues. Blanckenhagen, who had become a friend of Strauss by this time, told him this. And Strauss said he had never heard anything so true in all his life, coming out of the mouth of babes.

Ronna: He liked your insight.

Seth: I remember I was once with Strauss and Blanckenhagen and as I was leaving I said, "Well, in the last words of the *Republic*, 'Eu prattomen.'" And Strauss said, "That's it, that's the double meaning of justice."

Michael: Doing well and faring well?

Seth: This one phrase expresses the notion that we fare well by doing well—in the context, acting justly—and at the same time it recalls the difference between justice as minding one's own business and doing so well or perfectly. Plato had put a seal on the entire argument of the *Republic* in two last words. But Strauss had not seen it. And I just uttered it by accident.

Ronna: Without realizing what you were saying?

Seth: Without realizing that it said it all exactly in the way Strauss had seen it; but he hadn't connected it with this formula.

Michael: Did you ever think of Strauss as a model? I mean, when you later started teaching, or in studying things?

Seth: Well, I was always unbalanced in a way that he wasn't.

Ronna: In which direction?

Seth: In paying attention to the details.

Ronna: Even if you didn't see the larger argument, you would be working through the pieces that fascinated you?

Seth: Working them out. Strauss never did that, I don't think, in his courses.

Ronna: But don't you have to be willing to ponder the puzzle before you know how it fits together?

Seth: Well, I'm sure Strauss must have done it, but not in class, whereas I had no shame. Actually, there was a big difference between Strauss's tutorials and the lectures, very noticeable.

Ronna: Can you describe it?

Seth: He was much more reticent in class than he was in the tutorials. Years later, he would say in class what he had said in the tutorials but had not said at that time.

Ronna: He'd try things out in the tutorials?

Seth: Maybe that was it. He was much more cautious in public.

Michael: Was your Strauss everybody's Strauss?

Seth: I don't think so.

Michael: Did the students have disagreements they discussed?

Seth: I know there was a disagreement with Gourevitch, very early, who was suspicious of this historical scholarship, and saw it as contradictory, with regard to the antihistoricism.

Michael: That turned out to be Gourevitch's article, later on.[41]

Seth: Strauss thought that what he was doing was something like what Aristotle was doing in the first book of the *Metaphysics,* and Gourevitch thought it was much more like what Heidegger or Nietzsche was doing.

Michael: What about Bloom?

Seth: I remember the day on which he was converted. The difference between me and others, or at least between me and Bloom, is that I was converted at once without being converted, I had at that time no beliefs at all.

Robert: So no reason to resist?

Seth: No, and it all sounded extraordinarily plausible. Anyway, what I always thought was the point of conversion for Bloom—I never asked him if

---

41. Victor Gourevitch, "Philosophy and Politics," I–II, *Review of Metaphysics* 32 (1968): 58–84, 281–328.

it was really true—was in Strauss's course on Aristotle's *Politics,* where Bloom had argued in every class, about one thing or another.

Ronna: Quarreled with Strauss?

Seth: Yes. It had to do with the difference between the scientific horizon and the human horizon. Strauss was claiming that while the scientific horizon had changed enormously, the claim of science that the human horizon had changed was false. There was no evidence that anything further was known.

Ronna: Whereas Bloom thought there was progress?

Seth: Yes. So, on this particular day, Strauss made this point, and Bloom said, "What about infantile sexuality?" Strauss replied, "Oh, I think that any thoughtful nursemaid always knew that." The scales fell from his eyes. I always thought that was it, this very simple remark.

Michael: If you look at the way all the Strauss lectures began, it was always with the relativist problem, or the fact-value distinction. And it looks like, as a movement, it started in terms of a moral question that translated into a contemporary political issue. But was that a reason for your attachment to Strauss in the way it seemed to be for others?

Seth: No. All that was assumed, that these other theses couldn't be true. That seemed so obvious to me, for no reason at all.

Michael: So this has to do with the fact that other people experienced it as a sort of conversion. It looks as if they came to it with a position that had to be overcome.

Ronna: So what you were attracted to in Strauss wasn't necessarily what attracted others.

Michael: But you attended classes, you must have heard these things.

Seth: I never paid attention to that part. I remember he was amazing at giving hints as to how to read books. He would say something about how to read *Gulliver's Travels,*

Michael: What Bloom says about *Gulliver's Travels?*

Seth: Yes, that's from Strauss.

Ronna: What's that?

Michael: Just that it's ancients versus moderns. So book I is modern political practice, book II is ancient political practice, book III is modern theory or modern philosophy, book IV is ancient utopian politics based on political philosophy.

Seth: Right. Strauss had an enormous number of different books, all of which he knew in this way that he could say what they were about.

Robert: But in the way you mentioned before, that he hadn't really studied the whole *Odyssey?*

Seth: Well, in that case the importance of *physis,* which he had learned in some way from Reinhardt,[42] allowed him to connect his reflections on the nature of philosophy with this passage in the *Odyssey.*

Robert: Was there a particular point when people began to think of themselves as "Straussians"?

Seth: It became very big after 1955, after I left. A terrible thing happened in the spring of '52, which I don't really understand. Strauss had a tremendous double falling-out, with both Grene and Blanckenhagen. It was within a very short period, because they didn't meet until '51, at my birthday party given by Blanckenhagen, in order for Strauss to meet Grene. Strauss gave me as a birthday present his essay, "How to Read Spinoza," with a wonderful quotation from Cicero.

Ronna: What a great birthday present.

Seth: Right. Anyway, within a year something happened. It had something to do with the fact that the "Straussians," as they would now be called, had become so powerful it aroused resentment.

Michael: Who would have been in that group?

Seth: Well, Gourevitch and Bloom and myself.

Ronna: Was Gildin there?

Seth: Gildin came later. But there were people from St. John's, like Goldwin, in the political science department. Cropsey and Jaffa had come from the New School.[43] There was quite a group. And it obviously was causing tremendous tension. Blanckenhagen told me that this had happened. He had not yet broken with Strauss. I remember as a student being puzzled by what was really going on.

Ronna: Do you think you understand it now?

Seth: If you think of the two cases in which grown men confronted Strauss, it's interesting. The attraction lasts for a very short time before they go back to what they are.

Robert: Which two?

Seth: Grene and Blanckenhagen. In both cases, they felt this extraordinary electric effect. They were just like us, they had never heard anything like this.

---

42. Karl Reinhardt (1886–1958), author of books on Homer, Sophocles, and Parmenides.

43. Hilail Gildin, professor in the department of philosophy at Queens College, CUNY and editor-in-chief of *Interpretation.* His work in modern political philosophy includes a book on Rousseau. Robert Goldwin was a tutor and dean at St. John's College. Joseph Cropsey, professor emeritus in the department of political science at the University of Chicago, works in the history of political philosophy, ancient and modern. His books include studies of Adam Smith and Plato, among others, and he was co-editor, with Leo Strauss, of *History of Political Philosophy* (3d ed., Chicago: University of Chicago Press, 1987). For Harry Jaffa see above, n. 20.

This was particularly true for Blanckenhagen. It really turned him upside down.

Ronna: But only provisionally?

Seth: He turned right-side-up again.

Robert: What was it more specifically?

Seth: I suppose there are two ways of putting it. On the theoretical level, it was the problem of historicism: he wouldn't give that up. But looking at it in light of what we've been talking about, you could say that what he wasn't willing to give up was himself. He identified the problem with historicism, but that's not really what the issue was.

Robert: How would this show up?

Seth: He once was at a party and met a surgeon who asked him about his hump: "When did you get it? You must have had tuberculosis. Nine or ten?" Blanckenhagen said, "Yes." Then the surgeon said, "We can get rid of it. All you have to do is stay in bed for a year." And he said no.[44]

Ronna: This is who I am?

Seth: Well, it's complicated by the fact that he always thought he was going to die young. You had these two men who were very different, but both were always thinking of death. In Grene's case it was a kind of will to death, whereas for Blanckenhagen, it was based on the nature of his body. So every year was very precious. There was no will to die, just an acceptance.

Ronna: But he didn't die young.

Seth: No, you see, that's it. And Grene's still going strong.

Michael: Teaching is such a funny thing. You have to catch the person being taught at the age when the self is still being constituted. So when this big shock occurs, it's not so much that they don't go back to what they previously were; they really weren't anything. And in ten years, the reason they'll still be with it is that they won't want to give up themselves and what they are.

Robert: So Strauss's influence on Blanckenhagen and Grene looks as if it wouldn't be possible.

Seth: That's what's so strange. It was really like love, it had an extraordinary effect. But maybe it was a necessity that they right themselves.

Michael: It might be possible in rare cases for a perfect convergence to occur, in which someone's ready to learn something and someone's there to teach, and under those circumstances, someone might get turned upside down more in accordance with his own nature.

---

44. Victor Gourevitch, speaking at the memorial service for Benardete at NYU on 1 February 2002, recalled Benardete once saying that Blanckenhagen "wore his hunchback like folded wings."

Ronna: I thought you once mentioned a remark of Strauss's, that you could never convert a colleague or another adult.

Seth: I don't know if he said never, just that he had not convinced anybody of his own age. I think he said that before he met Blanckenhagen.

VISITORS

MARTIN BUBER

Seth: One spring, Martin Buber came to Chicago. He was to speak at Hillel House, and Strauss was asked to introduce him. I was sitting on a couch with Mrs. Strauss. Buber came in, looking very dignified.

Ronna: Venerable?

Seth: Very venerable. He sat right next to Strauss, next to the podium. And Strauss began this way: "I have the great pleasure to introduce Martin Buber, who is probably the greatest Jewish thinker since Mmm . . ." And after a long time it finally came out "Moses." Then he went on, "since Moses Mmm . . ." Everybody thought—

Ronna: Maimonides, at least.

Seth: Right. But Strauss continued, "Mmm . . ." and at last, "Mendelssohn." I flipped over the back of the chair. I thought it was the funniest thing I had ever heard. What happened was—you could see from Buber's face—when Strauss said "Moses," he blew up like a frog, and then he was slightly deflated when Strauss said "Moses Mmm . . ." and completely so by the end.

Ronna: What happened to Mrs. Strauss when you flipped over?

Seth: She held my hand, I think.

Ronna: That must have been very funny.

Seth: About two weeks later Blanckenhagen and I were at Strauss's house. At one point Strauss turns to Blanckenhagen and asks, "Do you know a student named Allan Bloom?" And Blanckenhagen says, "Yes." Strauss says, "You know, he's not the most intelligent student." And Blanckenhagen says, "No, but very intelligent." Strauss says, "But not the most intelligent." And Blanckenhagen says, "But intelligent." So they had this little conversation. What was the point of this? Strauss then told Blanckenhagen and me, "Well, this extraordinary thing happened to me the day after Buber's talk. Bloom was walking me home, and I stopped with great thoughtfulness and said to him, 'You know I think that Martin Buber is vain.' And Bloom said, 'Why, of course.' How did he figure it out? It took me two weeks to figure it out." I told the story to Bloom many years later and he said that what it meant was Strauss thought it possible not to be vain, and we never thought that.

Ronna: He had an elevated understanding of human beings?

Michael: Of the possibility of human beings.

Seth: Yes. Of course, I'm not sure that explains the contretemps with Blanckenhagen.

KARL REINHARDT

Seth: When Reinhardt was in Chicago Strauss discussed Aristophanes with him. Aristophanes is very simple, he said, it's really just *nomos* versus *physis* [convention versus nature]. Reinhardt was outraged, at least at first. Strauss, in telling me this story, said, "I don't see why anyone ever wrote esoterically. Even when they write things that are perfectly plain nobody ever understands."

Ronna: Do you have any idea why Reinhardt was angry or shocked?

Seth: That Aristophanes stood for the opposition between *nomos* and pleasure. This is connected with another thing. When Strauss began to study Aristophanes, he read some of the literature. One thing he read was a commentary on the *Frogs*, which he thought was quite good. And he said, "But of course it's held up by moralism. The Germans had to pay a terrible price for Hitler."

Robert: They were too moralistic because they had the burden of Hitler on their shoulders?

Seth: Right. Reinhardt made a very good comment. He said to Strauss that he thought all classical scholars were like adolescent girls when it came to good and evil. Then it turned out that he too was like that.

Ronna: Meaning?

Seth: Meaning it was black and white, no shading at all. It's amazing how true it is.

Michael: Do you think that is distinctive of classicists?

Seth: I thought it was, but I'm not sure. These people are interested in the noble, but when the noble is then identified with the moral, it comes out in this very innocent, naive manner.

KURT RIEZLER

Seth: Riezler came to Chicago and everybody knew about him.[45] So we all went to his first class, at night. He comes in—beautiful white hair, streaming back, wonderful face. He sits down at the desk. He looks at us, we look

---

45. Kurt Riezler (1882–1955), who taught in the New School philosophy department, wrote on Parmenides, art, and politics.

at him. At that point, he begins to grin and then asks, "Does anyone know who Plato was?" Everybody is silent. Not a word. Riezler tries again, and asks, "Well, does anyone know who Aristotle was?" So everybody left. No one came to his class after that.

Michael: Did anyone ever talk to Strauss about it?

Seth: I don't think anybody ever told him how disastrous this was.

Ronna: You were very generous, you gave him his one introduction.

Seth: I did think it was terrible at the time, but I wouldn't go back.

ARNOLD TOYNBEE

Seth: Shortly after I got on the Committee, Toynbee was invited, and that was the first big conference I ever attended. They had a very large oval table that occupied the whole room in the Social Science Building. It was so big that the dust in the middle of the table had never been cleaned. It got thicker and thicker because no one could reach their arms across this huge table. Anyway, everybody was there. Toynbee was very famous at that time.

Robert: Do you know what year this was?

Seth: It must have been 1949, or it could have been in the early '50s. What did they want to discuss with Toynbee?, why my specialty was not regarded by you as a special civilization. How come you left out the Hellenistic Age?, that was a separate civilization. There was this guy named [Marshall] Hodgson, who was a Quaker Arabist, whose speciality was the Assassins, and he says, "I want the Assassins to be a special civilization; it has all the criteria that you have laid down." Toynbee was very nice, because he did nothing but nod his head and said that if he ever revised it, he would take all these things into account. The response to Toynbee was typical of the Committee. But the height was Eliot's visit.

T. S. ELIOT

Seth: They had hired him to give a series of talks at Chicago on education, and then he was also to give a series of seminars for the Committee, to alternate with [Friedrich] Hayek. He didn't know that it was going to be alternating. He wasn't given a topic for the seminar. So at the very first meeting, which all the students and all the faculty attended, they had to decide what the topic would be. The topic they decided on was none other than poetry and philosophy. So that was the first meeting. Second meeting, this having been set as the topic, [John U.] Neff turned to Bloom, as the youngest student, to ask a question. He had no idea what to ask, he didn't know what was going on. So I cropped up and said, "Don't you agree with what Gorgias says, that tragedy is a deception in which the deceived are wiser than the undeceived?" And Eliot nodded his head and said, "Yes." Then Redfield senior said (low voice) "I don't know about that. I don't think if you are deceived you can be wiser . . ." They had this crazy discussion, about what Gorgias said. Then they decided that students should give papers on Eliot's poetry, that he would listen to. So whom did they choose? Mahdi was supposed to give the first paper,[46] then a woman mathematician. Mahdi's paper, no one understood.

Ronna: Was it about Arabic things?

Seth: No, about Eliot's poetry. And the woman's paper was about Eliot's conversion, in 1932 or whatever the date was, and there he was at the end of the table. It was a complete disaster. Hayek tried to rescue this, by saying he thought that poetry consists in the examination of everything that lies outside the intersects of ordinary language, like railroad tracks, but outside. Then the woman mathematician says, "Let me pursue that image. If we sort out the trains, we have the Limited going in one direction, and we have freight trains going in another, and cross signals . . ." It was the most extraordinary development of this image, Eliot sitting absolutely the same way throughout.

Ronna: Quietly?

Seth: Absolutely quietly. You thought you were in the presence of a New England preacher of the nineteenth century. That was the impression you got. At the end of the first session of the seminar, Mrs. Neff had arranged a party for Eliot, but she had failed to tell him. In the meantime, he had planned to go to another party with people who knew about him from St. Louis, and that was arranged by the wife of one of the members of the Committee. So when the first seminar ended, about nine or so, he got up. Mrs. Neff, who was a very old woman at that time, moved up to him on the left side, and this other woman moved up to him on the right side, and they began to pull on him. It was like Pentheus being pulled apart by the two Bacchantes. They were shouting at one another, about whose party he was going to. Exactly at this point Shils came up and tried to calm them down,[47] but Mrs. Neff paid no attention.

Michael: So whose party did Eliot go to?

46. Muhsin Mahdi, born in 1926 in Iraq, was professor of Arabic at Harvard from 1969–99 and before that at Chicago. He is a translator and interpreter of Alfarabi and leading scholar of Islamic political thought.

47. Edward Shils (1910–95), professor of sociology at the University of Chicago from 1938 to 1994 and an honorary fellow of Peterhouse, Cambridge, made contributions to social philosophy and sociological theory.

Seth: I don't know what happened, because I didn't go to either party.

Ronna: So this went on for a whole semester?

Seth: This went on for a whole semester. We finally got to meet Eliot at a party the Neffs had. Did I ever tell you about the apple strudel parties? There were these strudel parties that the students were invited to, at Neff's house, which consisted of apple strudel, heaped with whipped cream, and white wine. But it was always kept behind a Chinese screen in the second living room. Before you could get to it, you had to go through an excruciating, truly excruciating, confrontation with whatever bigwig was there. Everybody sat down, and the students were supposed to ask the bigwig questions.

Ronna: The *rite de passage,* for the strudel?

Seth: That's right. Everybody who had been there before knew that you kept your mouth shut, otherwise you'd never get to the strudel, because the guest might say something. The funniest occasion was when they had Louis Massignon, the expert on Arab mysticism, and Colin Clarke, who was an economist from Australia.

Ronna: Together?

Seth: They were both on the Committee for one term at the same time. So after they were introduced, some foreign student said that he had a question for Professor Massignon. The question is (in some kind of accent), "In my country, there is one party, party A, with many, many fertilizer and no land, and another party, party B, with many, many land and no fertilizer. Monsieur Massignon, What is the explanation? How can you solve this problem?" He wanted to talk to Colin Clarke, but he got it all mixed up. Oh yes, someone did ask Massignon a question. He talked about how terrible the Jewish terrorists were.

Ronna: In Palestine?

Seth: Yes, and someone said, "Well, aren't there also Arab terrorists?" And he said, "Yes, that's true. Yes. They blow up buildings too. But they do it gently."

Michael: So what happened at this particular strudel party for Eliot?

Seth: At that party there was champagne. He was standing in a corner, where I found him and we began talking.

Ronna: Do you remember what were you discussing?

Seth: Plutarch's translation, no, it was Amyot's translation of Plutarch, in relation to Shakespeare, or something like that. Anyway, I had a glass of champagne in my hand. I got so excited as I was talking to him, I was moving my hand back and forth very rapidly, and his eyes were glazed, wondering when this thing was finally going to spill all over him. He was nodding his head, therefore, agreeing with everything I said, he couldn't help himself.

Robert: How did the rest of his seminar go?

Seth: I remember his remark at the end of the last session. Neff, who was always sitting on his left, thanked him for having presided over these very stimulating discussions and so forth. Eliot, who had a part right down the middle of his head, put his head almost on the table so you could hardly hear him as he talked and said, "I don't know what others have learned from this occasion, but I have learned something: how a seminar is conducted."

Michael: It sounds like the Neffs had the most famous literary lights in the world trooping in every other semester.

Seth: I remember when the Rector of the University of Paris came. He was an expert on Spanish history in the second part of the eighteenth century, when nothing happened. It was very easy to be an expert.

Ronna: You could know everything.

Seth: Absolutely everything about this. But he was so drunk at the apple strudel party that he—who usually kept his mouth shut—said, "Sir, Spain has saved America three times." And he began to keel over. He said, "Once," and he couldn't remember. He never got through any of them. Everybody was startled, three times saved by Spain.

Michael: Do you think you learned something from these visiting dignitaries?

Seth: How absurd people are. That was the great lesson, you know. Everyone was really at their worst, I think.

Ronna: Because of the situation?

Seth: I think it must have been. All of this was supported by Mrs. Neff's money.

Ronna: It was her family money?

Seth: She was the heiress to a large Hawaiian fortune. They owned the Matson Line, luxury ocean liners, and the Honolulu paper. She was overheard to say once, "I think we shall have to renew the question of the Germans on the Committee."

Robert: Nothing ever came up of that?

Seth: No, no, she was as nutty as a fruitcake. She had a certain kind of charm, though, of somebody well brought up, who had spent her entire life slumming culturally, on the highest level. You know, they also invited Beazley once.[48] But there was no strudel party for him. This was the first time I ever heard about him and Lady Beazley. He was not knighted yet. He gave a

---

48. John Davidson Beazley (1885–1970), professor of classical archaeology and art at Oxford from 1925 to 1956, was an authority on black-figure and red-figure pottery.

wonderful lecture, called "The World of the Etruscan Mirror." He had a very high-pitched voice. He showed slides, and there was this picture on the back of an Etruscan mirror, of Heracles holding up the world. I still remember this extraordinary expression. He said, "There's Heracles, slightly muscle-bound perhaps, holding up the world, he grins and bears it." I was absolutely enchanted. I had never heard anything like it.

Ronna: He was British?

Seth: Yes. At the dinner, Lady Beazley was about to be introduced to Blanck-enhagen and she said in a loud voice, "If he is one of those Germans who came over after the war, I shall not speak to him." So they didn't meet, you see. Then they all sat down to dinner, and somebody was telling a story about a hedgehog. Blanckenhagen asked, "What's the German for hedgehog?" All these professors sitting around the table don't know. Then Lady Beazley said, "I know. But I haven't spoken German since 1933 and I don't intend to start now."

Chapter 2

ATHENS, ROME, AND FLORENCE

1952–54

GOING ABROAD

Seth: The Committee had arranged a Ford Fellowship for me, in 1953, because I said I wanted to study at the University of Florence under Pasquali, who was a great name.[1] But it turned out Pasquali had been killed that summer, before I came.

Ronna: In an automobile accident?

Seth: It was with a Vespa. Years later I learned the true story of Pasquali, from Momigliano,[2] who knows all things like that. Pasquali, even though he was not a Fascist, wanted to be a senator. Mussolini, who was tuned in to everyone's defects, knew this about Pasquali, and therefore never gave it to him. However, one month before he was hung upside down, he made Pasquali a senator. So the war comes to an end and Pasquali is a senator. He thinks that all the partisans are out to kill him. But according to Momigliano, no one's going to kill him, because they all knew of this silly ambition of his. But he went crazy, and they put him in a loony bin. He was there from the end of the war until the summer of '53. The day he walked out of the loony bin, he was run over by a Vespa. So I never got to study with Pasquali.

Michael: And you got this Ford Fellowship on the basis of wanting to study with a man who actually was in a loony bin.

---

1. Giorgio Pasquali (1885–1952), classical philologist.
2. Arnaldo Momigliano (1908–87), professor of ancient history at University College, London from 1951 to 1975, regular visiting professor at the University of Chicago from 1975 to 1987. He was a leading student of the writing of history in the ancient world, and published studies of Hebrew and Persian as well as Greek and Roman historiography.

Ronna: What did Pasquali work on?

Seth: He had written an extraordinary book called *Storia della tradizione e critica del testo,* which is a book about this big [hands stretched out wide]. It started out as a review of Paul Maas's book called *Textkritik,* which he had written for *Gnomon* before the war, maybe in '36 or something like that. Maas had given the rules for making up stemmata for codices. Then Pasquali expanded his review, discussing absolutely every counterexample, which turned out to be every author except three, in all of antiquity. It was an extraordinarily interesting and impressive achievement.

Ronna: So you wanted to do these philological things with him?

Seth: I thought I should learn modern philology. There was no one in Chicago who taught these things. Even though Einarson knew it, he would never teach this stuff.

JAMES BALDWIN

Ronna: So you went from Chicago to Italy in 1953–54?

Seth: The fellowship in Italy was the second one. There was an earlier fellowship in Greece, at the American School in Athens.

Robert: When was that?

Seth: I left Chicago in 1952. I traveled abroad by boat, on the *Normandy,* and had a wonderful time, because everybody at the table was so congenial. One of the passengers was James Baldwin.

Ronna: Now, how old were you then?

Seth: Twenty-two.

Michael: Was Baldwin well known yet?

Seth: He had just published his first novel, *Go Tell It on the Mountain.* We had long discussions on this long trip.

Robert: How long did it last?

Seth: Five or six days. Baldwin was going back to Paris. He hadn't written anything about the race problem. He was obviously very intelligent, but he gave an extraordinary impression of fear and uncertainty, and sort of bewilderment, really, about things. He talked about the fact that, when he was growing up, you could not go downtown.

Ronna: Where did he grow up?

Seth: In Harlem. It was impossible to go on Park Avenue or Fifth Avenue without being immediately picked up by the police. Somehow that had remained as the crucial experience. Then being deracinated in France somehow exacerbated that.

Ronna: He lived abroad permanently?

Seth: Yes.

Robert: Do you remember what you talked about?

Seth: The discussions turned on the question of provinciality. I had the impression at the time that he was not convinced that you could escape from it, or he was unwilling to escape from it. It was the whites who were determining his role, that's what we talked about. He was being determined by this other group. And therefore it was only a negative relation.

Michael: Does that show up in the writing?—that somehow there's an awareness of having certain themes forced upon him that otherwise wouldn't have been the case?

Robert: Of the things I've read, one gets the sense of someone who feels trapped. You were talking about fear, this experience of police; you can almost see that as an image for a more general problem.

Michael: Well, especially when one adds homosexuality.

Seth: That looked like another thing that was being determined by the society that had accepted him, the white society, that he was playing a role for them.

Robert: They had a place for that, if you could fit into it.

Seth: I thought he didn't know who he was.

Robert: That is the theme, as far as I understand it, of all his work, the problem of his identity, never being able to pin down in a decisive way exactly who he is. It's always oscillating. In so many ways, he is "white." You know, he's read by the white society, he's intelligent, he writes well; on the other hand, he is "black," but he doesn't really fit into that either. So there's this constant churning. Until finally, very late in his life—I forget the name of the book—he had been hounded by all the Black Power people, for being a traitor, and then, in one of those last books, he sort of caved in, although I remember thinking somehow it was a posture. One had the sense of this very unhappy person. I think of that sad face, those eyes.

Seth: Yes.

Ronna: The individual is an infinite flux and indeterminacy, then you have these kinds, black, homosexual, and so forth. That's supposed to give the individual some kind of identity, but it's inevitably alienating because it's not individual, it's a type.

Michael: Of course, there are always those things, but it's different from, say, family roles, which determine you vis-à-vis another particular human being. The fact that you're black or white may give a kind of general solidarity, but if you're a daughter or father, there's a particular relation that disposes you toward a particular human being.

Seth: That would make sense of the Christian martyr.

Robert: How so?

Seth: In other words, you're under the Roman Empire and you either have to confess or deny. And your answer is "I am a Christian." That looks totally determinate because of the imitation involved.

Ronna: Imitation of?

Seth: Imitation of Christ. But as it's understood by the would-be martyr himself or herself, that's what he is. It really shows up in Paul, the way it's described, "dead in Christ."

ENGLAND: JOHN DAVIDSON BEAZLEY, C. M. BOWRA, MAURICE POWICKE

Seth: On my way to Athens, I went to England first. I had $3,000, I think, from the Chicago fellowship, which was quite a lot of money. But it was given in four lump sums, and I spent all the money on books in Oxford before I ever got to Athens. I was supposed to pay my bill for food and board, but I didn't have any money to pay it. The director would call me in once a month and ask, "When are you going to pay the bill?" and I always said, "They haven't paid me yet."

Robert: You didn't tell them that they had already paid you and you had spent it all.

Seth: When I got to England, I had letters of introduction that Grene had given me to various people. One of them was Beazley, one was Bowra, and the other was Sir Maurice Powicke, who was a medieval historian.[3] Powicke was the first one I visited. I had tea with him and his wife. He said, "You know, everyone thinks that we British are hypocritical. But in fact, it just conceals our benevolence." Then I went to see Beazley, who was in the Ashmolean, where he had a special table.

Ronna: Had you met him already at Chicago?

Seth: No, I had heard him, but I had not met him. We talked about various things. Then, as I was getting up to leave, he said, "And how do you pronounce your name?" So I told him. And he said, "Where's the accent?" I said, "There isn't any accent." And he said, "Oh. A double spondee. Unique, I think. Goodbye."

Ronna: That was his contribution to your self-knowledge.

Seth: Isn't that amazing? Then I met Bowra, who gave me lunch at Wadham, where he was the warden. Years later he became vice-chancellor. The

---

3. On Beazley, see chap. 1, n. 48. C. M. Bowra (1898–1971), who was warden of Wadham College, Oxford from 1922 to 1971 and vice chancellor from 1951 to 1954, wrote on Greek lyric poetry and Sophocles. Maurice Powicke (1879–1963) was a fellow of Balliol College, Oxford.

first Sunday of the school term, the new chaplain of the university gave as his first sermon a denunciation of homosexuality at Oxford. The students immediately went to the vice-chancellor to ask him what he had to say. Headline of the Oxford paper: "Vice-Chancellor, Author of *The Greek Experience,* Absolutely Denies the Charges of the Chaplain." Author of *The Greek Experience.* This man, notorious as the center of the homosexual community at Oxford.

Ronna: Do you remember what you talked about with Bowra when you met him that day?

Seth: He was very amusing, as he was supposed to be. I do remember a funny story he told me about Beazley. He once met Beazley on the path of one of the colleges, and Beazley asked him what he had been reading. He had just finished Euripides' *Hecuba,* and he thought this was the very worst play of Euripides he had ever read. And Beazley said, "Whichever play of Euripides you read the last, you always think that's the worst."

THE AMERICAN SCHOOL IN ATHENS

EVA BRANN

Michael: Did you meet anyone interesting at the American School in Athens?

Seth: Eva Brann was there,[4] from Yale. She was the object of a rivalry between two women, both of whom were ten years older than the rest of us. One of them was named Judith Perlzweig and the other was Helen Bacon.[5] She's the one who did work on the *Seven,* she wrote on the *Symposium,* literary essays. Both women wanted Eva to be their disciple, to model herself after them. Judith Perlzweig was an extremely forthright person; she always said what was on her mind. Helen Bacon was the opposite, a very lady-like person. Eva didn't even know that they were competing over her. I had to tell her, at the end of the spring.

Michael: What did she say?

Seth: Oh, she denied it.

Ronna: She was more or less your age?

Seth: I think she was a little older.

4. Eva Brann, who has been a tutor at St. John's College, Annapolis since 1951 and served as dean of the College from 1990 to 1997, is the author of works on education, the imagination, and time, and has collaborated on translations of Plato's *Sophist* and *Phaedo.*

5. Judith Perlzweig Binder, senior associate member of the American School of Classical Studies at Athens, has done archaeological work on lamps from the Athenian Agora. Helen Bacon, associated with the American Academy in Rome and the American School in Athens, taught classics at Barnard College and wrote on Greek tragedy.

Ronna: Had Eva met up with Jacob Klein yet when you were with her in Greece?

Seth: Oh no, no. That came about through me.

Ronna: How did that happen?

Seth: When [Richard] Weigle, who was the president of St. John's at the time, called me in to say that I was fired, I told him I had just the person for them—Eva Brann. I made him write down the name. So they called her up. And Eva came and fell in love with the place.

ISTANBUL RELATIVES

Seth: When I went to England on my way to Greece and spent all my money on books, I decided to take the Orient Express to get to Athens, not knowing that it takes two days to go through Yugoslavia alone. So I shipped my big valise from London, and I had no clothes. I wore the same clothes for the whole trip. When I arrived in Athens and opened my suitcase, which had been beautifully baled with wire, it was empty. There was nothing in it. They had taken all the clothes out. So I had almost no clothes for the first three months. But then I was going to go to Istanbul to meet my relatives, who turned out to be in the wool business. So the first thing they did was to make custom-made shirts, and custom-made pajamas, and two suits. I had these beautiful hand-made suits when I came back from Istanbul to Athens. So naturally the first day I wore them to dinner. And Eva Brann took one look at me and said, "Now I understand, clothes make the man."

Ronna: Who were the Istanbul relatives exactly?

Seth: My father's brothers. They were younger and not eligible for the Turkish draft.

Ronna: Which is what motivated your father to leave?

Seth: That made my father's mother want to move; she was determined to keep him out of the Turkish army. So when he got to America in 1917, he immediately enlisted in the American army, to get his citizenship. His wartime duty was guarding the hospital in St. Louis.

Ronna: Was there still a Sephardic community in Istanbul?

Seth: Very small. It was totally isolated when I went, but it obviously was breaking down because my cousins spoke Turkish among themselves.

Ronna: Before that it was all Ladino?

Seth: Yes, and they still talked Ladino to their parents, but not among themselves. The uncles apparently still had a recognizable accent speaking Turkish. After five hundred years, they hadn't gotten it down right.

Michael: In what language did you speak to them?

Seth: English, I think, English or French. They were very knowledgeable in all languages about commerce.

Robert: Could you recognize them as being related to you?

Seth: I knew they were mine from this experience. When I was in Chicago, I got appendicitis. My father had to be notified so they could do the operation. After the operation, about 10:00 at night, in the absolutely silent corridors of the University of Chicago hospital, all of a sudden there was this shout, "Where is Benardete?" It was one of the uncles, who shouted just as if he was in the middle of a bazaar. He was on a business trip and had been sent by my father to see how I was. Okay. Years later I get on the plane in Athens. We're forced down into Thessaloníki, we can't get to Istanbul that day. There was some kind of Greek beauty pageant going on in the hotel where we were put up for the night. In the early morning we started up again for Istanbul. After the wind-swept icy air field, we have to walk a half a mile. I get off the plane and what do I hear—"Benardete!"

Ronna: It was your uncle again?

Seth: A different uncle. Shouting from the other end of the air field. A family trait.

WERNER JAEGER

Seth: I met Jaeger in Athens, in the spring of 1953.[6] He had never been to Greece before. He came, took one look at the Acropolis, and took to his bed. Never left his room again. I suppose he got stomach flu or something. But it seemed very extraordinary. Particularly because when he recovered he said that the great Boeckh,[7] when he retired, had been given money by students to go to Greece and he refused on the grounds that it couldn't be as beautiful as his expectation.

Ronna: It would never live up to his imagination?

Seth: Reality couldn't compete with that. On one occasion while Jaeger was in Athens we had a visit from H. T. Wade-Gery, the historian.[8] He was staying at the British School, which shared a tennis court with the American school, and he came over with his wife one night after dinner. We were all sitting in a big circle. And Jaeger began to talk aloud. He was really dreaming: "I wonder what the Greeks must have thought about the Thessalian *Tagoi*,"

6. Werner Jaeger (1888–1961), German classicist, became a professor of classics at Harvard in 1939. He is best known for his book, *Paideia: The Ideals of Greek Culture,* and for his work on Aristotle's intellectual development.

7. Philipp August Boeckh (1785–1867), classical philologist.

8. H. T. Wade-Gery, ancient historian, fellow, and tutor at Wadham College, Oxford.

which is a word for leader, "the Thessalian *Tagoi*, what they thought about their *megalopsuchia*, their *andreia* . . ." It went on and on this way. All of a sudden, Wade-Gery said, "Oh, I think they must have thought of them the way the British think of the Irish—a rough lot." Years later I met Wade-Gery at Harvard and he said, "I heard that you don't think very much of Jaeger." I said, "Well, neither do you." He had completely forgotten this remark.

Ronna: Did you learn modern Greek during the year in Athens?

Seth: A little bit. In the spring I organized a boat trip. That was thought to be extraordinary. Not just because I had done it, but because no one had ever done it, in the entire history of the school.

Michael: You mean, no one had ever gone to the islands?

Seth: No one had ever gone this way, which was the cheapest way of doing it, or the only way of doing it at that time.

Michael: You, of course, who had read Homer, were aware of the possibility of doing this.

Seth: It was such a small city at that time. I went to the president of American Express, and he arranged it.

Ronna: Where did you go?

Seth: We went through all the Cyclades.

Ronna: Were you working or reading?

Seth: I read Homer when I was there. Then when I got to Italy I decided to write on the *Iliad*.

ROME AND FLORENCE

Ronna: Did you begin working on the *Iliad* as soon as you got to Florence?

Seth: Well, the summer after leaving Athens, I stayed at the Academy in Rome, before going on to Florence.

Ronna: Were you working or traveling?

Seth: I was just reading in the library, as I remember. But some funny things happened. There was a man by the name of Hecht, who had been trained as an archaeologist at Yale but quit just before he got his Ph.D. He had been at the American Academy sometime before this and was carrying on an affair with the wife of one of the painters in residence. The painter found out one evening, and they had a fight in front of the big stairs. But Hecht had been trained as a boxer at college, and knocked him out. The next day, the director of the Academy asked him to leave. He then became an art dealer. He was the one who negotiated the Metropolitan's purchase of the Euphronius vase for a million dollars. So this is my genealogy of how these things happen.

Ronna: Who was at the Academy when you were there?

Seth: Well, there were the ladies from Bryn Mawr and Vassar, who used to grade my jokes. The lunches and dinners were in the portico of the Academy. And there were all these ladies who, although quite different, where recognizably of the same order.

Ronna: They were your age?

Seth: No, no, they were all in their fifties or sixties.

Ronna: What were they doing there?

Seth: They were Roman historians. There was Lily Ross-Taylor, who was like a sergeant-major.[9] She was so powerful that all her students from Bryn Mawr seemed very mousy. That was very noticeable, that she was exactly the opposite of everyone who was devoted to her.

Robert: So what was this grading?

Seth: I would constantly tell stories. And they would say B+, or that's an A– story.

LORD AND LADY BEAZLEY

Ronna: You mentioned that you met Beazley and Lady Beazley in Rome. Were they connected with the Academy?

Seth: No, no. Beazley lived in Oxford. He just traveled everywhere. In Rome I had met a Greek archaeologist, who is now in Australia, named Cambitoglou, a student of Beazley's.[10] So when Beazley came through Rome, we spent some time together. Beazley had a pet goose, which died. He had an assistant named Miss Price, and they were so heartbroken about the goose that they renamed Miss Price "Goosey." One day Cambitoglou was invited for lunch, and it was fish. So there was Miss Price—Goosey, Cambitoglou, Beazley, and Mrs. Beazley. The fish came in from the kitchen. The first thing Mrs. Beazley did was to very carefully remove all the skin from the fish, and pile it up on one plate. She turned to Cambitoglou and said, "You like skin, don't you?" He said, "No." And she said "Well, we'll give it to Goosey." So Goosey got all the skin of the fish and the best part was given to Beazley.

Ronna: Who was Lady Beazley?

Seth: She was the widow of an officer who had died in the First World War, and had married Beazley about 1920 or something like that. When they

9. Lily Ross-Taylor (1886–1969) was professor of Latin at Bryn Mawr College.

10. Alexander Cambitoglou, professor emeritus of archaeology and curator of the Nicholson Museum of Antiquities, University of Sydney.

were in Naples and Beazley was working, Lady Beazley said, "Jackie dear, why are you working so hard? After all, I already am Lady Beazley."

Ronna: Did you see the Beazleys often?

Seth: I remember once I was going with them to a restaurant in Rome. So we got in a cab. I was sitting in the front with the cab driver and the rest were in the back. I murmured something to the cab driver, and Lady Beazley said "Don't talk to the cab driver when we're driving!" She had very strict rules about everything. So they never went to a hotel which had an elevator.

Robert: Did you understand the grounds of this rule?

Seth: No. I mean, what difference did it make? They could always get a ground-floor apartment. They came from Jerusalem to Athens, you see. And the American School had booked them in a hotel with an elevator. So the first thing that Mrs. Beazley did was go over to the desk, pick up the phone and call up another hotel which didn't have an elevator. All these extraordinary rules.

Michael: Was it snobbishness? I mean, don't talk to the cab driver because you don't talk to cab drivers?

Seth: No, no, no.

Ronna: Danger?

Seth: Everything was danger, you see. That had something to do with the *kredemnon* she made.

Ronna: What's that?

Seth: We were on the patio of a hotel overlooking Rome, above a restaurant, and it became a little bit chilly. So Lady Beazley said "Jackie dear, you must put on your *kredemnon*." I said, "What's a *kredemnon*?" And as he was putting on this white tube of wool, which had straps over the shoulders, she said "Well that's an intelligent question. Don't you remember from the fifth book of the *Odyssey*? When Odysseus left the island of Calypso, his raft is overturned, and he is saved by a *kredemnon*, which was given to him by a goddess of the sea."

Ronna: Did you remember?

Seth: Yes. And she said, "Well this is something I knitted for the RAF during the war. Of course, I never did them in white. That was only for Jackie. The rest of them were in color. And of course they didn't have straps. I put on straps for Jackie because his shoulders are so broad." Here's this man seventy years old. There was *phantasia* working on a large scale here.

Ronna: Correcting the lines of perspective.

Seth: Right. Every one of these things that she knitted went to an RAF person with a little note saying, "This is a *kredemnon*. It is called a *kredemnon* because Odysseus . . ."

Roma: These soldiers on the front were hooked up with the heroic tradition of Homer.

Seth: Right, right.

Michael: So in the case of a plane crash, they had something to get them through.

Seth: The advantage of it not having anything on it was, if you put it, for instance, on the knee, if it got cold or anything like that, it could stretch to anything, or you could use it as a hat.

Robert: The all-purpose item, except for Jackie's.

Seth: This is connected, I think, with what Momigliano told me about him. The first time he met him, Beazley says to him, "Who was the best English king?" Momigliano says, "I don't know." And Beazley says, "Oh, I think it was Alfred." Momigliano said this was very typical of them, of the dons. Wade-Gery thought that the world had declined from 550 B.C. on. The only high point after 550 was the Battle of Thermopylae. And if you asked him, he could tell you exactly what the Spartans were thinking before the Persian attack. So these two, Beazley and Wade-Gery, fit in with Tolkien, who was the apologist. They had this little group. T. H. White was another one, and C. S. Lewis. They were impressed by the glories of the Middle Ages, in a very strange, child-like manner.

Michael: If you look at Tolkien's children's books, on the one hand, it's a celebration of the medieval, but on the other hand, it's bourgeois Englishmen. In a way it's just the nation for which Napoleon had such contempt. The real heroes are shopkeepers, these little Hobbits.

ELLIOTT CARTER

Michael: Wasn't it during this time in Rome that you met the Carters?[11]

Seth: The Carters were living at the Academy. He had a fellowship in music. The very striking thing was—which has proved to be constantly true—this extraordinary interest in things outside of music, like literature and so forth. Carter understood himself as belonging to the second wave of modernism, after Joyce, and Stravinsky, I suppose. So he was very much formed by modernism. But at the same time, like Eliot, he went back to everything before. He obviously had, in the previous ten years, worked out his theory about music and time, which was somehow the equivalent of Proust.

11. Elliott Carter (1908–), American composer, one of the major innovators in twentieth century music, whose compositions include symphonies, concertos, and string quartets. He is the winner of two Pulitzer prizes.

Ronna: Can you explain that?

Seth: Well, it wasn't the same theory. But he was trying to do something with time in music, where it never had been done before. In other words, one stage beyond counterpoint, where you have various lines responding to one another. But in counterpoint they're responding to each other on the basis of a grid that has been worked out before, whereas he has this responding at the time. That is supposed to be the true experience about time, constant change.

Ronna: And what Proust did for literature, he wants to do for music?

Seth: I think so. You know, he taught at St. John's.

Ronna: I didn't know that.

Seth: Many years earlier, when he knew Nabokov—Nicholas Nabokov, a cousin of Vladimir—who taught there. Nabokov was a great ladies' man. One of the students told me, she met him on the bus from Baltimore to Annapolis, and by the time they reached Annapolis, he had already proposed.

Ronna: So Carter taught everything that all the St. Johns' tutors taught?

Seth: I don't think he was there that long. It was when Scott Buchanan was there, when things fell apart.

Robert: So did he think that music was for the sake of something else?

Seth: He had a note somewhere, in one of his essays, on Plato's *Sophist*. He saw something in music like the discovery of the Stranger in the *Sophist*, where the paradigm they set up for understanding an art, namely fishing, turns out to be the paradigm for the sophist, not on that level, but in terms of hunting. Carter thought of that as the model for what he was trying to do. Something is set up and then you discover that it has another meaning as you go on in time.

Michael: Did you have conversations like this about music?

Seth: That's what I remember. He used to talk about the humiliating character of being a composer. One time we went to a concert being given by a visiting American conductor. The purpose of going was to talk to him afterwards and remind him of his existence, so that maybe at some time one of his pieces would be played. This was before he became very famous. It would probably be a terrible business.

Ronna: What about Mrs. Carter?

Seth: Mrs. Carter was originally a sculptress, and then had become devoted to him. There were pretty intense political discussions at the lunch table sometimes, which turned on the McCarthy era. Mrs. Carter would debate other people, who were taking right-wing lines.

Michael: Did you participate in these conversations?

Seth: I remember one occasion, in '52, when Eisenhower was elected, and one of the girls at the school in Athens said, "Oh, I never can return to America now." This was a girl from Ohio.

Ronna: Her image of the Eisenhower regime was . . .

Seth: That this was a tyranny beyond any other.

DISSERTATION ON THE *ILIAD*

Seth: When I got to Florence, I immediately went to a very expensive pensione. I should have gone to a cheaper place.

Michael: But you had just gotten your recent installment.

Seth: Right. Also, my relatives in Istanbul gave me a monthly stipend, which they put through an Italian bank. So I had quite a lot of money. I stayed in the Pensione Bartoletti. The most impressive feature of the room I had was that it had this stove in it, a wood stove, that said on it "The Brothers So-and-So, founded 1492." Of course, that was my year, the year of the expulsion of the Jews, and here it was on this piece of wood. It was extraordinarily cold. I used up a lot of money just heating the place.

Ronna: So you wrote the dissertation sitting in the room with the wood stove?

Seth: I sat in the room and read Homer from cover to cover, all the time. And I had all these notes, but nothing made any sense. So I said to myself, I better read it through as fast as possible.

Ronna: To get an overall impression?

Seth: Yes. So I read it in three days.

Ronna: In Greek?

Seth: Yes. Three days, eight books at a time. And I said, "My God, It's the *Symposium!*"

Ronna: The *Iliad* is?

Seth: Right, Diotima's account of the structure of *eros*. The *Iliad* has the first two layers, from Helen to—

Ronna: Patroclus?

Seth: To glory, through Hector.

Ronna: Oh, you mean it's Diotima's ladder of love (*Symposium* 211c–d)?

Seth: That's what it is. Once I realized that, I was able to write the dissertation in a month. I had made all these discoveries about the way he treated *anthropoi* versus *andres* [human beings versus men], what "hero" meant, things like that. That was the first part of the dissertation.

Michael: So, nobody really gave you any help.

Seth: No.

Michael: What did they think of it when you finally brought it back?

Seth: Grene immediately rejected it.

Michael: On what grounds?

Seth: He thought it was totally unacceptable, because it wasn't in conformity with Parry.[12] He was a strict believer in Parry.

Ronna: Did you discuss Parry's thesis in the dissertation?

Seth: I tried to show that it could not be true.

Robert: Can you fill me in?

Seth: A man named Milman Parry had gone to France on a fellowship from Berkeley, and had developed this thesis that the formulas in Homer were metrically determined and had no meaning in their particular context.

Robert: Was this developed post war?

Seth: No, before the war, but it became a doctrine in America after the war. It was not known in any other country except England, through Bowra, who had been at Harvard shortly after Milman Parry had been there, and he brought it back to England. It was not known in Europe.

Ronna: It had to do with oral poetry, right?

Seth: Right. He had gone to Yugoslavia and listened to bards. Anyway, I had all this counterevidence, I thought, that it couldn't be true. In the first book of the *Iliad,* Achilles uses the expression "great-hearted Achaeans," *megathumoi Achaeoi,* which is then repeated in Agamemnon's reply fifteen lines later, and never appears again in the entire *Iliad.* But the epithet "great-hearted" is constantly used of the Trojans. So it couldn't be arbitrary, because we have this metrical form, which could be fitted in any time he wants to use it, but he never uses it again. So it must be connected with meaning, the difference between the Achaeans and the Trojans.

Michael: That means after Achilles' withdrawal, something distinguishes them from the Trojans?

Seth: Right. But Grene didn't accept the plot at all. They knew I had done so much work on it, though, they didn't want to leave it just up to Grene. So, they said they would send it to Reinhardt. He read it and said he could not possibly judge it. This was so alien to him, he'd never seen anything like it. It didn't fit at all into Homeric scholarship.

Michael: This sounds like the beginning of your career as a misfit.

Seth: Well, they didn't know what to do, because Reinhardt hadn't said no. So they sent it to Bowra. And Bowra, to Grene's surprise, said yes.

Ronna: Did he give any comments?

Seth: I don't know.

---

12. Milman Parry (1902–35), a philologist best known for his thesis that the Homeric epics are works of a preliterate oral poetic tradition.

Robert: What about Strauss?

Seth: Strauss wasn't on the Committee.

Michael: Did he read it?

Seth: He read it, yes.

Robert: Did he say anything?

Seth: I think he said "You're probably right," or something like that. He hardly ever said anything more than that.

Ronna: But he told other people he thought it was good, didn't he?

Seth: I don't know, did he? Well, I do have a testimonial somewhere.

Ronna: What for?

Seth: A recommendation he once wrote, which he then sent me, where he gives all this praise, of a Straussian kind. I'll show it to you, if I have it.

Robert: But Strauss couldn't judge the dissertation because he wasn't on the Committee.

Seth: They asked him to be on it, but he said they were just a bunch of old beards.

Michael: He didn't say that to them?

Seth: No, he said that to me. He was in the political science department. That's why there are always these prefaces in the courses, "Why are we studying this in political science?"

Ronna: When you look back on the interpretation of the *Iliad* in your thesis, do you think it's right?

Seth: Well, I made a great mistake, which took me years to correct, when I realized I had not made a distinction between form and narrative causality. So I had got the form of the *Iliad,* that it was divided into three units—Helen, Hector, and the elimination of Ares and Aphrodite. It becomes purely human and cannot be connected with justice as originally understood, but has to be connected with totally human motives, which means fame and not right. Then they get combined in a very queer way when Achilles comes back.

Ronna: You noticed things like when the gods are present or not, and saw there is a pattern to it.

Seth: Right. I had seen a pattern through the model of Diotima's ladder of love. I knew, on that basis, that there had to be a shift at some point from an earlier phase to a second phase, but I didn't see why that has to happen when it does in the plot of the *Iliad.*

Ronna: Is that what you mean by narrative causality?

Seth: Yes. To see the patterns that the speeches make within the work is not of the same order. I had superimposed a form on the *Iliad* without asking the question whether Homer gave a causal explanation of why it changed from one level to another. What I hadn't yet discovered is what you might call the *logos* of the *logos*. And it seems to me very difficult to see that.[13]

Ronna: Did you write on the *Iliad* again?

Seth: In the appendix to the St. John's publication of the dissertation I tried to explain this mistake.[14]

---

13. This discussion of the *Iliad* is taken up again in chapter 6, pp. 117–18.

14. "Achilles and Hector: The Homeric Hero," *St. John's Review*, in two parts: spring 1985, 31–58; summer 1985, 85–114.

Chapter 3

ST. JOHN'S

1955–57

INTERVIEWS

N. O. BROWN, AT WESLEYAN

Michael: You spend two years abroad, come back to Chicago, and then you're off to St. John's. How did that happen? Did you have to interview?

Seth: Actually, I was interviewed before that for a position at Wesleyan. The president of Wesleyan at that time was a good friend of Neff. So every year one person from the Committee would get interviewed. But I don't think they ever hired anybody. They had Gourevitch, who had come from Wellesley. I don't think they ever hired anybody, precisely because Neff and the president had recommended them.

Ronna: That was the kiss of death.

Seth: Right. Anyway, I remember being interviewed by N. O. Brown. We had this strange conversation in which he told me he was writing this book, which became *Life against Death,* and that one chapter was going to be devoted to Hegel. I asked if he knew the Kojève interpretation of Hegel, and he said no. I said, "Well, let me write down the name for you. You'll find this very interesting." Not only did he find it interesting, but the very first sentence of this book is, "The standard interpretation of Hegel is . . ." And it's Kojève. It's so funny. One should always keep one's mouth shut. This is what happens.

MEETING WITH THE KLEINS

Michael: What about St. John's? Did you have an interview for that?

Seth: Yes, I still remember it so vividly. Somebody they hired couldn't come. So I was called late in May to be interviewed. There was an interview with a committee and then [Jacob] Klein took me to lunch, to meet Mrs. Klein.

Ronna: She had the final word on the whole thing?

Seth: I don't know. I remember it was a beautiful spring day. After lunch Klein said that he had to take a nap. And Mrs. Klein, after she had taken the dishes away, said, "Come into my garden." When she said those words, the shadows were such that I thought I was about to go into the world of the witches. Once I went through that garden gate, this was it.

Ronna: You would turn into a pig!

Seth: Or a mushroom.

Ronna: But you bravely followed.

Seth: I did.

Michael: Or were too much of a coward not to follow.

Seth: It was so extraordinary.

Ronna: So you sat in the garden with her for a while?

Seth: Yes, until Klein woke up.

Michael: What did you discuss with Klein in the interview?

Seth: It was quite interesting. Not the official interview, but afterwards. Klein asked me about my dissertation.

Ronna: Which was all completed at this point?

Seth: Yes. I was back in Chicago when this was arranged, in '55. Klein asked me some very shrewd questions about the *Iliad.* The one I remember most vividly was, "Tell me about horses." And I said, "Oh, you know about horses." So I told him all about Lady Wentworth and how the horses were to be understood, and so forth.

Ronna: Did you tell us about her?

Seth: Lady Wentworth wrote *The Book of the Arabian Horse,* which I happened to have read. I had first read these treatises of the early Christian era called *Medicine of Horses.* I wanted to find out why there was an implicit comparison between horses and men in the *Iliad,* why they have the same attributes. Lady Wentworth was the granddaughter of Byron, who introduced with her husband—no, it was her mother with her husband—who introduced Arabian breeding into England. They were Arabists, naturally. Lady Wentworth's father was a minor English poet, who had the capacity to see stars in the daytime. He was apparently a great ladies' man. Platonic relationships. Whenever he went to a party, he would say to some woman, "I've fallen in love with you." Anyway, Lady Wentworth wrote this extraordinary remark somewhere, about the character of a race horse, that it has to have the body of a boxer and the legs of a runner. This is a very delicate balance, between this huge chest and spindly legs. I used that as the model for Achilles, because Achilles is the combination of the two Ajaxes. And that shows that he's of a different order than anybody else.

Ronna: Not a single type.

Seth: He embodies a contradiction.

Ronna: So Klein understood these things?

Seth: That's the strange thing about him. When I was there, the dean's office used to be on the first floor of the main hall, and there was a coffee shop below it. I was sitting there one noon, with some students, and all of a sudden Klein came down and beckoned me to follow him up to his office.

Robert: So this was after you were hired?

Seth: After I was hired. He immediately lay down on a couch, handed me Hesiod's *Theogony*, and he said, "What do you make of this?" He showed me the passage in which Night has given birth to Eris [Strife], but just before giving birth to Eris she's given birth to Philotes, or love. Klein asked, "How do you explain that?" So I thought for about ten seconds and I said, "Sex." And he said, "Oh, that's what you think." Closed the book and dismissed me. That was his way.

Ronna: Do you think he had an opinion?

Seth: I think he did probably have something, but he would never tell. It's just like Bloom's experience with him, many years later. Bloom went and gave a talk on *Gulliver's Travels* there.[1] There was a question period, in which Klein didn't say anything until the very end. And then he said, "Mr. Bloom, I have one question: How come there are no clocks in Lilliput?"

Robert: And Bloom answered?

Seth: Bloom said he didn't have an answer.

Robert: And that was it? Klein didn't offer anything further?

Seth: If in fact he had an answer, it was a typical *Meno* kind of answer—"By Zeus, I do not know." His interpretation of every book was based on noticing something like this.

Michael: Well, if you take it in the most favorable light, you could say, Klein asks Bloom about clocks, which is clearly significant, because Gulliver is said to have a watch, which he brought with him to Lilliput, so your attention is called to the fact that they don't have clocks. If you can't answer that question, then, it means you don't really understand what's going on. It does instill a kind of modesty with respect to the book as a whole. Your problem is, you answered the question he asked you!

---

1. "An Outline of *Gulliver's Travels*" was published in *Ancients and Moderns: Essays on the Tradition of Political Philosophy in Honor of Leo Strauss*, edited by Joseph Cropsey (New York: Basic Books, 1964).

Seth: Even when you did answer, I'm sure that Klein had something much more in mind. But this formula, "By Zeus, I do not know," was not only the basis for his interpretation of the *Meno*. It became the model for the whole meaning of St. John's. Klein told St. John's that this was what St. John's meant. It was the *Meno*. So what everybody learned was "By Zeus, Socrates, I do not know."

TUTORS AND COURSES

Michael: You mentioned at one point that you read the *Philebus* with Klein and some other St. John's tutors. Do you remember who they were?
Seth: One was Bart, one was a man named McGraw, and the other was Winfrey-Smith.[2] They were all very much molded by Klein. Winfrey-Smith, Klein told him, was the fourth Christian since the beginning of the world. There was Paul, there was Augustine, Kierkegaard, and Winfrey-Smith.
Ronna: Was there anything to it?
Seth: I think Klein held this up for him and Winfrey-Smith tried to live up to it.
Robert: He should now aspire . . .
Seth: To this form.
Michael: Did Klein do this with everyone?
Seth: Yes, but this is the only one I remember.
Ronna: Did he give you a model?
Seth: I don't remember that.
Robert: So he gave everyone these eidetic identities.
Seth: Yes, these super-selves. That's why—this is my theory—Winfrey-Smith married the daughter of S. J. Perelman. It's the natural consequence of Klein's eidetic analysis, that the fourth Christian in the world should marry into the family of a comic writer.

Robert: Did you teach Plato at St. John's?
Seth: No, that's only in the freshman year. They have a seminar. They do it historically, even though it's totally nonhistorical.
Robert: How so, nonhistorical?
Seth: The first year is the ancients, the second year is the early Christians and the medieval up to the Renaissance, the third year is, I think, the Renaissance,

2. Robert Bart, tutor at St. John's from 1946 to 1990 and dean at Santa Fe from 1977 to 1982. Hugh McGrath was a tutor from 1948 to 1989. J. Winfrey-Smith, a tutor from 1941 to 1984, wrote on Aristotle and Machiavelli.

and the fourth year is moderns—but there's no history. In principle they could do it in any order. Klein took it as an achievement of St. John's if somebody thought that Dante wrote in Greek. That was deliberate. At the end of the second year, for the sophomores, Klein would give a lecture on the history of mathematics, a summary of his book.[3] This was the only history given at St. John's. It was amazing the way Klein remade the school in his image. It already had a great books program, but based on the influence of Thomism.

Michael: So it was trivium and quadrivium.

Seth: That's right, based on the notion that the real Renaissance was the twelfth century. But when Klein came he told them what the program meant. There was a split between the ancients and the moderns, which could be understood in terms of his book, by which they should be guided.

Michael: So what do you remember teaching at St. John's?

Seth: I taught French, Greek, and Euclid, plus a freshman seminar in the first year.

Michael: What was that like?

Ronna: He was desperately trying to catch up the night before!

Seth: Right. I made the greatest progress in Euclid.

Ronna: You came to learn some things?

Seth: About the character of how these proofs are put together, and why it's important to do it in such a manner that the reason for it being true becomes clear. So that's what I stressed, the necessity for elegance of proofs, so that you can have clarity about what's going on.

Michael: That is interesting.

Seth: The French was more or less a disaster. I was in French, while everybody else was in Greek, you see. We read *Phèdre*.

Robert: Is that something you were free to decide?

Seth: No, no. But actually the *Phèdre* turned out to be rather interesting.

Ronna: Do you remember why?

Seth: Well, I immediately realized that this was Racine's presentation of the difference between Paganism and Christianity.

Robert: The difference being?

Seth: He makes one slight shift in the story at the end, which is when the monster comes out of the sea to destroy Hippolytus. The narrator says, "Hippolytus faced the monster with useless courage. But everyone else took refuge in a neighboring temple." This is Augustine's view of ancient virtue, that it really is a claim to having a power which you don't have in yourself,

---

3. Jacob Klein, *Greek Mathematical Thought and the Origin of Algebra*, translated by Eva Brann (Cambridge: MIT Press, 1968).

whereas everybody else relies on God. And then it turns out that what I re-alized must have been true, because Racine gave up writing pagan plays and went to Port Royal and wrote Jansenist plays, with Biblical stories. This was a turning point.

Ronna: So it doesn't sound so bad. You were working hard and learning something.

Seth: No, it was interesting. It was a lot of work, though. And I don't know if the seminars were very useful. These were difficult books, after the *Iliad*. Students need much more guidance.

Michael: You had a co-teacher?

Seth: Yes, Winfrey-Smith. He had learned the Klein technique, which meant that you didn't say anything.

Ronna: Do you think the tutors had more to offer and just didn't do it? Or they didn't learn as much as they could because they knew they weren't go-ing to have come up with anything to talk about in class?

Seth: Oh, they had enough to say, I think. But the whole context was really against it.

Robert: What did you teach your second year there?

Seth: The second year I taught Greek, and senior seminar.

Michael: Senior seminar is just. . . ?

Seth: It's moderns: Darwin, Freud, I don't remember exactly.

Ronna: If someone had some expertise, like you have in Greek, you couldn't just teach that.

Seth: Well no, because, you see, the whole thing was based on the notion that you were never supposed to learn anything.

Ronna: I thought it was just the opposite.

Seth: No, you're never supposed to learn anything.

Michael: "By Zeus, I do not know."

Ronna: Oh, I see, you never become an expert.

Robert: You're always trying to live up to the standard of knowledge of ig-norance.

JACOB KLEIN

Ronna: When did Klein come to St. John's and how did he end up there?

Seth: I think he went in '37 or '38. He somehow met Buchanan and Barr.[4] Apparently there was a lot of opposition to him.

---

4. Stringfellow Barr (1897–1982), president of St. John's College, Annapolis, from 1937 to 1946, and co-founder of its great books program, together with Scott Buchanan (1895–1968).

Ronna: But he must have been politically astute, because he really took over, didn't he?

Seth: Well, I went there in '55, when he was already dean, so apparently it had all been settled. That's a long distance since '38.

Robert: Where was Klein from?

Seth: He was born in Russia.

Robert: Do you know when he left, or why?

Seth: At the time of the revolution, I suppose.

Robert: So he would have already internalized the language before he left?

Seth: Presumably. He once talked about the fact that he had experienced Russian education, Belgian education, which was French, and German education, and he thought the Russian education was best.

Robert: Did he say why?

Seth: Well, it very much agreed in impression with what [Myles] Burnyeat said, in the *Times Literary Supplement*. Did you read that? He went to a Leningrad seminar, where an old professor was going through the *Laws*, and it had taken fifteen years. Burnyeat was very impressed by the competence of the students. He thought their knowledge of Greek was superior to anyone in England. Isn't that amazing?

Ronna: This was recently?

Seth: About two years ago. But then he said it was done in this very rigid manner, where the professor gave explanations of everything. There was no conversation with students.

Ronna: We don't have translations of Russian ancient philosophy scholarship.

Seth: Remember Momigliano learned Russian to read Russian scholarship in classics.

Ronna: Not surprising!

Seth: Momigliano, who knew this stuff—I mean, he read everything—said that the Russian Marxist historians were always amused by the naive Marxists and [F. W.] Walbank. They didn't take him seriously as an ancient historian.

ADVICE FROM KLEIN AND A GUEST LECTURE

Seth: While I was at St. John's I got the galleys from the University of Chicago Press for my translations of Aeschylus.

Michael: There were two plays, weren't there?

Seth: Yes, the *Persians* and the *Suppliant Maidens*.

Ronna: Did you get anyone to read over the translations?

Seth: They were read by Grene and [Richard] Lattimore.

Michael: Did you have anything to do with Lattimore?

Seth: I met him once before I left in '52. Then when I came back to the States in '54, I was traveling on a steamer and ended up somewhere in Virginia. I went to see him at Bryn Mawr and had a conversation with him. I don't remember much about it, except that he was very dried up. He's the brother of Owen Lattimore.[5]

Ronna: Who's that?

Seth: Owen Lattimore was accused by McCarthy of being a secret agent, the controlling communist agent of all spies in America.

Ronna: Was it ever corroborated at all?

Seth: No. But Lattimore was an expert on inner Asian frontiers of Mongolia and obviously had very strong communist sympathies; he accepted the Chinese Communist line about what they were doing in China.

Robert: So you were working on the Aeschylus translations while you were at St. John's?

Seth: No, they were completed before then. But they sent the galleys to me there, along with an advertising questionnaire, about how to sell the book. I got it in the mail box, and the dean's office was right above. So I showed it to Klein and he gave these very funny answers, which I wrote in. One of them was, "Under what circumstances would this book be read?" And Klein said, "In all weathers."

Ronna: Rain or snow.

Seth: So I sent this in and they wrote back, "We are not amused." Ten years later, I got another letter, "We are amused." A new business manager had come in, and he went through the old papers.

Seth: Klein was once invited to give a speech at Hampton, a black college in Virginia, but he declined and gave it over to me. He must have known what was coming. After I arrived, they took me to a room and I rested before dinner, then we went to the lecture room. There was a huge crowd, because it turned out it was their regular Friday night assembly, to which the entire college came, hundreds of people. Everybody on the stage except myself, all the men, were dressed in ROTC uniforms, including the president. It was a military school.

---

5. Richard Lattimore (1906–84), professor of Greek at Bryn Mawr from 1935 to 1971, was a scholar and translator of Greek literature and the co-editor, with David Grene, of *The Complete Greek Tragedies* (Chicago: University of Chicago Press). Owen Lattimore (1900–1989) was a China scholar and director of the Page School of International Relations at Johns Hopkins University from 1938 to 1950.

Michael: What were you supposed to lecture on?

Seth: I was to talk about the *Iliad*. All of a sudden the organ began to play; everybody stood up and began to sing a hymn. All I had was this copy of the *Iliad*, so I sang the opening words: *"Menen aeide thea."* Then they stopped and I was introduced. I had written the speech out on the back of an envelope, à la Lincoln. I had certain points that I was planning to make. I put my watch out as I began the speech. Well, after I had gone through all the points I had on the envelope, I looked at my watch and only twenty minutes had gone by. So I said, "Now let me go through this again in deeper detail." Then I went through the whole thing again, and looked at the watch, and that was forty minutes. I did it three times, using the same formula, elaborating things and so forth. And it was all being recorded.

Robert: This is the form and the dynamic of the argument!

Seth: Right. Later the secretary of the department sent me a transcript of it, and said, "Oh it reads much better than when I heard it."

Michael: Do you still have the transcript?

Seth: No, but they took a picture for the student newspaper, which they sent me. I don't know if I have still have it. There I am in my Istanbul suit, holding onto the lectern. They had taken it at such an angle that I really looked like a preacher, in that black suit.

THE CAPLANS

Seth: There was an old Russian Jewish couple at St. John's, the Caplans [Fannie and Simon]. Caplan once told the story about how he came to understand the fragility of civilization. He had gone back to Russia and saw a book he wanted to buy, but the price was too high. He tried to argue the price down, and this push-cart dealer said, "You know, if you don't buy it, it will be turned into cigarette paper." This was his example of how everything was very fragile.

Robert: What did Caplan work on?

Seth: He wrote a commentary on Polybius, in three volumes.

Ronna: Was he still teaching when you met them?

Seth: He was still teaching. But he seemed very old to me, older than Klein. His wife was like a girlish revolutionary. She must have been in her sixties, but she retained her idealism, from before the war. The man had a quizzical expression on his face at all times. His head was always tilted at an angle, so he looked extremely skeptical. At the same time he was always very kind, and judicious, it seemed. Anyway, he was most famous for this remark. Some issue about the chapel had come up in relation to the college, and he said, "Gentlemen, you must always remember College Avenue runs tangent to Church Social." It was a perfect line for St. John's, with regard to geometry and beauty.

Ronna: Did they have mandatory attendance at chapel?

Seth: I wouldn't be surprised. This was in the '30s.

Ronna: Did it have a church affiliation originally?

Seth: It must have. Everything was affiliated.

MRS. KLEIN

Robert: Didn't Klein meet up regularly for a while with Isaiah Berlin? I thought that came up in the *New York Review of Books* piece, from the book of conversations.

Seth: It was during the time Berlin was an envoy for Churchill in Washington. In late '41 to '44, I think. At some point in this period Klein married Mrs. Klein. She was the ex-wife of the son of Husserl, who drove a taxicab in Washington.

Robert: Gerhard Husserl. He wrote a dissertation on law. When I was in Germany, it was in all the libraries.

Ronna: But he never became an academic?

Robert: I guess not.

Seth: Mrs. Klein looked as though she was born to the social manner that would fit with someone like Berlin. But . . .

Ronna: She married Jacob Klein.

Robert: How long ago did she die?

Seth: Last year.

Robert: Was there an obituary?

Seth: In the college paper.

Ronna: Where was she born?

Seth: She had the same background as Blanckenhagen, Baltic German.

Ronna: She was not Jewish?

Seth: No. Her father was a very important professor of chemistry in Göttingen. That's where she was psychoanalyzed by Lou Salome. She mentioned to me later, after I left, that she got inquiries from people who wanted to look at her father's work, which turned out to be important in some respect. The funny thing is, sometime after Klein died her attitude toward him changed.

Ronna: From what to what?

Seth: When I knew her, I thought she always took a very ironic stance toward his relation to the college, and also his funny behavior.

Ronna: Like what?

Seth: Well, he had an obsession about always cleaning everything. He would never touch a door handle without wiping it, and when he sat down to dinner at his own house, the first thing he did was to wipe the plate with his napkin. Mrs. Klein would get absolutely furious. She had just washed the dishes.

Ronna: So how did she change in her attitude?

Seth: Well, I was thinking mostly about her understanding of his relation to the college. When I first knew her, it seemed as if she thought there was something perverse about it; but when I met her once after his death, she totally denied that. His relation to the college had become something very important.

Robert: The only time you had contact with her after leaving St. John's was after Klein died?

Seth: Yes, when I gave a talk there, on the *Republic*.

Robert: What did you present?

Seth: It was not their teaching on the *Republic*, I remember that.

Ronna: They protested your interpretation?

Seth: Not really. It was all at an enormous distance.

Ronna: Do you remember when Klein gave a lecture at the New School on Leibniz?

Robert: I remember that lecture. It was in 1973, I think.

Ronna: I asked a question that had to do with how Leibniz accounted for error. I was sitting in the first row, and he came right up to me and started, "Well my dear . . ."

Robert: He seemed very frail. I remember thinking, his skin was like China. It was so stretched, translucent.

Seth: Didn't we see Momigliano that way?

Robert: Remember that? We met him at Princeton, for that talk he gave. Peter Brown showed up, and Saul Kripke was there.

Seth: His skin was that of somebody about to die. It had a kind of beauty to it. But it was a death mask. Very disturbing, but very beautiful.

KLEIN AND STRAUSS

Ronna: Did Klein ever talk about Strauss?

Seth: I remember, many years later, he put up tremendous resistance to Strauss's interpretation of the cave.

Robert: On what grounds?

Seth: That it wasn't the city, but it was a description of the womb. Of course, the prisoners are said to be there from childhood, not from birth. That's the basis of the image. So you have to—this seems to be typical of Klein—take that out and look at the picture of the description of the prisoners, and realize that they must be hunched up exactly like a baby in the womb. So he resisted Strauss's view about the city. Years later, after I left St. John's, I met Gurwitsch in Cambridge.

Ronna: Aron Gurwitsch?

Seth: Yes. He knew Klein, so when I met him he asked me, "What is Klein doing?" I said, "You know, he does these very extraordinary things. For example, this interpretation . . ." Gurwitsch wouldn't entertain it for a moment. It was at a party, so he was polite. But the contempt he expressed for this interpretation is something I'll never forget.

Michael: I once told you, I think, what Gadamer said about Klein? This was in Germany, in '71. A bunch of us were at a Gasthaus and we started talking, about Klein and Strauss and the rest of them. Gadamer got into the conversation about Klein and said, yes he admired the first book, the Greek mathematics book, enormously but that the *Meno* was a book written for the American mind. This was not meant to be a compliment.

Seth: No, no, right.

Ronna: Klein's interpretation of the cave is interesting, because he always seems to back off from the political implications.

Seth: That's it. This has to do with the whole dispute about the Nazis, and a remark of Strauss's.

Robert: What was that?

Seth: "I'm not as moral as Mr. Klein." That really shocked Klein.

Robert: How did this come up?

Seth: When I was at St. John's, I think that Bart, one of the tutors, told me this. Then I met Strauss in New York once, when he was on his way to St. John's. I met Irving Kristol at the same time, in some hotel. I don't recall what the occasion was. I remember Strauss saying to me, "You know, I think I'm as moral as Klein. But not theoretically."

Ronna: Moral in my behavior, but not in my understanding of things?

Seth: Right. Then, many years later, there was a meeting at St. John's, in which Strauss said something like that, not in exactly the same terms.

Robert: How did it go there?

Michael: Are you talking about the "giving of accounts"? Strauss again shocked Klein by saying something like, "I think you're more consumed with morality than I am," which took Klein aback because he always thought that Strauss was the one.

Seth: Right. There was this very funny occasion. It was the first time I ever met Klein, in Chicago. Strauss had some students of Klein, from St. John's. So Klein came to give a lecture, downtown. There was a party for him at Strauss's house, and there were Strauss's students and Klein's former students and so forth. It was one of these railroad apartments, so there was a kind of doorway between one place and another. Strauss was in one room, with several students around him, and they were having a serious discussion. In another room, Klein was talking with some alumni of St. John's. The year before, St. John's had gone co-ed and they were interested in what this entailed in terms of the change in character of the college. All of a sudden they heard a voice from the other end of the apartment: "And what about vice?" Strauss must have overheard their conversation. Klein laughed and said, "Oh, there's that too." But he wasn't interested in it. What was striking though, was the tone in which Strauss said it, which had a double character to it. On the one hand, it was very funny, on the other hand, it had a moral tone. And I think that Klein understood only the moral part. I don't think he got the emphasis that Strauss had given to the word, "vice."

Ronna: Do you think that this understanding Strauss had of himself was accurate?

Seth: Which?

Ronna: Amoral theoretically.

Seth: Yes, I think that that's so.

Ronna: Whereas Klein had a strange combination of mathematics and morality, without the political.

Seth: Yes, right. So very much like the *Republic,* in other words.

Ronna: And the traditional understanding of Plato.

Seth: Right. I think Klein never understood the fact that there is always a double argument in Plato.

Michael: Although he did understand that there was a hidden argument.

Seth: Yes, but not a double argument.

Michael: Can you explain that a little more?

Seth: Well, in other words, as he saw it, there is a hidden argument based on what was being said, but you don't have to pay attention to the fact that the dialogues are constructed in such a way as to show the very nature of what is being discussed. The dialogue is an imitation of reality because it shows that reality has this double character to it, with two strands not necessarily leading in the same direction, though attached to each other. It looks as if Strauss understood that relatively early—I don't know how early—but Klein did not.

Ronna: Is there some specific content to this double character that always holds, or is it different in different cases? Do you have a good example of it?

Seth: Well, one could think of several examples. But if you take the image of the *Republic*, about *periagoge,* the turning around, I think that Strauss and Klein understood it differently. Klein took it very much like a conversion, in which you're turning away from obscurity toward the light.

Robert: And it's a liberation.

Seth: Yes. Whereas Strauss, I think, understood it as turning back to the darkness, and seeing there wasn't as much light as you thought there was.

Ronna: After already having seen the light?

Seth: You could say that the way out of the cave described in the *Republic* seems to be the model for the first level of the argument.

Ronna: Mhmm. And that's where Klein stops?

Seth: Yes.

Michael: When you first met Klein, did you understand this difference between him and Strauss?

Seth: I remember talking at great length one evening, after I'd been at St. John's for a year, to Kennington and [Dwight] McDonald in New York about Klein, praising him over Strauss.

Ronna: What did you think Klein's strength was?

Seth: I thought he had some kind of insight into soul.

Robert: Do you remember what made you think that at the time?

Seth: I suppose it was this magical quality. You know, he could turn to the blackboard and draw a perfect circle, for instance. He was able to turn his arm like a compass. Everybody else's breaks at the bottom, but he would stand exactly right, so he could draw perfect circles.

Chapter 4

HARVARD

1957–60

JOINING THE SOCIETY OF FELLOWS

Robert: From St. John's you went to Harvard as a junior fellow? How did that come about?

Seth: Blanckenhagen, who was a visiting professor at Harvard, recommended me for the Society of Fellows. As a consequence, they interviewed him. That's why it's so very difficult for someone who's not a Harvard person to get it. They're likely to interview the person who makes the recommendation, so if you write from the West Coast, there's almost no chance that they'll take the person you recommended. So they invited Blanckenhagen to dinner and interviewed him. He said to them, "Well Benardete is really quite good, but he needs to be polished. And he can only be polished by Harvard." He devised a perfect scheme for getting me in. My interview at Harvard was with W. V. O. Quine and Arthur Darby Nock; then there was a biologist, [Frederick] Hisaw, and [Wassily] Leontieff, the economist.

Robert: These were all senior fellows?

Seth: Yes, you're interviewed by the senior fellows before you meet the junior fellows at the dinner.

Ronna: Senior fellows are permanent?

Seth: Yes, they elect themselves. But Nock was the main interviewer.[1] I was beginning to work on Sophocles, I think. So we had a long discussion, in

---

1. Arthur Darby Nock (1902–63), professor in classics at Harvard from 1929 to 1963, was a scholar of religion in the ancient world.

which Nock said at one point, "How can you say that Sophocles was political? Don't you remember that anecdote in Athenaeus?" And I said, "What about the other part of the anecdote?" And Quine said, "No more of this."
Ronna: Were you both thinking of the same thing?
Seth: I suppose he thought he knew what I was referring to.
Ronna: It wasn't just bravado.
Seth: No, I had something in mind and he accepted it. But it was so funny, Quine saying, "Now wait a minute, you can't keep this up."

ARTHUR DARBY NOCK

Robert: Who was Nock?
Seth: Nock was an interesting guy, in a way. A man from Cambridge, England, who had been brought over by [A. Lawrence] Lowell in the early part of the thirties. He was an Anglican, but had lost his faith. He was very reactionary, in a blustery kind of way. He talked in an almost unintelligible fashion, keeping up the speech of Oxbridge, even though he had been more than twenty years at Harvard—the same way that [Harry Austyn] Wolfson kept up his Yiddish accent, despite having been at Harvard since he was an undergraduate. But when you'd hear him, you'd think he just got off the boat. So these two were maintaining their own integrity over against this enormous institution.
Robert: Exactly.
Seth: Nock had his own room in Eliot House, where I lived too. Nock was much more intelligent than he seemed to be. He was the expert on the syncretistic religions of the Hellenistic period, so Christianity and everything before. One of these very, very learned men, like Momigliano; well, half as learned as Momigliano, but that kind of extraordinary knowledge. And not stupid at all. But he had developed a habit of being just a silly duffer. He walked in a very funny manner, like a duck, which was apparently an imitation of his teacher at Cambridge, J. T. Shepherd,[2] who had walked that way. And he had exactly the same neurosis as Klein: he wouldn't touch door handles. He had all these crotchets, you know. After Jane and I were married, we went to have dinner with him in his room, and I remember how difficult it was to understand him.
Ronna: You mean just his speech?
Seth: [After an imitation] We could hardly understand a word. He was a bachelor. There was one story that made him famous as a character at Har-

---

2. Fellow of King's College, Cambridge and translator of Sophocles.

vard for the rest of his life. During the war Harvard was taken by over the V-12 program.

Ronna: What was that?

Seth: The officer training program. You went to college at the same time as you were trained as an officer. But Nock was allowed to keep his rooms. So one summer night, a new MP was making the rounds of all the rooms in Eliot House to make sure all the doors were open and everybody was in their bed. And he came to a closed door. So he pushed it open, and flashed his light in. There was Nock, sitting stark naked in the middle of the room surrounded by blue books, grading them. The MP said, "Jesus Christ!" And Nock said, "No Sir, just his humble servant, Arthur Darby Nock."

Ronna: That sounds like it should be a scene in a Severn Darden movie.

Seth: It became world famous. Once Nock gave a lecture at Yale, at one of the medieval colleges with huge fireplaces. They had set up the lectern right in front of the fireplace. Nock was so drunk that he fell over backward and half the lecture was up the smokestack. He was still talking.

Ronna: He didn't notice?

Seth: No, he didn't notice that he was horizontal. So he was taken to his room after this to sleep it off. And at midnight, all of a sudden there was a knock at the head of the college's door, and there was Nock, saying, "Now let's get down to some serious drinking."

Ronna: He was ready to start all over again.

Seth: Right. But the interesting thing about Nock was the elaborate façade he had.

Robert: Was there an explanation for that?

Seth: Somebody who didn't want to be hurt, I suppose. That came out in the following manner. One evening, about midnight, I met him at the entrance to Eliot House. He had just come back from the funeral of the wife of the university chaplain, whose name was, I think, Buttrick.[3] He was very upset. He talked about half an hour, in a perfectly human way. Then he suddenly noticed that he had done so. And very slowly, right before my eyes, he began to pull the pieces in place. Within five minutes he had this elaborate rococo style that he put on again.

Ronna: This constructed persona.

Seth: Yes. It was the most extraordinary thing I've ever seen. Very hard to describe. It really had to do with his gestures, the way he had become a fussy old man.

---

3. George Arthur Buttrick (1892–1980), a professor in the Harvard Divinity School, was minister of Harvard's Memorial Chapel and chief editor of *The Interpreter's Bible*.

Robert: He was aware that he had let it down and now was pulling it back up.

Seth: Right. The woman who died had read my dissertation, and he asked her, "Is he any good or is he crazy?" And she said, "Let him in." So that's how I got in.

Robert: Who was that?

Seth: The wife of the chaplain, Buttrick.

Ronna: Whose opinion obviously counted.

Seth: For him, yes. I'll tell you how much. Buttrick died, Mrs. Buttrick died, then Nock died, relatively young. He looked much older than he turned out to be. We went to his sixtieth birthday party and it was probably about a year and a half after that that he died. But he looked more like eighty. Quine said he looked like that when he came in 1932.

Ronna: It was part of this thing.

Seth: Right. Anyway, on the tombstone, on one side it says "The Reverend Buttrick and his wife" and on the other side it said, "Arthur Darby Nock, their friend." Just as though he was like a dog.

Ronna: Attached to this couple.

Seth: Isn't that strange?

Ronna: Were there common seminars among the fellows?

Seth: No, no. But we did meet a few times a week. We had one meeting with the senior fellows on Monday night where there would be guests if anybody was passing through. And then there were luncheons, on Tuesday and Friday, I think.

Michael: So did you learn anything from anybody else during this period?

Seth: I didn't learn anything from them. You had to make a tremendous effort, which I wasn't willing to do, to make connections.

Robert: But was there nobody during those years as a junior fellow who really impressed you?

Seth: Well, there were two mathematicians. One was named Monroe, I think. One was a very good friend of Eva Brann's. They were obviously very smart, and both had an intuitive understanding of mathematics. That is, what Diego said that he got five years ago, they had from day one.[4] That was the impression they gave.

Ronna: So these meetings with the other fellows were not very interesting?

Seth: Well, it was always entertaining. There was one very funny evening, in which I was trapped at one end of the table. The table was a horseshoe

---

4. Diego Benardete, Seth's younger half-brother, teaches mathematics at the University of Hartford, Connecticut.

table, a very beautiful piece of furniture. The chairman of the senior fellows sat right in the middle of this horseshoe, and the others sat on both sides of him. I was at one end with Nock, Hisaw, and [Charles] Gulick, of Goodwin and Gulick, the Greek grammar, who was ninety-five and could only distinguish between light and dark at this time. At one point he said, "Old Professor Goodwin used to say"—this takes you back to 1870, at the latest—"Old Professor Goodwin used to say that there's not a man between the ages of nine and ninety who's not interested in the opposite sex." At this point Arthur Darby Nock jumps up and says, "And that's true of them too. Why just the other day I was being seduced by an eighty-five year old woman."

Ronna: You were just sitting there taking it all in.

Seth: I was sitting there, thinking I have to scribble this down. Then Nock began to sing a ditty about "What can we do with a virgin sturgeon?" The evening ended with Hisaw telling a story about a friend of his who had just undergone a prostate operation: the doctor put his liquids under a microscope and had him look through it, and when he saw a lone sperm wriggling its way across the field he said, "There goes the last of the Mohicans." Nock always wore a vest fastened with a gold chain. When he jumped up and announced that a woman had tried to seduce him, the chain popped open. He was absolutely so delighted.

CLASSICISTS AT HARVARD

Seth: The master of the house, Finley, turned out also to have this elaborate façade, of a different manner.

Ronna: Is this F-i-n-d-l-a-y?

Seth: No. This is John Finley, the son of the former president of CCNY and the chief editorial writer for the *New York Times*, who had been president of a college before.[5] He was a classicist. And he had this extraordinary image-making ability. So Harvard was to Radcliffe as the *Iliad* was to the *Odyssey*, or Odysseus was to Penelope. He would go on and on like that. He would visit the captain of the football team on Friday night and say, "This reminds me of book ten of the *Iliad*." It was totally spurious, from beginning to end. One day I was talking to him about something and it suddenly all vanished. He talked in a very intelligent and sober manner.

Ronna: So this was another person with an elaborate façade?

5. John H. Finley (1904–95), master of Eliot House and professor of Greek at Harvard, wrote on Thucydides, Pindar and Aeschylus, and Homer. His father, John Huston Finley, was president of Knox College and of CCNY, and senior editor of the *New York Times* from 1920 to 1940.

Seth: Extraordinary.

Robert: Who were the other people in classics at the time?

Seth: Besides Finley, there was Hammond, who was in Roman history, and there was Sterling Dow, a down east guy from Maine.[6] His most famous lecture was given at the Hellenic Center in Washington, about scholarship. It was an hour talk: you need a pad of yellow foolscap, two sharp yellow pencils, and 3 × 5 cards.

Robert: And you're ready to roll.

Seth: There was a man named Calvert Watkins, who was an Indo-European expert.[7] He was taking this course, "Persian," in which he was the only student. At that time Harvard had classes on Saturday. He told the teacher that he was not going to be there the next Saturday. And the teacher said, "Well, you'll just miss that lecture." Sure enough, when he came back, they went on to the next topic.

Michael: So did you have much interaction with these people?

Seth: It was such a closed society. I did get to know a man named Wendell Clausen, a classicist from Amherst who had come to Harvard as a visiting professor the year I came, I think. He was then hired, and stayed. Oh yes, the other person was Whitman.[8]

Ronna: Cedric Whitman? Didn't he write about the "heroic tradition"?

Seth: Yes. He wrote on Sophocles, Homer, also Aristophanes. The influence was a combination of Finley and Jaeger. Jaeger was also at Harvard.

Ronna: He was an old man?

Seth: Not so old. I told you, didn't I?, about when I met him in Athens, where he took one look at the Acropolis and then never left his room again?

Michael: Yes, that was funny. Did you have an explanation for it?

Seth: I guess the reality fell so short of his imagination. I think I told you about Wade-Gery's reaction to him in Athens. Years later, when Wade-Gery was at Harvard, he read my Herodotus book. I asked him what he thought about it. And he said, "After reading it for two hours, I decided it wasn't nonsense."

Michael: Well, I think that's a pretty good description of it.

---

6. Mason Hammond, professor emeritus of Latin, is a Virgil scholar. Sterling Dow (1891–1972), an archaeologist, was a professor in the classics and history departments.

7. Watkins became a professor of linguistics and classics at Harvard.

8. Wendell Clausen, professor emeritus of Latin, is a Virgil scholar. Cedric Whitman (1916–79), professor of classics at Harvard from 1947 to 1979, is the author of *Sophocles: A Study in Heroic Humanism* (1951) and *Homer and the Heroic Tradition* (1958).

OTHER FELLOWS

WILLARD V. O. QUINE

Michael: You said Quine was at your interview. Did you get to know him at all?

Seth: A little bit. But he was very hard to know. There was a senior fellow named Purcell, who had a Nobel Prize in physics.[9] It had just been announced, must have been Sunday or Monday, that the Russians had put up a satellite. I was talking to Purcell, and Quine came over and said, "Oh no, they didn't do it. They just did it all by mirrors. They just made a little model." Purcell, who was on the Presidential Advisory Board for Science, said, "Oh no, they did it. In fact they had a rocket so powerful that you can walk through it with swinging doors." Then Quine believed that they had done it. His initial reaction was as a Republican from Ohio.

Robert: It was all fake.

Michael: Did you have other conversations with Quine?

Seth: At one point I had just read a book by Erwin Strauss, I can't remember the title.[10]

Robert: Something about phenomenology?

Seth: I think so. The first book, in German. I was talking to Quine about it, saying that it gave a very powerful analysis of the difference between habit and understanding, with the example of driving a car: if in fact habit took over, you wouldn't be paying attention and would make a mistake. The character of understanding is the conscious rejection of alternatives. And therefore it's very different from a rat in a maze, where there isn't any preservation of what was rejected. I thought it was very powerful. Quine said, "Yes, that's true but it's too complicated."

Ronna: What did he want?

Seth: He wanted it very simple; he wanted Skinner.

Michael: I once heard a very funny account of a Skinnerian learning how to drive, a behavioral account of what it would mean to learn how to drive on Skinner's terms. You'd be dead a hundred times before you learned how to open the door.

Seth: This reminds me of Chomsky's famous article, criticizing Skinner.

Robert: What was that?

Seth: Skinner wrote a book on language and behavior and Chomsky wrote

---

9. Edward M. Purcell (1912–97) won the physics prize in 1952.
10. Erwin Strauss (1891–1975), German phenomenological psychologist.

a very good review, revealing of the character of psychology, in which the arguments turned out to be of two types, one perfectly in accord with common sense and the other based on the latest research. So the paragraphs alternated in his argument. The funniest example of Skinner's was of how you'd get somebody to say "pencil." You'd put him in a room that had pictures and models of pen and pencil sets everywhere, of different shapes and sizes and colors, and a microphone in the room would keep on saying "Pen and . . . Pen and . . ." And Chomsky's argument against this was, he'd say, "Let me out of here!"

JAAKO HINTIKKA

Robert: Who were some of the other junior fellows?
Seth: Hintikka was a junior fellow with me. This was a year or two before Quine took over all of English philosophy through *Word and Object*. Grice was in town and he was the cynosure of everyone. I went into the cafeteria, and there were Rogers Albritton, Hintikka, and Grice sitting at a table.[11] Hintikka invited me over, and I sat down and listened to this conversation which they were in the middle of: Grice said, "You see, if I had set the conditions at five minutes to twelve which prevented you at twelve o'clock from leaving a room, then you couldn't leave at twelve o'clock." When Albritton expressed puzzlement, he said, "Well, suppose if I put a wall in front of the door after you had entered the hut, then you wouldn't be able to leave." Then Albritton said, "Well, I believe you about the first, but I don't believe you about the wall." And I turned to Hintikka and said, "What are they talking about?" "Free will." Then the conversation changed, and Grice asked me, "Which would you prefer to be, good or nice?" I said, "Good, of course." He said, "Really?" And Albritton said, "Well, you know there are people like that."

DANIEL ELLSBERG

Robert: How about Chomsky? Wasn't he a junior fellow when you were?
Seth: He had left, I think, two years before I came.
Michael: So who else was there?
Seth: Well, the one who became most famous was the Pentagon Papers guy.

11. Rogers Albritton, professor of philosophy at UCLA, works in the fields of metaphysics, philosophy of language, and philosophy of mind. Jaako Hintikka, professor of philosophy at Boston University, has made contributions to the philosophy of language and philosophical logic. Herbert Paul Grice (1913–88), did work in the theory of meaning and communication.

Robert: Daniel Ellsberg?

Seth: Ellsberg was a junior fellow. He was connected with the Rand Corporation.

Robert: That's right, because it was as an employee that he originally started getting familiar with all this stuff in southeast Asia.

Ronna: What was his field?

Seth: Economics.

Robert: But his big thing was mathematical theories, isn't that right?

Seth: I don't know that. He was connected with a senior fellow who for a short time was the head of the Institute at Princeton, an economist, who was in the Kennedy administration, I can't remember his name. But Ellsberg revealed himself to be an absolute monster by a question he asked the junior fellows, about nuclear extermination. He was asking everyone whether we would press the button if we had to. And the expression on his face, when he contemplated these mega-deaths, was something to behold. I had an eerie feeling that this was a guy totally unscrupulous.

RENATO POGGIOLI

Seth: One of the fellows was Renato Poggioli. He was brought in by Harry Levin and his famous line was always, in accent, "I agree with Harry."[12]

Ronna: Whatever he says.

Seth: Right. He talked like an Italian journalist, with a cigarette hanging from his lower lip, spreading ashes everywhere, always ending with this remark, "Very well, you see the point."

Ronna: What was his field?

Seth: Russian literature. A student at Harvard told me the following story. He was being examined for his Ph.D. oral. And Poggioli says to him, "Now tell me about Italian erotic poetry of the sixteenth century." So the student replied very properly, that there wasn't such a thing, that whenever they did that they wrote in Latin. At this point Levin says, "But Renato, what about Aretino?" "But Harry," says Poggioli—Poggioli had said, "Very well, you see the point"—"But Harry, Aretino, he is not erotic, he is obscene." He was such a perfect conversationalist. Because whenever you said something to him, he would say, "Very well, you see the point." You felt as though you were on a cloud.

Ronna: Perfect understanding.

Seth: Perfect understanding, of something or other. I remember Blanck-

---

12. Harry Levin (1912–93) was a professor of comparative literature at Harvard.

enhagen was able to give the impression of great wisdom by saying, in accent, "Well, you know, I really don't know."

Michael: I suppose, if it's worth commenting on the fact that you don't know something, the implication is that most of the time you do know.

HARVEY MANSFIELD

Ronna: You met Jane while you were a junior fellow? What was she doing?[13]

Seth: Jane got her Ph.D. from Harvard in 1958. Then she was an instructor for three years in a program on history and literature.

Michael: You must have met Mansfield during this time too.[14] Can you remember how that happened?

Seth: He must have been attached to Eliot House. He was either beginning to teach or finishing his Ph.D., I don't remember.

Robert: With whom was he working?

Seth: Friedrich was his sponsor at Harvard.[15]

Michael: He was not connected in any way with Strauss at this time?

Seth: I can't remember whether he had met up with Strauss on the West Coast.

Michael: Wasn't Strauss in Stanford for a year? [at the Center for Advanced Study in the Behavioral Sciences]. I think that was when Mansfield went out to see him. In one of your articles, in the early Hesiod article, I think, you said you had just read Hesiod with Mansfield.[16]

Seth: Right, that was after Jane and I were married. Mansfield and Christian Wolf came over one day a week and we read it.[17] Mansfield would come early and have a conversation with Jane. But he was rather quiet in our discussions.

THE HERODOTUS PROJECT

ARNALDO MOMIGLIANO

Ronna: When you got the Harvard fellowship, were you expected to do a particular project?

---

13. Jane Benardete, Seth's wife, professor emerita of the English Department of Hunter College, works primarily on American literature.

14. Harvey Mansfield, professor in the department of government at Harvard, whose work in political philosophy and political science includes the translation and interpretation of Machiavelli and Toqueville.

15. Carl Joachim Friedrich (1901–84), professor of political science and government at Harvard.

16. "Hesiod's *Works and Days:* A First Reading," *Agon* 1 (1967): 150–74.

17. Christian Wolf is a professor in the department of music at Dartmouth.

Seth: I was working on Herodotus.

Ronna: Wasn't it the Herodotus work that led you to meet Momigliano?

Seth: Yes. Somebody in California, where he was living at the time, had shown him my Herodotus study, which was still in manuscript. Then at some point he came to Cambridge, and was staying in the rooms of the Society. Jane and I were already married, so it must have been 1962. Anyway, I went to see him and we had this knock-down fight about Herodotus. It was really something.

Ronna: What was the cause of the fight?

Seth: He wanted to understand Herodotus as the father of history, meaning history as we do it now. And I was claiming that that's not what he was doing. He had no intention of being the founder of . . .

Robert: This empirical discipline?

Seth: Right. He was doing something else. We were each bringing all kinds of pieces of evidence. It ended amicably enough, because he admitted in the end that maybe that had not been Herodotus's intention. He was taking it from the point of view of the future, and maybe that in fact was not how to understand him. So that was sort of a concession.

Michael: Well, he's the father of history and a bad historian. But Momigliano didn't think that.

Seth: No. His argument was that the really impressive thing about Herodotus was that he was the first to devise historical narrative. This was an extraordinary achievement. If you look at kings' accounts on inscriptions in the Near East, there's nothing like this, in which a story is being told, things are fitted together in proper sequence. And this is really the model for what it means to tell about historical events. I had discounted that as not being important. I was thinking that there doesn't seem to be so great a difference between that and the story of the *Iliad*.

Michael: It's like the difference between pretending to tell the truth and admitting that you're not. It's not the same as Hesiod's lies like the truth. So there does seem to be something to it. Herodotus presents his story as though it's an account of the real, and Homer doesn't do that.

Seth: That's true.

Michael: Can you tell us your reason for dedicating *The Being of the Beautiful* to Momigliano?

Seth: Bloom told me that Momigliano wanted to see it published and had recommended it strongly. The funny thing was, it came out the same year that Iris Murdoch dedicated her novel to Momigliano.

Ronna: What a pair! Do you know how Momigliano got a copy of your Herodotus manuscript?

Seth: I never found out where he got it.

Michael: Did he know Strauss?

Seth: No, he never knew Strauss. Didn't I tell you the story about Strauss writing him a letter? I met Momigliano. Then I went to Chicago to see Strauss and told him I had met Momigliano. And he said, "You know, he never replied to a letter I wrote him." I asked, "What was the letter about?" Strauss had read an essay of Momigliano's which stated that the Stoics in Roman times had separated moral virtue from wisdom. And Strauss wrote him a letter saying, "Where?" So the next time I met Momigliano, I said, "You know I met Strauss and he remembers that you never replied to his letter." Momigliano said, "I couldn't find it any place. So in embarrassment I never replied." In one of Strauss's letters, there is a wonderful remark about Momigliano's account of him, in a long article Momigliano wrote in *Historia Italiano*.

Robert: One of these genealogies?

Seth: Yes. Momigliano thought he had pinned him down as this Rabbi. Strauss was overjoyed.

Ronna: He thought he had escaped his net? So Momigliano thought of him as pious?

Seth: Not necessarily pious. But he thought he could understand him, not in terms of philosophy, but through this rabbinical background.

Robert: Did you discuss Momigliano with other people?

Seth: I remember Bloom was very impressed by Momigliano's remarks, which he thought were very acute, but didn't understand what he was doing.

Ronna: What kind of remarks?

Seth: I don't remember exactly. One was to the effect that Britain paid a very high price in the Puritan revolution by postponing an appreciation of Shakespeare.

Michael: Oh, I remember that remark. It was about Rousseau: Rousseau was the price we had to pay for the postponement of the appreciation of Shakespeare. I never quite understood what he meant either.

Ronna: Remember Peter Brown's reflections on Momigliano?

Michael: I thought it was by Grafton.[18]

Seth: Grafton wrote too. But Brown's was for the British Academy.

Ronna: I liked the description of how he went around with all the different vests and suit jackets and hundreds of pockets with little notepads and bibliographic notes in every one, thousands of yellowed sheets of note paper.

---

18. Peter Brown, fellow and tutor in classics at Oxford and scholar of ancient history. Anthony Grafton, professor of history at Princeton, wrote on Renaissance and early modern Europe.

Was anything of Momigliano's particularly influential for you? You like the formula "alien wisdom," don't you?

Seth: Yes. What's interesting about it is that Momigliano was not an ancient, for a number of reasons, but one of them was that they were not cosmopolitan. They thought they were perfectly capable on their own and didn't need alien wisdom. So they didn't learn other languages. This had to do with his failure to understand the decisive importance of philosophy. Once that distinction has been made, you don't have to travel anymore.

Ronna: You mean, the distinction between *nomos* and *physis* [convention and nature]?

Seth: Yes. On the other hand, it's certainly very puzzling that there is this failure to see things that seem so obvious to us now, like that Persian must be connected with Greek and Latin. They didn't know that. So, on this historical dimension, there's a failure, as Momigliano sees it.

Michael: Would you say that in some way he represents just how far, at its very best, scholarship can go? Isn't it hard to imagine him as other than an academic?

Seth: Well, it's complicated by the fact that he's an alien academic. He was one of the very few who did Hebrew, Roman, and Greek things.

Ronna: Like [David] Daube?

Seth: Like Daube. Very unusual. So in one sense, he is necessarily an excrescence on *Altertumswissenschaft*, which is what he practices, because he has a peculiar perspective on the scholarship. So he saw the failure of the Roman Empire connected with the good of the Roman Empire, insofar as it broke down the distinction between stranger and citizen.

Ronna: He and Daube are alike in rising to the top of this other world that they emigrated into.

Seth: But in the case of Momigliano, never satisfied with his recognition. Even in my hearing, he talked of collecting honorary degrees. He wanted a kind of recognition from everybody that in the nature of things can never be granted. Somebody has to resist somewhere. Also he kept so many opinions to himself about what he thought of people. So he seemed much more friendly to many more people than in fact he really was, and he never let on.

Ronna: Did he always feel alien, do you think? Or did he at some point feel assimilated?

Seth: In the case of teaching in England, I think he once said to me, as long as you were yourself, they didn't care who you were. What they didn't like was anyone who pretended to be them.

Ronna: Do you remember what Daube said about Momigliano?

Seth: I do remember mentioning to Momigliano, after I first read Daube, that I noticed this extraordinary left-wing tendency that came over Daube's work.

Ronna: During the time he lived in Berkeley?

Seth: Well, it showed up clearly in the book on civil disobedience.

Robert: *Civil Disobedience and Antiquity*.

Seth: It didn't seem to be in total conformity with law, and seemed to have a source which wasn't in his previous work, so I wondered where it was coming from. Momigliano of course immediately knew that that was true.

Ronna: Because he was falling in love with a woman in Berkeley.

Robert: And was enthusiastic about the student rebellion.

Seth: You saw that in his work too?

Robert: In his writing, and it was confirmed by things he said to us. He thought of himself as a friend of the feminist revolution, endorsed it wholeheartedly.

HERODOTUS AND THE BEGINNING OF PHILOSOPHY

Michael: While you were working on Herodotus at Harvard did you give talks or papers?

Seth: Yes, at a radio station. Oh no, not a radio station. There was a thing called the Lowell Lecture Series that could be done by junior fellows at the Boston Public Library. So in the spring, it must have been in the last year, I gave six talks on Herodotus.

Robert: Did you write them up?

Seth: Yes. They were early versions of my book.[19] I remember there was a radio station that called me in to ask whether they would be interesting enough to be recorded.

Michael: And you said?

Seth: No!

Ronna: Why did you choose to write on Herodotus? Did you already have an insight into what you were going to do with it?

Michael: Presumably you had just finished with the *Iliad* and you were led into it by Homer?

Seth: I'm not sure. That might have been one thing. But there was something else. Strauss had made this crucial observation about the interpreta-

---

19. *Herodotean Inquiries* (The Hague: Nijhoff, 1969); new ed. with "Second Thoughts" (South Bend: St. Augustine's Press, 1999). About the lecture series at the Boston Public Library, Harvey Mansfield adds: Harvard had a bus that transported people from the university to the public library. We used to all pile into the bus, which had a sign on it, "Herodotean Inquiries."

tion of the story of Gyges, that Herodotus was not Gyges. So it occurred to me that this must somehow be the beginning of philosophy.

Ronna: That Herodotus could look upon the things . . .

Seth: The things that are not his own without shame.

Ronna: Why is he other than Gyges?

Seth: Gyges is the one who lays down this rule that he is not supposed to look upon the wife of Candaules. Then I noticed that there is a massive contradiction in the language. The story is about Candaules' wife being thought to be the most beautiful of women. But when Gyges formulates the prohibition he says, "The beautiful things were found long ago, of which one of them is: only look at your own." So there is this massive contradiction about the *kalon* [the beautiful], which interested me. I think that's where it started.

Ronna: Your study of Homer was leading you at the same time to Herodotus?

Seth: Well, there was the problem of the *Iliad,* in book II, his interpretation of the Trojan War. I thought Egypt might provide the clue to Herodotus's understanding of Homer—that Homer is to Egypt as the beautiful is to the law.

Ronna: The Homeric revision of the Egyptian gods, translating the lawful into the beautiful?

Seth: Right.

Robert: You said you were thinking of Herodotus as the beginning of philosophy, and you link that with liberation from shame. Did you at the time think of yourself as doing philosophy in working out this interpretation of Herodotus?

Seth: Only in a very mechanical manner. I thought that Herodotus was the coherent text for pre-Socratic philosophy, that you could use Herodotus to get into pre-Socratic philosophy, because he was making use, in a coherent argument, of what they had discovered.

Robert: What the pre-Socratics had discovered?

Seth: Yes, namely the character of *physis* as opposed to *nomos.*

Michael: So there's a sort of systematic treatment of *nomos* after the discovery of its distinction from *physis.* In a way it's like Platonic philosophy, then, turning toward these things that the others just knew enough about to turn away from.

Robert: But relying on them, on the other hand, because otherwise you wouldn't be able to thematize *nomos* as *nomos,* since you wouldn't have the basic contrast.

Seth: Right. It was Plato, though, who led me to my original understanding of Herodotus.

Michael: How so?

Seth: I thought I discovered a key to the structure of the work in Plato's divided line (see *Republic* VI.509d–511e)—that the segments of the divided line provide a model for the pattern in books II through IV of Herodotus. But I didn't see that there was a development taking place in the course of those books, so I wasn't really working out Herodotus's argument.

Ronna: A development independent of the pattern?

Seth: Yes. Actually, I think I made a similar mistake in the other thing I was working on at the time, Sophocles' *Oedipus*.[20]

Michael: Is that when you wrote your first article on the *Oedipus*?

Seth: Yes, very reluctantly.

Ronna: Why were you so reluctant?

Seth: [Joseph] Cropsey wrote to me, to tell me they were thinking of doing a festschrift for Strauss.[21] He asked me if I wanted to contribute something to it, and I thought I was too young.

Robert: But then you agreed? What made you decide on the *Oedipus*?

Seth: It seemed to me that I got an understanding of Sophocles through Herodotus, combined with the *Republic*.

Ronna: Can you explain that?

Seth: I realized that the title, "Oedipus the Tyrant," was in fact the key to understanding what was going on.

Ronna: And the *Republic* helped you understand the tyrant?

Seth: Right, book IX. Then Herodotus has the same thing, about being lame as a sign of the tyrant.

Ronna: So you thought about that.

Seth: Yes, and saw that it turned on the question of incest.

Ronna: The incest issue is in Herodotus?

Seth: Yes, because of the extraordinary fact that he uses *eros* only in two ways, either the *eros* for tyranny, or for illegal passion. The key example is when he uses the verb about Candaules in love with his wife; it's thought to be very odd, *eros* for your own wife, and it leads to this transgression of the law. It's very striking that *eros* is restricted in this way.

Ronna: So you noticed that in Herodotus. And you knew its significance in the *Oedipus*?

Seth: Yes. But in that case, again, I had discerned a pattern—a form that was the essence of this particular problem—but I didn't connect it with the action of the play.

20. This discussion is taken up again in the sections on Herodotus and *Oedipus Tyrannus* in chapter 6, pp. 117–23.

21. Benardete's essay, "Sophocles' *Oedipus Tyrannus*" was published in *Ancients and Moderns* (1964; see chap. 3 n. 1).

Chapter 5

BRANDEIS, NEW YORK UNIVERSITY, AND THE NEW SCHOOL
1960–2001

BRANDEIS, 1960–64

HERBERT MARCUSE

Ronna: After Harvard you went on to Brandeis? How did you get the job there?

Michael: Was it in the classics department?

Seth: They didn't really have a classics department. They had a foreign language department.

Robert: Brandeis at that time wasn't even that old. It's post war, isn't it?

Seth: Right. When I came up for tenure, I had moved to another department, Near Eastern.

Michael: Do you remember who hired you?

Seth: A man in Spanish. I remember noticing—this was my first professional job, because at St. John's I wasn't really hired—that the faculty who were under him made up all sorts of magical properties in order to justify his being chairman.

Ronna: They had to look up to him?

Seth: Yes. He was a perfectly ordinary person, but was somehow made larger than life. I remember attending a Ph.D. oral defense with Marcuse and Diamandopoulos.[1] I think the student was in history of ideas, but Greek philosophy was part of it. Marcuse asked this student a question about

---

1. Herbert Marcuse (1898–79), who emigrated to the United States in 1934 and began teaching at Brandeis in 1958, was a social theorist and political activist known especially for his influence in the 1960s on the new left. Peter Diamandopoulos was a dean at Brandeis University and later president of Adelphi University.

Burke that was so tendentious he told you by the way he had formulated it what the answer was. The student answered exactly as he was expected to and Marcuse was beaming at how smart he was.

Michael: You don't remember what the question was?

Seth: No.

ERIC HAVELOCK

Seth: At one point they were trying to get Havelock to come, to give them prestige.[2] His wife was at Vassar and he was at Yale at that time. He was negotiating with them to get a double appointment. They asked him what his conditions would be, and the first one was, fire Benardete.

Michael: Why this ill will?

Ronna: Did you ever meet him?

Seth: He had been at Harvard. But I just met him, I didn't know him.

Robert: In the meantime he had moved on to Yale?

Seth: Yes.

Michael: Didn't Strauss write a review of Havelock?[3]

Seth: Yes, but Havelock claims he never read the review, although everybody at Yale read the review. Everybody who hated Havelock read the review.

Ronna: That was a funny piece.

Seth: Yes, very funny. Strauss once wrote me a letter about it, saying "This was the only time I took out a ruler and rapped somebody over the knuckles."

Ronna: He treated him like Protagoras in it, isn't that right?

Seth: The contemporary Protagoras.

Robert: But you left before he ever got to Brandeis?

Seth: He never went. It was just a negotiating ploy.

Robert: Meantime, it had the effect of your being ousted?

Seth: Well, after a lot of complications, I was offered tenure, but by that time I had taken the job at NYU.

---

2. Eric Havelock (1903–88), professor of classics at Harvard from 1946 to 1963 and at Yale from 1963 to 1976, was especially interested in the oral tradition of Greek poetry and Plato's response to it.

3. Strauss's review of *The Liberal Temper in Greek Politics* is reprinted in *Liberalism Ancient and Modern* (Chicago: University of Chicago Press, 1968; repr. 1995), 26–64.

NEW YORK UNIVERSITY AND THE NEW SCHOOL, 1964–2001

HOWARD WHITE

Ronna: How did you get to NYU?

Seth: There was a position open. And I knew one of the people here, named Casson.[4]

Robert: Oh, he is a friend of my former colleague at Lang College, Jean LeCorbeiller.

Seth: I had met Casson in Athens.

Michael: And when did you begin teaching at the New School?

Seth: I was hired by Howard White in 1964 to teach a course on the *Republic* that [Hilail] Gildin was supposed to teach—he must already have been at Queens. So I taught the course, and I never told anybody that I wasn't Gildin. Many years later, somebody met Gildin and said, "I was a student in your course on the *Republic* at the New School. You know, it wasn't very good."

Ronna: Had you known Howard White earlier?[5]

Seth: I met him through [Richard] Kennington. When I came to town, he was dean at the New School. He was married to the daughter of [Kurt] Riezler and had all these paintings.

Michael: Where did the money come from?

Seth: Riezler had married the daughter of a Berlin art dealer, that's where the collection came from.

Ronna: Did you come to know Howard White at all?

Seth: He was strange: on the one hand, very modest, on the other hand, very proud, somehow at sixes and sevens, not straight.

Ronna: He would teach courses on Plato and Shakespeare?

Seth: Shakespeare and Bacon, always from a very odd angle.

Ronna: He did have students, didn't he?

Seth: Yes, he had quite a number of students.

Michael: Wasn't he a Strauss student when Strauss was at the New School?

Seth: Yes, at the same time as Kennington and [Harry] Jaffa, and someone else, a man whose name begins with M?

Michael: Magid?[6]

4. Lionel Casson, professor in the classics department of New York University and author of a book on ancient seafaring.

5. Howard B. White (1912–74), dean of the Graduate Faculty at the New School, wrote on Shakespeare and Bacon.

6. Henry Magid taught philosophy at CUNY from 1960 to 1972.

Seth: Yes. I think those four.

Michael: You said Howard White was at sixes and sevens. Can you think of a story that exemplifies what you mean by that?

Seth: I remember that he thought of himself as being the bridge between the University-in-exile and the American system. So as dean he was going to preserve whatever they had contributed. But that was absurd. He wasn't in that tradition at all, he hadn't absorbed that. He could only be a bridge as it were intellectually, but he wanted to be it culturally.

Ronna: Is there such a thing? If you mean by "culturally" someone who is deeply rooted, who has a foot in each camp, is that even possible?

Seth: No, I don't think so, you see. But he thought that he in fact embodied it.

Michael: It sort of fits being married to Riezler's daughter.

Seth: I was surprised later reading Strauss' memorial speech, and the appreciation of Riezler it expressed.[7] The basis for that was not at all obvious to me. It reminds me of how hard I found it to understand why Strauss thought Reinhardt was so important.

Ronna: Why was that?

Seth: It had to do with the question of whether the distinction between *physis* and *nomos* came from philosophy or from the sophists, which was important to Strauss at the time. But Strauss admitted, "It wouldn't mean the same thing to you as it did to me." That made me realize the disparity between the experience that leads to some kind of insight and the conclusion that is then transmitted, that you can never really make up for that experience.

Ronna: Do you think it's ever possible for the teacher to work through some experience, come to a conclusion, transmit the conclusion to a student, then for the student to bring to it something more?

Seth: I was thinking about that essay in the *TLS* by Gerald . . . the historian of science?

Robert: Holton?

Seth: Gerald Holton, about quantum physics—that everybody in the first generation of quantum physics was Platonically grounded in the sense that it was so puzzling to them; they couldn't help but face the extraordinary difficulties. But in two generations it had become just a technique and the philosophic issues had totally vanished.

Michael: But you'd think it could work the other way. If it took such an

---

7. "Kurt Riezler," in *What is Political Philosophy? and Other Studies* (Westwood, Conn.: Greenwood Press Publishers, 1959), 233–60.

effort for the discoverer to break through, he might not have much steam left for elaborating on the conclusions, and another generation might make something more of it, though I can't think of an example at the moment.

Ronna: Well, in a way, you could understand the whole notion of a second sailing this way. If you read it historically, as a development from the Pre-Socratics to Socrates, couldn't you say it's a version of this other direction?

Michael: Or you might say you could understand the relation between the Greek poets and Plato that way. You've often said you can't understand them without Plato. Well, it might be that Plato in a way did understand them better than they understood themselves, but not without what they'd seen.

Seth: So the formula for that, if it's true, would be the relation between the *kalon* and the true.

Ronna: The *kalon* is the insight?

Seth: Yes, that might be what Socrates means in the *Apology,* when he speaks of the poets.

ARON GURWITSCH

Robert: Were you able to teach what you wanted at the New School?

Michael: I remember a remark you once mentioned of [Aron] Gurwitsch's, when you said you were interested in teaching the *Protagoras.*

Seth: And Gurwitsch said, "That's what we read in school."

Michael: At which point you reconsidered.

Seth: And decided to teach the *Sophist.*

Robert: So when Gurwitsch made that disdainful comment about Klein's interpretation of the cave, it wasn't only about Klein, but about Plato.

Seth: When the Europeans used to run the department, they would invite me once a year to discuss the schedule. At one point, when [Hans] Jonas was chair, he turned to Gurwitsch and said, "Well, it's your turn to teach a seminar. What will it be on? What will we call it?" Gurwitsch said, very slowly, "Intentionality." And the smile on his face was like the cat that had licked the cream. This was total knowledge. This was the only thing. It was extraordinary.

Ronna: I had a course with him, in one semester, beginning with Descartes and of course everything was a mumbling version of Husserl.

Robert: Leading up to intentionality.

HANNAH ARENDT AND JACOB TAUBES

Ronna: Did you ever have any dealings with Hannah Arendt?

Seth: Only at a party at Jonas's, when I asked her about [Karl] Jaspers.

Robert: What did you ask her?

Seth: It was about Jacob Taubes, whose name had come up in the conversation.[8] On one occasion, Taubes came to St. John's to give a talk about history. It was all Kojève, but the one name he didn't mention was Kojève. Somebody in the question period asked him, "Isn't this just Kojève?" And Taubes said, "What difference does it make where I buy my ideas from?" I told that to Strauss shortly afterwards and he said, "Yes, but he should have asked, 'What if you steal them?'"

Ronna: He would absorb things and repeat them?

Seth: Without knowing it, in some way. The famous story is that he was at Jerusalem, lecturing on Wednesday, and [Gershom] Scholem was giving lectures on Monday, which Taubes attended. Taubes became quite well known, and Scholem was told that he should visit his class. So he attended on a Wednesday and heard the lecture that he had given on Monday. Shortly afterwards, Scholem was invited to Berlin to receive an honorary degree and give a talk at the Free University, where Taubes teaches. The rector of the University at that time was good old Otto Georg von Simpson, from the Committee, who was now back in Germany. He was talking to Scholem and said, "You know, we very much regret that you refuse to take an honorary degree, but we quite understand." And Scholem said, "No, you don't understand. I just won't take a degree from a university that hires Jacob Taubes."

Ronna: Nothing to do with anything of world-historical importance.

Seth: No, just Jacob Taubes. You know, he was at one time married to Susan Sontag.

Ronna: We heard him speak in Tübingen, one of those Tübingen lectures where about six hundred people came out.

Robert: Yes, I remember. It was utterly unintelligible.

Seth: He was the leader in Berlin of the student rebellion.

Robert: I knew nothing about his background. But that helps explain why he was touted as a hero.

Seth: He had stolen letters from von Simpson's desk, and published them in the student newspaper.

Robert: When Taubes was a professor?

Seth: Yes.

Robert: How did he get as far as he did?

Seth: He wrote a very famous book, published in Switzerland, on gnosticism. It had something to do with millenarianism, eschatology. Then he was

---

8. Jacob Taubes (1923–87), philosopher of religion, for whom political theology was a central theme.

constantly attached to religion departments. But he never could stick anywhere.

Robert: He died about two years ago. I asked you about Hannah Arendt and
you were saying there was a party at which you were talking about Taubes.

Seth: And it was very revealing, her opinion of Taubes was based entirely
on a remark of Jaspers.

Ronna: Do you remember what that was?

Seth: Jaspers had used some compound German word for a "fake." I looked
it up afterward, but I can't remember now what it was. It was very striking
that it was not her own judgment she was conveying.

Ronna: That fits with the excerpts in the *Times* from her correspondence
with Jaspers.

Robert: Did you ever have any words with Arendt about Strauss?

Seth: No.

Robert: Didn't they know each other as students?

Seth: I didn't know that. Once there was a dinner party at the Carters'.
Blanckenhagen was there, Jane and I, Dwight McDonald. Sitting next to me
was the harpsichordist, Sylvia Marlowe. Arendt's piece on Eichmann was
coming out in the *New Yorker.* Dwight McDonald was saying that the New
York Jewish intellectuals had ganged up on her. Sylvia Marlowe said, "As the
only Jew here, I agree with you." I said, "You're not the only Jew here." She
turned to me and said, "What's your name?" And I said, "Benardete." She
said, "But what was your name before you changed it?" If you have a name
like "Sylvia Marlowe . . ."

Ronna: Right.

Seth: Then Blanckenhagen said, turning to McDonald, "But you must say
about the articles, they're not human." Meaning humane. McDonald said,
"Well, I suppose that neither Hannah nor I am human." Everybody changed
the subject. He wanted to make a witty remark. But it came out in this funny
way.

Michael: Did you know McDonald well?

Seth: No, I just met him a few times at the Carters'.

Michael: But you knew his son.

Seth: I knew his son at Harvard. He was a classmate of the son of Mary Mc-
Carthy and [Edmund] Wilson—they had grown up together—who became
a professor. I once made Dwight McDonald buy my Herodotus book.

Ronna: How did you do that?

Seth: I think we were at a party at the Carters', talking about books, and Herodotus came up.

Ronna: So you said, "I happen to have written a book."

Seth: And he said he wanted to buy it. So I sent him the book and he sent me the money.

THE *NEW YORK REVIEW OF BOOKS*

Seth: The editor of the *New York Review of Books*, [Robert] Silvers, is a friend of the Carters'. He was once at the Carters' and saw my Herodotus book on their table. The consequence of this was that the guy who lived his life exploiting Stravinsky—

Robert: Robert Craft?

Seth: Right. He wrote an article in the *New York Review of Books* in which there's a footnote to *Herodotean Inquiries*. What it means, I have no idea. But that led to the request for me to write a review of Fränkel's *Early Greek Poetry and Philosophy*.

Ronna: I remember sending the book to you, from New York to Martha's Vineyard, one summer.

Seth: Right. So I wrote the review. They wanted it to be done again. So I did it over.

Ronna: What did they want you to do differently?

Seth: Add quotations. But I also revised it. Then I never heard anything from them. Until suddenly, it must have been three years later, a messenger boy came to the door with the proofs for this article that was going to be printed.

Ronna: It was very urgent.

Seth: Urgent, the next week. And it was not anything I had written. It was the two pieces combined.

Ronna: Completely crazy.

Seth: Totally. Bloom loved it. "Oh this is wonderful. This is the way you should always write."

Ronna: Did you ever find out who edited it?

Seth: Somebody who sat there for three years, trying to make sense of my two reviews.

Ronna: It only made sense to him combined. And they published that?

Seth: Yes. The consequence of this combination, by the way, was that the piece begins with a mistake. It refers to Diehls instead of Diels.

Michael: You mean Diels and Kranz?

Seth: Right. It was a reference to *Die Fragmente der Vorsokratiker*. So Martha Nussbaum wrote me a note and said "How could Diehls come in here?" I wrote back and said, "One day I'll explain it." [Harold] Cherniss also wrote to me about it. "But," he said, "I don't understand what you mean" . . . what was it that he didn't understand? Oh yes, the problem of how philosophy could come after the poets talked about "lies like the truth." How come philosophy didn't precede poetry, if philosophy goes after the truth?

Ronna: That sounds like an interesting problem.

Seth: I thought it was. It looks as though the poets were post-philosophic.

Ronna: What do you think now?

Seth: The piece I wrote recently on Hesiod is supposed to explain it.[9] So many years later I came up with an answer for Cherniss.

Michael: You said he always used to send back a response immediately.

Seth: He'd say, "I'm sorry not to have replied earlier. I received it at 9:30 this morning."

Michael: That is very clever. He never had to read things.

ENCOUNTERS WITH MADMEN

ELECTRIC BLUE

Seth: One night, after class at the New School, we were coming down from the Cedar Tavern, on the second floor. It was a very mild night. And there was a man standing right at the door dressed in blue, from his hat to his shoes, bathed in neon light.

Ronna: I remember that. It was in the early seventies.

Seth: I know it was after '69, because this guy was in a class I gave in the theater department at CUNY, which I was invited to give, along with the Polish literary critic, Jan Kott, and [Richard] Schechner, who had done "Dionysus '69." We gave three talks on Euripides, at CUNY, on the *Bacchae*. I was rationality itself.

Robert: In that group.

Seth: So as we were coming out of the Cedar Tavern that night, this guy says to me, "Oh, I owe everything to you." I said, "How come?" And he said, "Well, I took your course on the *Antigone* and I wrote a book called *Elizabeth the First, A Secret Jewess,* which is now translated into Hebrew and Braille, and I'm about to write another book, inspired by your thought, to prove that Odysseus came from Odessa.

A FORMER WEATHERMAN

Michael: Wasn't there one occasion at NYU where you had to call the police?

Seth: Yes, it happened right here. I was giving a course on Greek tragedy.

---

9. "The First Crisis in First Philosophy," *Graduate Faculty Philosophy Journal* 19, no. 1 (1995): 238–48; reprinted in *The Argument of the Action* (Chicago: University of Chicago Press, 2000).

On the first day of the term, a man asked whether he could sit in. And I said fine. Toward the end of each class he would ask some question which was very hard to answer. But about a month after the course had begun, he began to take over, and talk at great length. At the end of one class I had to tell him to keep quiet. He said, "I'm going to follow you to your next class," which I taught right afterward. I said, "You haven't been invited to that class." He said, "I'm going to stick to you anyway." So he came up here to the seminar room, where the class was being held. I said, "Well, I have to call the police." And I called the campus police. Two people in suits and one in uniform came up, and listened to this conversation we were having, in which he said to me, "What is the one word which you alone can tell me, which can solve both Heidegger's problem and my own? Rosa Luxembourg was the only woman who solved the feminist problem of the twentieth century," and so on. It took the policemen some time to figure out . . .

Ronna: That he was crazy.

Seth: Right. But after they figured out that I was the professor and he was the crazy one, they said to him, "Come with us." He refused. But they were very wise. They didn't know how he would react, so they wouldn't touch him. They called the New York City police. Then three New York City police came. And we had this conversation again. It became wilder and wilder. The policeman began to talk to this fellow and call him "Socrates": "Okay, Socrates, you come with us." Then the university policeman called a psychiatrist. When the psychiatrist came, the guy said to me, "Well, you know what you've condemned me to—homosexual rape." "Rape," says the psychiatrist, "now that's very interesting." The rest of the talk was about Pre-Socratic philosophy and Heidegger, he couldn't care less; but as soon as he heard the word "rape," he zoomed in like that.

Robert: This is my bailiwick.

Seth: So we were inching our way toward the elevator, which was then operated by hand. The New York policemen were trying to draw him there. I had noticed that he was constantly calculating how crazy he could behave, on the basis of my reaction and everybody else's. It was very self-conscious. So we were outside the office door of a former colleague of mine, Mrs. Trell.[10] All of a sudden, her door flies open and she comes rushing out, with eyes blazing out of her head, shouting at the top of her lungs, "I could kill him!" He took one look at her, and they led him away. That was real madness. It turned out she was talking about a mislaid package.

---

10. Bluma Trell taught in the New York University classics department from 1959 to 1979 and part time until 1989.

Michael: You never heard from this person again?

Seth: Yes, I did. He called me up later and asked, "Now what was wrong?" And I said, "You weren't polite." He said, "That's all it is? Politeness?" And I said, "Yes," and hung up.

Michael: You gave him the word. He wanted one word.

Seth: It turned out that he had been in the underground, and in fact had just surfaced and had taken on an assumed name. So he was totally disoriented, in coming back to "reality."

Ronna: From the '6os?

Seth: Yes, he was a Weatherman.

Ronna: And decided to reenter reality through Benardete's Greek tragedy class. I remember one guy who used to come to your classes at the New School, with a huge microphone. It had an arm that extended right up to your face. It was terrible.

Seth: Right, I remember that.

Ronna: We speculated a lot about it.

Seth: He was putting everything on a huge master tape.

Ronna: It was the *Statesman*. I think people were attracted by some sense of the esoteric, that you were finding meanings where others, . . .

Seth: Where no man had trod.

Ronna: They thought they found a kindred spirit.

Seth: It must be something like that. The last one was this guy from Israel, who wrote me a letter he slipped under my door. He had been attending classes here and at the New School for about two years. Then he put something under my door to announce that he was God and I was his prophet. And I was supposed to spread the word. If not, he would do something terrible.

Robert: What?

Seth: Either kill himself or kill me. I don't remember which.

Michael: How long ago was this?

Seth: Fifteen years ago, maybe? I must have sobered up in the meantime.

Michael: Well, you know, all these people who bothered you fifteen years ago have now become tenured professors.

Seth: And now they're bothering everybody else.

JULIUS THE CZECH PLATONIST

Seth: About ten years ago, I had just finished the first term on the *Republic*, and the philosophy club here at NYU asked me to give a talk on it. So I planned to give a talk on the structure of the argument in the first book. I got a phone call and somebody told me that a visiting Czech, a man named Julius who had been involved in the Charter '77 group, wanted to come to the talk. So he was there in the audience. I was talking about the absolute incoherence of the demand that Glaucon makes on Socrates: he wants Socrates to show justice in itself and also its effect on the soul independent of rewards, and he isn't aware that these are two different questions. Julius protested this distinction. We had to take out the Greek text and I showed it to him, but it was clear he couldn't understand it. So we shouted at one another for some time. Then I went on to Glaucon's statue and said that it is perfectly absurd. Then [Thomas] Nagel, who had come to the talk, got into the discussion and said, "Oh, but philosophers do this all the time, make up impossible situations." And I realized that this had to do with the bat.[11] Anyway, the next day I got a call from Nagel, saying that this man, Julius, while he was here as a member of the Humanities Council on a fellowship, wanted to attend some Greek classes. I said I was doing Sophocles' *Trachiniae,* and he could come. So he showed up and didn't say anything the first week. The second week we went out to the Cedar Tavern and he told me his life story. He had gotten a Ph.D. from Charles University in '67 or so, and then had taken a two-year fellowship, somewhere in California, I think. It was unclear whether Prague was supporting it or some American institution. Then he went back and the Russians moved in, so he decided not to teach. He went into a factory, married and had a child. Sometime in the course of this factory work he decided to learn Greek, on his own, which immediately explained to me why he didn't really know it. He became devoted to Plato, read everything he could, and developed many theories, the character of which was that, unlike all other accounts of Plato, his was based on the text. He was complaining about the fact that it was not accepted in England, when he made these very simple points.

Ronna: At Oxford?

Seth: Yes, and elsewhere. And I said, "Well, I think that's perfectly natural." He had a friend working with him in the factory in Prague, and at some point he said to this friend, "You know, our sons are getting older and not getting a good education. Why don't I teach them Plato?" And his friend said, "Fine." So the two sons and the two fathers met together once a week and Julius talked to them about Plato. Then other people in Prague heard about it and joined the group. As it grew, a spy showed up in the group. He didn't mention who it was, but he knew. He decided that he would write a

---

11. This is an allusion to Thomas Nagel's influential article, "What Is It Like to Be a Bat," *Philosophical Review* 83 (1974): 435–450.

series of letters to the universities in Europe saying, "I am Julius, studying Plato with this group. Could you send some of your distinguished people down to participate?" Somehow this caught on at Oxford, and they made an enormous effort to do it. Everybody came to Julius' seminar on Plato— [Myles] Burnyeat, [G. E. L.] Owen.[12] [Jacques] Derrida came and was stopped at the border. It became a very big thing. And the secret police wanted to stop it. One week they arrested everyone and put them all in jail, where they had the seminar. The secret police were really furious at this. They began stopping the professors for hours at the border and detaining them. They became more and more vicious, until finally they had two thugs beat up Julius's wife, who was a television writer, and crack her skull.

Michael: Wasn't there also a story about being parked inside the apartment?

Seth: Right. He decided when this happened that he would have to give it up. But before that, two secret agents stood in his apartment at the doorway twenty-four hours a day, relieved every eight hours or so. They were not acknowledged by anyone in the group. Meanwhile they smoked constantly, and the cigarette butts grew to a huge pyramid at the doorway. Everyone who went into the apartment had to step through this pile of cigarette butts and past the two agents. When he finally called a halt to the meetings, after his wife was attacked, the agents disappeared. The next day he was called in by the head of the secret police. In Prague, the office of the secret police is in the same building where they talked to the prisoners. So while he was being interrogated on the third floor, he could hear through the elevator shafts the screams from the cellar. The head called him in and Julius said to him, "What about the two secret agents who are in my apartment?" The man said, "What secret agents?" And Julius said, "Well, you know, I wasn't the only one to see them. Foreigners saw them." "Oh," he said, "those secret agents." Julius told me, that's the whole point, to make you believe that what you know is not true. Then he said, "As a consequence of this they gave me an exit visa, and I couldn't come back. So I left with my wife and we went to England, where I was welcomed with open arms and I lectured everywhere."

Renna: On Plato?

Seth: On this experience. He was connected with Charter '77, and it looks as if he was really in on it from the beginning. At the same time, however, he would go to the philosophers' meetings and the philologists' meetings and say to these Oxford dons, "You don't know any Greek. You've misinter-

---

12. Myles Burnyeat, fellow at All Souls College, Oxford, works in ancient philosophy. G. E. L. Owen (1922–82), a scholar of ancient philosophy, taught at Oxford, Harvard, and Cambridge.

preted Plato. This is what Plato says." When he went to England, he had been promised that he'd be made a lecturer in ancient philosophy. This offer fell through. And he said to me, "You see, the Czech secret police got to them." They had really turned his head.

Ronna: They were everywhere, all-powerful.

Seth: They were manipulating the Oxford dons. I fortunately managed to avoid asking about any opinions he had of Plato, because it is clear that I would have thought they were just as nutty as the English thought. Anyway, at the next meeting of the *Trachiniae* class he insisted upon talking and I told him to shut up and he left.

Ronna: He was really intrusive?

Seth: Yes. I immediately realized as he was going out the door what was going on. I was got at by the Czech secret police! Years later I was at a party at the Carters' and I met Richard Wollheim.[13] I asked him, "Do you know a guy named Julius?" "Oh," he said "that crackpot, yes." So I said to him, "You know he told me that he was promised a fellowship. How come it didn't happen?" And Wollheim said, "He turned out to be quite impossible. We couldn't give it to him." So I asked, "Did you ever tell him?" And he said, "No."

Michael: British understatement once again.

Ronna: I guess you'd expect someone to draw the right inference.

Michael: But it shows they didn't give very much thought to the world he had come out of. How could you expect him to draw the right inference when he had spent his life with police at his door.

Seth: Also, they thought it was so important that he agree with them. Although they admired him for the politics, they drew the line academically and wouldn't allow him into the club.

---

13. Richard Wollheim (1923–), professor at University College London and Berkeley, whose work is in philosophy of mind, aesthetics, and history of philosophy.

Part Two

REFLECTIONS

Seth Benardete, New York University, c, 1990. Courtesy Michael Platt

Chapter 6

FROM PATTERN TO DYNAMIC

DISCOVERING THE IMPORTANCE OF PLOT

THE *ILIAD*

Michael: When we were talking about your dissertation, you said you later came to see the mistake in your original reading of the *Iliad*—that you had the structure of the poem, but without explaining it through the plot.[1] Can you say anything more about how you understand that difference?

Seth: Well, in the first version, I had a formal Platonic pattern that I had imposed on the plot, on the basis of Diotima's ladder of love (*Symposium* 211c–d). But I didn't ask the question, How come the combat between Paris and Menelaus is replaced by the combat between Hector and Ajax? On the basis of Diotima's schema, you can go from one to the other because you see the same pattern.

Ronna: Would you go so far as to say that the schema kept you from seeing the dynamic of the plot?

Seth: It never occurred to me that there would be a dynamic. I didn't see that the challenge to Agamemnon, which Achilles lays down in the first book, but which is rejected, is then picked up in the third book by Menelaus, who realizes that, in order to justify his claim to Helen, he has to accept the principle Achilles introduced.

Ronna: What is that principle?

Seth: The principle of natural right, which is not based on law. When Menelaus accepts the challenge from Paris, it means he gives up his legal right to her, and says "I have to earn it." But that was the principle that

---

1. See chap. 2, pp. 69–70.

Achilles laid down to Agamemnon in the beginning, which had been rejected. I hadn't seen that in fact it worked its way into Menelaus. Consequently, the shift to the second layer, that is, to another understanding based
on natural right, was in fact initiated by Achilles; but Achilles has to learn
that he in fact has this principle in himself. I knew, from the Diotima model,
that there had to be a shift in motivation at some point, but I didn't see any
necessity for that to come in the ninth year of the war. Only later did I pay attention to what the plot indicates—that Achilles needed nine years to grow
up at Troy before he comes to know that he is the number-one guy.

Michael: This understanding of the way plot works seems to be a really
crucial element in everything you've done since I've known you.

HERODOTUS

Ronna: You suggested earlier that you felt you repeated the mistake of your
Iliad reading when you came to Herodotus.[2] But I wonder if or how that
affects your understanding of the structure. Would you still say that the
model is the divided line?

Seth: Yes, right. Book II, Egypt, is the level of *dianoia* [thought]; book III is
pistis [trust], that's Persia; then book IV is *eikasia* [imaging], that's Scythia and
Libya. There's the same sequence, by the way, in Lucretius, II, III, IV. So it
might be a widespread pattern.

Ronna: This downward movement?

Seth: Yes, right.

Ronna: What about book I of Herodotus? Is that *noēsis* [intellection]?

Seth: No. Book I is the way into the problem of the next three books; it's
about why II, III, and IV are necessary in order to understand Greece. You
can show that the problem of true *logos* and *pistis* comes up in Book III.

Ronna: Explicitly?

Seth: Explicitly, as characteristic of the Persians. They learned to tell lies,
first under Darius, who proposes that you tell lies for the sake of some good
and therefore you tell the truth for the sake of some good. So he destroys the
nomos for the sake of tyranny. It's very explicit. There's a man who, although
put under tremendous pressure to lie, tells the Persians the truth and then
commits suicide. Immediately afterwards Darius makes this remark and it's
all over. The pattern can be seen in the language. Words of likeness and simi-
larity are most dense in book IV. In book II, everything is based on the problem of two, two things that don't fit together but do belong together.

2. See chap. 4, pp. 99–100.

Ronna: Male and female?

Seth: Yes, or water and earth, permanence and change, body and soul. The self-contradiction within Egyptian *nomos* is based on the recognition of these two things, which they have no capacity to put together.

Robert: So what was missing from the interpretation of Herodotus based on the divided line?

Seth: Only years later did I see what it means that the pattern is broken at III.38. That's when the tyranny of Polycrates on Samos comes in, right after the burial question comes up. It marks the end of the holy law, then you begin looking at things in light of the political. I realized I must have been wrong in just seeing book IV as patterned over against II. Book IV does represent the level of *eikasia;* but it belongs to the political which has been introduced in contrast to the sacred, after III.38. So it has to be understood in terms of Greek freedom.

Ronna: It's part of a pattern but there's also been a development of the argument?

Seth: Right, right. But I didn't understand that originally, that there was a second thing, which would have led me to work out the argument.

Robert: Is that what you had in mind when I asked you earlier whether in studying Herodotus you thought of yourself as doing philosophy, and you said, only in a mechanical way?

Seth: Yes. I saw this pattern in Herodotus, the divided line as the basis for books II through IV, but I didn't connect it with the movement of the argument. I didn't pay enough attention to the turning point at III.38, where something new takes place when the priest disappears and the political begins.

Robert: Are you suggesting that symmetry-breaking is the key to knowing there's more than just pattern, there's also dynamic or motion?

Seth: I think that's right.

Robert: And you want to say that you weren't really doing philosophy as long as you were just getting patterns without the dynamic of argument?

Ronna: It sounds more like a development in your understanding of what philosophy requires rather than—

Robert: That it's not philosophy to begin with.

Seth: Well, that might be true if you looked at it backwards. But I didn't think of myself that way.

Michael: It sounds as if Plato played a crucial role for you in unlocking these other writers.

Ronna: You've suggested that in the case of both Homer and Herodotus.

Robert: You took the divided line from the *Republic* and used it as a pattern to understand Herodotus; but does that mean you didn't understand the divided line itself as part of a Platonic argument?

Seth: No, not at all. I took it, more or less, the way everyone takes it.

ANTIGONE AND *OEDIPUS TYRANNUS*

Seth: When I came to the *Antigone* a similar thing happened. I began by reflecting on the difference between the private and the public. That was my reinterpretation of Hegel; but I thought you had to construe the play in more of an ancient manner than Hegel had.

Ronna: So all along you were getting guidance from the philosophers.

Seth: And therefore I wasn't philosophizing.

Ronna: What do you think was missing in your original understanding of the *Antigone?*

Seth: I saw that the play raises an Oedipus-like riddle: Why does the daughter of the incestuous marriage become the upholder of the sacred law of the family? But that's an eidetic problem independent of the plot of the play and it wouldn't make any difference whether she died or not.

Ronna: So, on the one hand, you have this puzzle, on the other, the plot, and they turned out to coincide?

Seth: No. The very fact that it ends with Creon shows they don't coincide. They must be very different orders of things, and you have to do something to put them together. But I didn't see that originally.

Michael: When do you think it was that you came to realize the kind of mistake we've been talking about?

Seth: I think I made the reflection on the defect of my *Iliad* interpretation when I saw I had made the same mistake in the *Oedipus* essay, the one for Strauss's festschrift. I had written it in the early '60s, when I was a junior fellow, but it didn't come out until 1964.

Michael: And you had come to see your original interpretation of the *Oedipus* as mistaken by the time you wrote about the play in "On Greek Tragedy"?[3]

Seth: Yes.

Robert: How was the original interpretation mistaken?

Seth: It was the ninth book of the *Republic* that had given me the key to the *Oedipus.* You could understand what it means for the *idion* and the *koinon*

---

3. In *The Great Ideas Today* (Encyclopaedia Britannica, Inc., 1980); reprinted in *The Argument of the Action* (Chicago: University of Chicago Press, 2000). On the earlier *Oedipus* essay, see chap. 4, n. 21.

[the private and public] to break down, or in the case of the tyrant, that desires would be identical with reality. Sophocles has set it up in such a way that one sees there is a necessary connection between the riddle of the Sphinx and the two crimes Oedipus commits, but that's totally independent of the plot. That's as it were the truth of the plot, but it doesn't require any unfolding,

Ronna: Any causal sequence.

Seth: You could do anything in order to show that that was so. So you can get rid of the story and say, this is what the story really means, consequently, you don't need the plot.

Robert: So you have structure without explanation of it, that's what it sounds like.

Seth: Right.

Michael: But you had used the notion of a "limping third," so you knew already that paradigms never quite fit. I remember when I talked to you about *Politics* II, and suggested that Aristotle's own division into three follows Hippodamas's division into three. You pointed out to me that even in the way I chopped it up it was very hard to make a class division into three and maybe that was intentional, and you used this expression a "limping triad," which is obviously a reference to the *Oedipus.*

Seth: Well, in fact the *Oedipus* is an eidetic analysis, à la *Sophist* and *Statesman,* where he sets up triads that never work. It's very much like Platonic *diairesis* [division].

Ronna: Would you say that your concern with the problem of that pattern almost kept you from paying attention to the plot?

Seth: Yes, because it looks as though it's such a powerful interpretation of the *Oedipus* that you don't need anything else. It gives a solution that does not require anything puzzling. It's paradoxical but it has a form to it. It's coherent, and it's meant to be. It's a form based totally on the counterfactual. So you can put together Oedipus's fate and his character in a perfectly simple way.

Michael: Which was what you unraveled in the second piece.

Seth: Right. The formula was: Had he known what he was, he would have done what he did. So there isn't any problem. What seems to be totally imposed is the unfolding of himself. I remember this very distinctly. The key to the *Oedipus* from this point of view is that the word "polis" disappears half way through. It constantly appears for 800 lines, then the chorus says, "May not competition disappear from the city." After that there's no "polis" for the next 800 lines. So the play begins as a political problem, turns into a family problem, and finally becomes a problem of self-identity. It looks as if you're moving progressively away from the polis.

Ronna: To the self?

Seth: To the self and parents. Then you have to turn it around and see why they are the same problem precisely because of the character of tyranny.

Ronna: Did you understand this the first time through?

Seth: Yes, but then I realized many years later, in rereading it, that the difficulty with this interpretation is that you don't need the play in order for it to hold. You could have any story.

Ronna: To exemplify this structure?

Seth: Right, anything could have happened.

Robert: As long as you moved from city to family to self.

Seth: Yes, that structure had a curious way of illuminating Oedipus independent of the action of the play. So you could take every scene as showing different aspects of Oedipus and it doesn't make any difference what the sequence is, because they're all going to turn out to be coherent.

Michael: If it made any difference, it would only be in a performance of the play, on an altogether different plane.

Ronna: With the structure alone, you wouldn't understand the causes of the transformation, in this case the disappearance of "polis."

Seth: And you can't understand why Oedipus had to blind himself.

Ronna: How does that fit in?

Seth: The interpretation based on the structure of tyranny, although it might be true in a certain way, doesn't look at the way Oedipus himself explains his self-blinding. His own explanation turns on his parents in Hades. It's a totally different dimension. It doesn't seem to have anything to do with tyranny. It turns on something, hinted at right in the beginning, that they didn't bury the corpses from the plague, and only the women lament. At the end of the play, Oedipus asks that Jocasta be buried, and that's directly connected with this funny thing about Hades, shame. But it doesn't seem as though it fits in. Then, once you look at the line of the action, everything explodes, nothing seems to be coherent.

Ronna: That's when you made your discovery of two possible plots, two different sequences?

Seth: Yes. The crucial thing is that, if I was right in the first place, Sophocles could have had Oedipus leave Delphi and wander around for five years and then come to Thebes. His father would have been dead for five years, there would have been many deaths caused by the Sphinx, he would have solved the riddle, and then this play would have unfolded in exactly the same manner.

Michael: But Sophocles goes out of his way to make it inexplicable.

Seth: Right. In other words, it turns out that he has embedded the self-opacity of Oedipus in the self-opacity of Thebes. That I had not understood originally. There is this double level of self-ignorance. The self-opacity concerning the murder of Laius is the first thing. Oedipus must have come to Jocasta when she was in mourning, but she never mentions the fact that Laius had just died.

Michael: It's even worse than that, isn't it? It's not even clear that she knows Laius is dead.

Seth: Right. And they do not at all connect Oedipus with the prior events. The beauty of the play turns out to be that on the form level you have total necessity, the unfolding in time of what was true from the beginning; but the context in which this unfolding is taking place is totally at random. No one had ever done that before. In other words, you have absolute fate with regard to the central character, but everything else is at random and everybody is out of their minds.

Robert: But you want to say that in working out this new interpretation you weren't just taking the pattern you already had and adding something on to it. It's not form analysis plus something else.

Seth: No, there's a real undermining. Sophocles wrote a play which has a very queer character to it; he traps the audience in a way that puts them in this funny position like that of Oedipus. They cannot possibly understand what's going on, but they think, because they're already familiar with the story of Oedipus, that they know what's happening.

AENEID

Ronna: You've suggested the role Plato played in your understanding of the pre-Platonic poets. But you've also studied post-Platonic poets, the Latin writers. Is there any sign that somehow the same thing is being done in a more self-conscious form post-Platonically, whereas in the other cases Plato must have made explicit something he learned from his predecessors?

Seth: Well, that's interesting. The odd thing is, if you take the *Aeneid* as being the paradigm case of a post-Platonic work, it also echoes Homer. Everybody is more or less agreed that Aeneas has no character. There's a passage in the *Aeneid* where Aeneas has gone to a Greek who has settled in what is going to be Rome and the king tells him that he doesn't have the forces to help him against the Latins, and he should go to the Etruscans. Then Virgil in three lines says, a messenger was sent to the king of the Etruscans, the request was made, and the forces were granted. This is in narrative. Then you think about that and you wonder, why couldn't the whole story be told that way?, since it's all known beforehand, where Aeneas is going. So the *Aeneid* would in fact be one line: Aeneas left Troy and founded the city that was meant ultimately to be Rome. That's the story. Nothing happens to him. It's all been preordained. The poem could be reduced to this. And that seems to be Virgil's reflection on what it means to come second, after Homer and Plato.

THE *LOGOS* OF THE ACTION IN THE PLATONIC DIALOGUE

Michael: What we've been discussing about pattern and plot is obviously connected with why Platonic dialogues are dialogic. Otherwise, in an interpretation of Plato, you could simply give the meaning of the dialogue and dispense with the action.

Seth: But it's interesting. I had imbibed too early Strauss's claims about *logos* and action and hadn't realized what it really meant, except that there was a formulaic manner in which you could superimpose the argument onto what was happening in the dialogue. I didn't understand that there was in fact an argument *in* the action. If you don't see that, it just looks as if you have the repeated modification of a theme as the dialogue goes on.

Ronna: I see the culmination of this in your *Phaedrus* book.[4] When I was studying the *Phaedrus* originally, I was preoccupied with the necessity of the structure, parts and whole, and I thought that's what Plato meant by logographic necessity. I remember what a surprise it was for me when I read your book and realized you were saying logographic necessity was something different from the animal as a model of whole and parts (*Phaedrus* 264b–c). It took me a long time to see what that could mean.

Seth: The animal is this form analysis.

Ronna: Right, and I took that to be the same as logographic necessity. But you associate logographic necessity with a temporal, or sequential dimension.

Seth: Right, that's the real action.

Robert: The becoming . . .

Ronna: Which has a causality to it . . .

Seth: And also has a *logos*. In other words, the mistake is when you take the details of the dialogue as a constant modification of the themes of the dialogue. But the consequence is that nothing really changes. There's an enrichment of the modular way, but in fact it turns out there is another development.

---

4. *The Rhetoric of Morality and Philosophy: Plato's Gorgias and Phaedrus* (Chicago: University of Chicago Press, 1991).

Ronna: That's the dynamic?

Seth: Right. So that turns out to be something that already was in Homer, and in tragedy. This was not something invented by Plato; he must have realized that they had done this very odd thing, which is most conspicuous in the case of the *Oedipus,* because there you get total incoherence of plot, which brings you immediately to what the deeper issue is.

Michael: So this is somehow the same as to say that "The surface of things is the heart of things"?[5]

Seth: Yes, but it's interesting because I knew that very early, but I never really understood what it meant. And Strauss didn't explain to anybody what he was doing.

Michael: But you do think he was doing the same thing?

Seth: Oh, I have no doubt that that's what he was doing, but I'm not sure it was clear to anybody what the principle is. He had set up, from the *Hiero* book on, that there was a sort of standard formula by which this could be done, the setting, the characters . . .

Ronna: The title . . .

Seth: Right.

Michael: But you didn't originally see how all of that is connected with the action of the work as you now understand it?

Seth: I think the first time I began to understand that in Plato was probably the *Republic.* I remember being struck, teaching the *Republic,* how it was like a machine, with the argument unfolding in this extraordinary manner.

Robert: The way you describe the initial position, which you later saw as mistaken, it sounds as if at least one important part of the mistake is holding something too fixed. You take something as fixed, which gets manifested in this form.

Ronna: The skeletal structure?

Robert: It's what the Germans call a *Roster.*

Ronna: Your use of the "template" in the *Phaedrus* and *Gorgias* is an interesting case of this. You take something like the relation of Gorgias, Polus, and Callicles, or the relation of the three parts in the chariot image of the soul, which looks like a rigid structure, but then it turns out there's a motion to that structure which explains what it is.

Seth: Right, right.

Michael: And without which it turns out to be unintelligible.

---

5. "The problem inherent in the surface of things, and only in the surface of things, is the heart of things." Leo Strauss, *Thoughts on Machiavelli* (Seattle: University of Washington Press, 1958), 13. Benardete refers to this "golden sentence" in "Leo Strauss's *The City and Man,*" *Political Science Reviewer* 8 (1978): 1.

Seth: What I learned from Plato about how this works turned out to be the key to the understanding of everybody else.

Ronna: So you came to see something like this at work in poetry only with the help of Plato?

Michael: But you've suggested how much Plato must have learned from the poets.

Seth: That's true. And in fact, when you take the formal pattern from Plato, it can be misleading for the interpretation of the other works, if you haven't put it together with the dynamic. So, all of *Oedipus* is in the ninth book of the *Republic,* about the dream world and the tyrant. But if you simply apply that directly to the *Oedipus* you get this formal analysis.

Ronna: Without the plot.

Michael: But when you understand the connection between argument and action in the Platonic dialogue, it's so clear that you can go back to the way you did it the first time and use the action as a guide to what's going on in the argument. And maybe that's not possible in a poem where you only have action and the theme is not really presented in the work itself in the same way that it is in a Platonic dialogue.

Seth: It's interesting about philosophy, that it has this power to free itself from the dynamic to such an extent that you can get it, but then in fact there is a concealed element to it too.

Ronna: Do you think every philosophic work has this dynamic aspect, even if only in a concealed way?

Michael: Well, it seems to me that whenever you really start getting interested in something, it's probably not an accident that you start to discover something that runs at least parallel to this. But you're really of mixed feelings, aren't you, about whether it occurs after the ancients, in some modified form, say in Rousseau, or in Descartes?

Seth: I don't know really. I think it has to do with experience. One has to have gone through these steps in reading the author for oneself. But it does look as though this is the nature of philosophic thinking itself. So what shows up in formal terms in literary criticism, that is, the distinction between form and action, is identical, or at least can be matched with the natural steps of thinking.

Ronna: Is this a way to understand "second sailing"?

Seth: Yes, I think this discovery of the action is a second sailing. Maybe you always have to do something like what happens in the *Republic,* where you make the move to the invention of the perfect city only in order to step back from it.

Robert: You construct a model, which eventually has to be undermined?

Seth: Well, you might say, in other words, that mathematical physics is the paradigm for the first stage of philosophical thinking.

Ronna: Why do you say that?

Robert: Because what you do is, you take a domain and you provide this *Roster*, this form, but you give no account of it, you don't explain the form.

Ronna: Mathematical physics stands for the tension between structure and cause?

Seth: For structure without cause.

Michael: And the second sailing is a correction of that. But isn't there something illusory about trying to pinpoint the moment at which one makes the second sailing? It looks as if it is a continual state of undergoing, rather than something that happens once and then you're beyond it.

Seth: The real question—you might say the Platonic question—is: Is the trap door in a Platonic writing an imitation of the trap door in nature?

Ronna: Can you say anything more about that?

Seth: Well, if the Platonic dialogue, and ancient poetry, always have to do with the oddity of the individual, what is being reflected in these imitations is the fact that something is being disclosed in a particular that is incapable of being disclosed in any other way. It looks as if the Platonic enterprise is based on a thesis about the nature of the world—that there is something I would call the encounter with the question, which can't be determined by a formula or concept. The problem in nature would have to come up experientially, as it does in the reading of the dialogue, even though it's been designed; otherwise the dialogue wouldn't be an imitation. There isn't any thread that you can pull on that will open it up, even after you have this principle.

Ronna: That's why you like that line in *A River Runs Through It*, right?[6]

Seth: Yes.

Michael: If we go back to your first *Iliad* interpretation and the later one, one way of stating the difference is that, if you simply concentrate on the structure, you think you're dealing with particulars, but in fact you turn them into paradigms. Achilles becomes paradigmatic, and then it's shorthand for something which you can express more completely. But in fact that's very different from following the plot so you see the relation of the pieces insofar as they grow out of one another and they're necessary because of what came before.

---

6. "All there is to thinking," he said, "is seeing something noticeable which makes you see something you weren't noticing which makes you see something that isn't even visible." Norman Maclean, *A River Runs through It* (Chicago: University of Chicago Press, 1976). Benardete uses this line as the epigraph for his book *Socrates' Second Sailing: On Plato's Republic* (Chicago: University of Chicago Press, 1989).

Seth: But it looks as if there must be a false mapping of the true nature of philosophy onto this formal pattern, so that it reflects it in some way, which is not totally spurious. That's the way Heidegger thought of it, as totally spurious. That's not the Platonic way.

Michael: The question seems to be whether there is something on the level of a philosophic argument that runs parallel to what happens in the *Odyssey* or the *Iliad.* Could you find something comparable in an Aristotelian treatise, or Descartes, so that the unfolding of the argument is meant to be taken as an action, just as the unfolding of the plot is meant to be taken as an argument in Homer? It looks as though the esotericism of the tradition in the West necessarily involves something like this combination of argument and action.

Robert: But the key is that you always want to tie thinking to a unique particular, not just a particular, but a unique particular, an individual.

Seth: That is, you want to tie thinking to nonthinking, and that's very hard to do.

REPUBLIC

Michael: It occurs to me that in a way paradigm fits with the kind of writing one does when one is reading something quickly oneself, in contrast with teaching, when you do a seminar over the course of fifteen weeks and constantly reevaluate what came the previous week; that seems to be connected with being able to see the *logos* of a text unfold. I wonder if there was any correspondence between the shift you made from paradigm to the unfolding of the argument and teaching seminars.

Seth: I think that it may have had to do with teaching a text twice. That was probably the crucial experience.

Robert: I was thinking about comments you made after teaching the three-semester course on the *Republic.* You said it became possible to look at other things in a way you couldn't have without the understanding you arrived at through the *Republic.* It sounded as if working on the *Republic,* both giving the course as well as writing the book, was a kind of turning point.

Seth: I suppose it was, because of the way it turned out that the paradigmatic understanding of it is absolutely coincident with the *logos* understanding of it. Plato is driving through this apparently simple principle and making it undergo transformations, so that you can see how he is constantly pulling things out of the same form.

Ronna: Could you sketch the difference between what you're calling the paradigmatic understanding and the *logos* understanding? Does it have anything to do with the city in speech versus the city in deed?

Seth: Well, there are two things that are very striking in the *Republic*. On the one hand, you have the two Thrasymachean principles that are driven straight through the dialogue.

Ronna: The precise?

Seth: The precise and anger, which are manifest together in Thrasymachus, and then show up in the structure of the city. So, on the one hand, you get mathematics in book VII, and on the other hand, you get a class structure, which is based on the centrality of Thrasymachus's pseudo-anger.

Michael: That's the *thumoeides* [the spirited]?[7]

Seth: I think so.

Ronna: But they coincide only in him and otherwise are split?

Seth: They seem to be split, because it looks as if the thumoeidetic without the eidetic, as it were, is completed in book IV, and as though V, VI, and VII, about philosophy, have left that behind. And then, lo and behold, it turns out that this other thing that Thrasymachus had introduced—

Robert: The precise?

Seth: —was being pushed through to the end.

Ronna: But it's not accidental that these two principles show up in Thrasymachus, is it?

Seth: You don't know that it's not accidental. You don't know why, on the one hand, you should get a fictional passion and a demand that seems as if it's unreal. It does look as though they must be connected in some way, but you don't know exactly how they're connected. The thing they have in common is this ideality. Or, there is this ideality, on the one hand, and there is a fiction, on the other, and then the question is, what is the connection between the two?

Ronna: And that's what has to be worked out in the course of the dialogue?

Seth: It's interesting. Strauss had seen the two strands, but he experienced them separately.

Ronna: You mean, at different times in studying the dialogue?

Seth: Yes. The one he knew from Alfrarabi was the thumoeidetic. What he originally did was to figure out how it showed up in the whole analysis of the soul and so forth. Many years later, before writing *The City and Man*, he came to the *technē* argument. And then he saw that they were somehow connected.

---

7. See Benardete's discussion of this term in *Socrates' Second Sailing*, 55–56.

Ronna: Did you realize this yourself and then say, "Oh that's what Strauss saw!"?

Seth: No, I learned from him that this really is the crucial thing. What I thought I did on my own was to see how Glaucon, picking up Thrasymachus's objections, formalized into a massive problem what had apparently been only a speck on the horizon in Thrasymachus's account, that is, the relation between eidetic analysis and the good, concealed by the fact that Glaucon uses *eidos* with regard to the good.

Ronna: That doesn't sound like a concealment.

Seth: Glaucon asks two questions, What is justice? and Does justice make you happy? Then he gives an analysis of the good that has nothing to do with justice, but he doesn't know that. So he separates them out in this a funny way. He first gives an analysis of the good that is slightly incoherent. Then he gives a triple account of justice, but this is totally independent of his account of the good. And he doesn't know that is so, so he forces Socrates to face a problem which, as he formulates it, cannot be answered, or looks as though it cannot be answered.

Ronna: That problem being?

Seth: Since his analysis of justice depends on goods he had not mentioned at all as being good, it looks as though the argument is over before it starts. So you have to reformulate Glaucon's question in a way that he didn't even know it could be formulated, which is that the goods he set up are good independent of justice or injustice. He didn't know that that was what the issue was. He wanted a proof by Socrates that you could not be happy, i.e. have the goods that he had outlined, unless you had justice. But that's not what Glaucon thought the issue was. He thought he wanted a proof as to why the goods that come from injustice are not good, and in fact make you unhappy. That's a different issue.

Ronna: Are you saying Socrates revises his question in order to bring this out?

Seth: Once Glaucon asks his question, Socrates has to answer it, and that's why the city is introduced, to look at something in which there will be an argument about justice independent of the question of the good.

Michael: So does Glaucon reproduce the order of the city without realizing that's what he's doing?

Seth: The way I had formulated it finally was that Glaucon turns out to be looking at the statues, the shadows on the wall of the cave, and asking Socrates, who, if he had these statues, would be happy? And Socrates proves that's quite impossible. By taking this intermediate stance, between being outside the cave and being entirely within it, Glaucon poses what appears to be an impossible problem. He takes it for granted that justice is of a certain kind, which is in fact an idealization of the images in the cave, and therefore doesn't stand independent of it. And at the same time—

Ronna: He wants the real goodness of it to be shown.

Seth: Right, having shown that it's totally spurious. The amazing thing is that Socrates solves Glaucon's impossible question by the analysis of the cave.

Ronna: He shows it's not impossible after all?

Seth: The three highest goods according to Glaucon were health, sight, and understanding, and Socrates proves that you can't have them unless you're just. So there are three arguments at the end in book IX: pleasure, justice, and seeing.

Ronna: The tyrant is stuck at home.

Seth: He can't go abroad, he has a necessarily false understanding of pleasure, and he cannot think. So the interesting thing is, a pseudo-problem that Glaucon set up has in fact a true answer to it, because it is not so impossible as it seems to be.

Ronna: How did the good show up in the discussion with Thrasymachus?

Seth: What's so interesting about the first book is that you have Thrasymachus representing these two principles, which are mysteriously related. Then Socrates introduces the good.

Michael: At the end of book I?

Seth: When he tells Thrasymachus that the real issue is, What is the best way of life?, and you want to prove that you can't have it unless you're just, or you can't have it if you're unjust. So it looks as if there's a slide in the argument, which makes Socrates dissatisfied with the argument against Thrasymachus, because he has to argue three different positions.

Ronna: Three different positions?

Seth: The first question is, What is justice? The second question is, Can you be happy independent of justice? And then, Does justice make you happy? Something like that.

Ronna: But the question of the good life is something that Socrates introduces.

Seth: Socrates introduces it initially because Thrasymachus gets into a difficulty with regard to his own paradigmatic analysis of regimes. A value-neutral interpretation of the three kinds of regimes turns out only to be applicable to the tyrant.

Ronna: How is that?

Seth: In other words, Thrasymachus says that each kind of regime lays down laws in accordance with its own interest, but that can't be true unless there's only one man at the top. Otherwise there's some kind of compromise, and that's the gangster group. So Socrates shows that what looks like an oligarchic interpretation of Thrasymachus, with wealth as the key, turns out to hold true only of the tyrant, and therefore it is not a neutral analysis of political life, but makes the tyrant central.

Ronna: He's the standard.

Seth: Right, without explaining how there could be political life. So Socrates really has a very complicated task. He has to show that Thrasymachus is in some way right to have made this move to the tyrant as being crucial to the understanding of the city. And at the same time, it's a misunderstanding of the relation between regime principles and regime advantage.

Ronna: Regime principles being?

Seth: Whatever they say, freedom for democracy, or money for oligarchy, that's the principle, that's not the advantage. Thrasymachus had identified them and claimed that they always coincided. That's what it meant for everybody to work for the advantage of the rulers, which is the same as the principle of the regime. So there's a very complicated argument to show that that is never the case, that you can't have a regime in which the advantage is identical with the principle.

Ronna: Except tyranny?

Seth: Then it becomes really quite interesting, because it turns out it's very hard to know what the advantage is in the case of the tyrant. Thrasymachus can't supply it, except money, which doesn't make any sense. So Socrates has to give an analysis of the tyrant which shows that he is revealing of the structure and the internal character of the city, independent, as it were, of the tyrant as an individual.

Ronna: And the good shows up in the notion of the advantage of the ruler?

Seth: Right. The analysis of the tyrant has to be in some way central because of the fictional character of the city. The dream-like character of the city is somehow revealed individually in the tyrant, who absorbs this to the highest degree, and is the true believer of the city. So Thrasymachus turns out to be right, but the consequence of his being right is that he has no goods.

Ronna: Because it's unreal.

Seth: Yes, right.

Robert: What was really important for you, in coming to understand the *Republic,* was the way patterns or paradigms, on the one hand, and dynamic, on the other, are so utterly wrapped up with one another?

Ronna: That might conceal the difference.

Seth: It did conceal it. Since the *Republic* at its high point is very paradigmatic—the structure of the soul, the structure of the city, the sun, the divided line, and the cave—it looks as though everything is being set up in terms of paradigms. So it would be possible to look at each one of them and interpret them in themselves.

Ronna: They have a structure, and the structure reverberates in another version of the same.

Robert: They're self-contained, which is exactly the way people so often treat them.

Seth: So it looks as though you are invited to give a paradigmatic interpretation of everything. But then you don't see how one of them leads into the other. The crucial thing is to see that the move from the soul-structure to philosophy is based on the soul-structure. It might seem as though it's been abandoned, and therefore as though a deduction is being made from these higher principles, whereas in fact it turns out that what is being worked out is a nonphilosophical interpretation of philosophy based on a false interpretation of the soul.

Ronna: I wonder if you could say that the most prevailing misunderstanding of what philosophy is for Plato, based on an interpretation of the *Republic*, is due to not seeing the dynamic, which shows that the false understanding of the soul is really generating the account of philosophy. It's an important example, then, isn't it, of the importance of recognizing the plot of the philosophic argument?

Seth: I think so. One of the first things I remember from Strauss was how you could understand the whole *Republic* in terms of moving from the moral dimension of the first analysis of poetry to the metaphysical dimension of the second analysis of poetry, and the reason for that is the intervention of philosophy in between. So you have, as it were, this schema, which is obviously true, without knowing the basis for the argument.

Ronna: So you do have a kind of whole on that first level. What you're missing is something else.

Seth: You have to realize that you're not abandoning what you started with, but you're really pulling out what was there to begin with though you didn't know it.

Michael: So this has to do with the double way in which *thumos* [spiritedness] comes into the argument as a whole. On the one hand, it is clearly present on the moral level. But on the other hand, there's a connection between this moral phenomenon and the theoretical books in the middle. So the very notion of *eidos* is linked up with some sort of positing and it's only intelligible on the basis of what you thought was a purely moral principle. The intervention of philosophy in the middle is only possible on the basis of the first four books, and that in turn is responsible for what comes later in the argument. If you take the poetry issue, at first glance it looks as though you've got poetry in book III and again in book X, after philosophy intervenes, and you're much more interested in the question of the truth of poetry in X, in contrast with the moral implications in III. But in fact there's an argument through *thumos* which makes you see that in a way it's the same.

Seth: That's signified by this very queer thing, that what Glaucon found to be missing in the "city of pigs"—couches and tables—turn out in book X to be the examples of . . .

Robert: The "ideas"?

Seth: Right. Socrates says, that's the city in truth, and you want the city in falsehood. So you know that something very funny has happened—that they must be related somehow. You end up with "making" on the divine level at the end.

GORGIAS

Seth: I think the difference between the pattern and the argument might have become most manifest to me in working on the *Gorgias*.

Robert: You mean with the series of frames as it moves through Gorgias, Polus, and Callicles?

Seth: Yes. Unless you see that there is a constant transformation going on—so species that had originally been arranged as distinct collapse into one another—there are two things you can't understand: how in fact justice and rhetoric are connected, and why this argument has to be so long.

Ronna: What do you mean by species?

Seth: The *Gorgias* was a key for me in seeing how the relations between the beautiful, the good, and the just can be worked out. It's by mistaking what their character is that Gorgias, Polus, and Callicles get generated.

Ronna: Isn't there some kind of containment, so it's all there in some sense in Gorgias, then it's refracted through Polus and then again on another level through Callicles?

Seth: But it goes through a sequence of transformations in the course of that movement.

Ronna: Was it just in writing the book on the *Phaedrus* and *Gorgias* that the real dynamic of the argument first became clear to you?

Seth: I think I worked it out teaching the *Gorgias* a second time.

Robert: I was in that course, in the mid-eighties, and remember how different it was from the one you gave about ten years earlier, even the way you began. The first time, what was so important was the Peloponnesian

War and the theme of war. It's not as if that was absent the second time around. But from the very beginning, the important question was: How do you put together Gorgias, Polus, and Callicles into an ongoing argument?

Ronna: The structure and the movement of the *Gorgias* seem clear as long as you look at the segments with the three interlocutors; but once you get to Callicles, it isn't so obvious why the conversation goes on as it does, in contrast with the *Republic,* for example, where you think you see the distinct moves that have to be made.

Seth: And, lo and behold, it turns out to be the *Republic.* But the crucial thing I understood from the *Gorgias* is that you only get the thrust of the argument if you keep in mind the problem of eidetic analysis.

Ronna: What is the problem of eidetic analysis?

Seth: Namely that, on the surface, you start with a fully articulated Platonic realm of concepts that either do not overlap at all or they are identical.

Ronna: Either isolated entities or simply one.

Seth: Right. But the way in which the paradigms are presented, there is no suggestion on the surface that they in fact have these funny overlaps, which makes it impossible for them to be understood as separate, the way they are presented, or identical, the way the argument is going.

Ronna: Are we talking about the beautiful, the just, and the good?

Seth: Yes. Once you see that Polus identifies the beautiful, the just, and the good, all sorts of things follow when the good is identified with pleasure. Pleasure goes inside the just and the beautiful, and then you can see the next move by Callicles, and so forth.

Ronna: When did you start making diagrams to try to express this? In a way it is hard to spell these things out. You try to make it visible by these frames and vectors.

Seth: The interesting thing about the diagrams, which must be really a key to *de Anima,* is that they are only effective if they're in motion. If you're in a class and draw it on the board, it's exactly the act of drawing that allows the students to follow. The diagrams never seem to have the same effect on the page.

Michael: That's true, I think. If someone watches you drawing, they can see the layers, how one expands into another. When you put it on the page it's not really layered, you don't know what comes first. That has to be put in somehow.

Ronna: The process of drawing the layers is an imitation of the movement of the argument.

Seth: This is really key for Aristotle's understanding of intellection. Imagine coming into a room where on the blackboard there is a triangle and a line drawn parallel to the base. Somebody says, "What is that?" and you say, "It's a line parallel to the base." Then Aristotle comes in and moves the line, saying, "Look, I want to prove that the three angles of the triangle are equal to a straight line." Draw this line, and then you see it. You don't follow it if you don't see it being drawn.

Ronna: You've got to start making movies.

Seth: "The moving finger writes . . ."

TIMAEUS

Robert: You first wrote on the *Timaeus* before the book on the *Republic*. Did you come to a different view of the relation between those dialogues after writing the original *Timaeus* article,[8] once you came to understand the dynamic of the argument in the *Republic*?

Seth: I got a new understanding of the *Timaeus*, I think, once I saw the importance of the double account of space.

Ronna: What's the double account?

Seth: Timaeus first gives an account of the transformation of matter through the elements, which is presented according to hypothesis. That's where you get the whole notion that the "this," which you're pointing to, is space.

Ronna: Say, fiery space?

Seth: Right. Then he gives a second account which is not understood that way, but is in fact a dialogue. Somebody asks you a question, What is that?, and you have to give an answer. It's only then that the question of truth comes up. So he makes a distinction between scientific discourse and dialogic discourse, and dialogic discourse is grounded in space, not in the temporal order of number.

Ronna: How is the space of dialogue characterized?

Seth: It involves the facing of the other in which there is reversal of left and right. And I think that has to do with the notion of the friend.

Ronna: This reversal of left and right in space cannot be deduced from pure number?

Seth: And it cannot be understood in terms of mere relations of body.

Robert: But you want to say that this mirroring, and the issue of handedness, have something to do with the friend?

Seth: Yes, and it suggests how the *Timaeus* is the ground for the possibility of the *Republic*.

---

8. "On Plato's *Timaeus* and Timaeus' Science Fiction," *Interpretation* 2, no. 1 (summer 1971): 21–63.

Ronna: How does that work?

Seth: There are two levels to the argument of the *Timaeus*. On the first level, Timaeus has to account for the city in speech being realized, and in order to do that he has to put it in space and time, so he has to give an account of space and time. The cosmology has to do with the realization of the city. But his account turns out to be a likely story, and not about the realization, because it's not a real cosmology. So you have to go to a second level, and what you discover is that in fact it's an account of the possibility of the dialogic city of the *Republic*.

Ronna: Does this have something to do with the disorder of the narrative sequence, that he has not, and apparently cannot, put the account in the proper order?

Robert: The notion of proper order is parasitic on the nondialogic conception?

Seth: That's right. It assumes that there's a direct approach to the beings. Timaeus gives a totally false account of the transformation of the elements, where they transform into each other perfectly. Then he says he's made a terrible mistake. In fact only three of the elements do this, but earth does not. And therefore there's the possibility of cosmos only because there's disorder. The first account would allow there to be order, but no cosmos.

Ronna: Why not?

Seth: Because the elements would separate out into four. All earth would go to earth and all fire to fire. You would have a striated universe, but you wouldn't have a cosmos.

Ronna: One phase of Empedocles' universe.

Seth: Right, to get a cosmos you have to introduce this disorder.

Ronna: And you want to ask, what guarantees, or what is the ground of disorder? Or what precludes perfect order?

Seth: That's right. And the answer is, you are not the other.

Robert: And space is the truth of that.

Ronna: I can see that there must be something like this going on. It couldn't be that the *Timaeus* is the ground for the reality of the city in speech of the *Republic*. You know there must be a step beyond that.

Robert: Has anyone understood anything like this?

Seth: You know what [A. E.] Taylor says? That what the *Timaeus* shows is that Socrates is an idealist who had no experience of political things, hence he could not describe the city at war.

PHAEDRUS

Michael: I would have thought that the *Phaedrus* would be very important for this idea of the *logos* of the action, since you're really talking at some level about how Platonic dialogues are put together, and the *Phaedrus* is the dialogue about dialogues. It seems to be concerned with the fact that the way to knowing something can't be known at the same time as the thing you're attempting to know.

Seth: It does look as if the *Phaedrus* is the point from which one can generalize, if the interpretation is right, that this is the principle underlying all writing and thinking.

Michael: You taught the *Phaedrus* before the *Gorgias* class, right?

Seth: Yes, but the first time I taught it, I had not seen the movement. I remember I gave a lecture on it in which I was able to show what the structure was, and what the relation was of the hyperuranian to the Olympian gods and to the soul. The formula was that Plato was proposing the Platonic dialogues as the new Olympian gods to replace the old ones. They would be the new dispensation. But I had to teach it again, at NYU, before I saw the dynamic in the argument.

Ronna: Can you reconstruct what that is?

Seth: In my original understanding, Lysias's speech is the charioteer, Socrates' first speech the white horse, and Socrates' second speech is the black horse.

Ronna: That's the pattern?

Seth: Right. But the crucial thing in discovering the motion of the argument is to see that the second speech is in fact the truth of the first speech.

Michael: Which means that the beautiful is the truth of mind.

Ronna: But each stage is also something independent?

Seth: Right. Then there's an inversion of the prior section when it's absorbed in a subsequent section. This is something I didn't say, but one could say that the assertion about the beloved—seeing himself in the image held up by the lover and falling in love with that without knowing what it is—is in fact the paradigm of all understanding. You have to go through these two phases: you're perplexed before something without knowing what it is, then there's a second phase in which it totally turns around. This is first and second sailing. A problem presents itself, which is an image of the true problem, but not recognized as an image; it's taken in itself, and that leads to some perplexity. Then in undergoing the crucial philosophic transformation, it is seen to be something quite different, though related to what you began with.

Ronna: Is *eros* also paradigmatic in the way the erotic pairing of self and other reveals an internal structure of the self?

Seth: Well, if this interpretation of the *Phaedrus* is right, it looks as if something like the *Lysis* is necessary, in order to explain what Socrates would be on his own.

Michael: How so?

Seth: In other words, Socrates necessarily becomes obscure because of this constant fabrication of himself in pairing up with whomever he is pairing up with. So that in a way he vanishes or he only appears in some fictional form.

Michael: He only appears as a lover of this *X*?

Seth: Yes. It looks as if you need another account that will show what it means for Socrates not to be linked up, to see whether that has a structure to it which doesn't have this character.

Ronna: And you think the *Lysis* supplies that?

Seth: My guess is that it does.

SOPHIST AND STATESMAN

Ronna: The *Sophist* and the *Statesman* are, I think, the works on which you've written the most. They were the first things on Plato you wrote about, then the book on the trilogy, and now they're the subjects of the most recent Plato pieces you've done.[9]

Michael: In calling the book *The Being of the Beautiful,* you highlighted something in these dialogues—the *kalon* [the beautiful]—that seems to have been central for you for a long time.

Seth: It's interesting that that book, when I first wrote it, had a different title.

Ronna: Wasn't it "The Condemnation of Socrates"? That's how I first read it.

Seth: Right. The change of the title depended very much on my understanding of the *Hippias Major.*

Ronna: Which became the introduction?

Seth: Yes.

Michael: From the first essay on the *Sophist,* what is it that really changed in your understanding of the dialogue?

9. The early articles are "Plato's *Sophist* 231b1–7," *Phronesis* 5, no. 2 (1960): 129–39 and "*Eidos* and *Diaeresis* in Plato's *Statesman*," *Philologus* 107, nos. 3–4 (1963): 193–226. The book is *The Being of the Beautiful: Plato's "Theaetetus," "Sophist," and "Statesman"* (Chicago: University of Chicago Press, 1984). The more recent essays are "The Plan of Plato's *Statesman*," *Metis* 7, nos. 1–2 (1992): 25–47 and "On Plato's *Sophist*," *Review of Metaphysics* 46, no. 4 (June 1993): 474–80.

Seth: The hard part of the *Sophist*, I thought originally, is the understanding of same and other. The first time through, I thought it could be understood in terms of logical operators—the other is the negation, the same is the identity operator. But then I realized this didn't look as though it was connected with the problem that was set up.

Ronna: Of who the philosopher is?

Seth: The question of image. It didn't look as though it could answer the question of how to draw the distinction between an image and class formation. That was what the real difficulty was.

Ronna: In the original *Statesman* article, you were interested in the problem of class formation, in *eidos* and *diairesis,* isn't that right?

Seth: Yes, that's interesting. In the *Sophist,* too, I started with a recognition of the breakdown of *diairesis,* without knowing that that was the principle of *diairesis.* So the development started with the recognition of the fact that these schemata did not work.

Ronna: But you don't think you understood why originally?, or you didn't understand the generality of this breakdown?

Seth: I had detected a systematic series of errors on the part of the speaker without seeing that these errors were necessary.

Robert: You saw the breakdown of an expected pattern?

Seth: Which revealed something about a problem, but what I didn't realize is that it could not have been done otherwise.

Ronna: That thinking had to proceed this way.

Seth: Yes, right. In the case of the *Sophist,* I knew that he had not in fact solved the problem. That's what I claimed, that he could not get out of the difficulty he had raised.

Ronna: You were accusing Plato?

Michael: Or the Eleatic Stranger?

Seth: In the book, I only got as far as to see that the analysis of soul cathartics is an analysis of Socrates. But I didn't see until many years later that this gave the clue to the relation between eikastics and phantastics [the two arts of image-making in the *Sophist*].

Ronna: Doesn't this come out in the last *Sophist* piece?

Seth: That's what I wanted to show. Kennington made a remark many years ago which had lodged in my mind—that somebody talking about the *Republic* had failed to give an account of what an image in *logos* would be. I remembered that. Then I realized about the *Sophist,* years after writing the book, that the real difficulty is that it is all based on visual distinctions and the Stranger never says what an eikastic or a phantastic speech is. I had seen that eikastic speech is identical with the problem of eidetic formation, because Theaetetus says what an *eikon* in speech is, namely "another such." And that turns out to be the same as forming a class, where each member is "another such." But I had never asked the question, what is a phantasic logos?, because the Stranger doesn't say what it is. I later came to the conclusion that it is an eikastic speech misunderstood.

Ronna: This is false opinion?

Seth: Right. Therefore the problem is identical with Theaetetus's failure to understand that Socrates and the Stranger are one and the same.

Ronna: Do you say that in the latest *Sophist* piece?

Seth: Yes. In other words, the Stranger comes in as the philosopher who is to give an account of Socrates as the sophist, the sophist being a *phantasma* of the philosopher, which he then does precisely in this analysis. Theaetetus falsely says, that's the sophist. And the Stranger says, I don't think so. Then it turns out, Socrates is the philosopher and not this *phantasma*. The *phantasma* must be Theaetetus failing to see that the image is in fact the reality of Socrates, rather than an image of the sophist. That's what a *phantastikos logos* is. The problem then is, how can the Stranger explain to Theaetetus what it means for him to have made such a mistake?

Ronna: This seems to be connected with the question I've been thinking about, what Socrates is concerned with when he says he fears that the Stranger is a refutative god. "Refutative god" sounds like the description Socrates gave of himself as midwife in the *Theaetetus;* so what does it mean that Socrates should fear the Stranger has come to watch over him, when the Stranger seems to be the incarnation of Socrates as he described himself in the midwife account?

Seth: Well, the Stranger in fact withdraws from being the full philosopher in order to represent Socrates as the full philosopher.

Ronna: The Stranger puts on a mask?

Seth: And therefore splits.

Ronna: Between?

Seth: Sophist and statesman, to reveal that Socrates is their unity, and therefore will always be mistaken for one or the other.

Ronna: Is that to be understood as a refutation of Socrates?

Seth: Well, one result of the split is to make Socrates necessarily look as if he is Aristotle's Socrates.

Ronna: Concerned with the human things only?

Seth: Right. That's what Theaetetus falls for: Socrates takes care of the soul, the Stranger takes care of being. The entire analysis of Socrates is totally

false, although the conclusion is true. So it's really an image. The whole eidetic analysis is completely wrong, but the characterization is true.

Ronna: How could that be?

Seth: It's interesting. The Stranger gets Socrates, but under false pretenses.
To get him under right pretenses would be to collapse him into the Stranger,
and make him into the reality which the Stranger is able to copy.

Ronna: This became clear to you this last time through in a way you don't
think you understood in writing *The Being of the Beautiful*?

Seth: I had not seen before that there really was an answer to the question
he had raised. The *Sophist* is an account of the indeterminate dyad as being
the central form of all philosophical analysis.

Ronna: Just the *Sophist* alone, not together with the *Statesman*?

Seth: Well, the *Sophist* turns on this formal category, the other, which is in
fact standing for the way eidetic analysis necessarily breaks down. That's
what the other is. So Plato has a category inside the argument that illustrates
what he is talking about, as opposed to everybody else, who believes that
things are just what they are. The Stranger therefore refutes all of Pre-
Socratic philosophy, you could say, by showing how they all made a Thrasymachean error about precision. Everybody was a Platonist before Plato.

Michael: This would seem to describe your own misreading of the *Sophist*.
You discovered that the division turns out to be false, but you didn't see why
it was false. The discovery of its being truly false is the discovery of what
we've been calling the plot or the argument.

Seth: Right.

Ronna: Did you come to this layer of understanding through the *Statesman*?
At least you wrote the *Statesman* piece first, I think.

Seth: But I'm not sure it was connected with it. I didn't really formulate
what it means for Socrates to say that the philosopher will appear as the
statesman, which means, of course, that the sophist is at the very heart of
philosophy, because he's the one who always turns out to be the other. So it
looks as though they've made a mistake, but then it turns out that, no, that's
the truth, everything is the other. So the elusiveness of the sophist turns out
to be the elusiveness of being. And that fit what I already knew about the
character of the *kalon* from the *Hippias Major*, though I hadn't realized it.

Michael: That the *kalon* is somehow perfect in itself while necessarily
pointing to something else?

Seth: That that is the mark of being. It's amazing how consistent it all is. It's
very disturbing, because it didn't look that way going along.

Ronna: When you look at it from the outside, at various versions of your
readings, it looks like an incremental deepening of your understanding; but

you're suggesting now that it's really a Platonic *periagoge*, a radical reversal in which you totally replace a prior understanding.

Robert: You understand that a *diairesis* breaks down, and it's not just partial but you see this breaking down all over. But you don't understand, initially, the way it's incorporated into something else. So it's not as if the observation of this breakdown is abandoned, right?

Michael: That seems to be the difference between your first *Sophist* article and the book. The really hard thing to understand is the difference between the book and the most recent version. It does look as if in the book you're not only giving an account of where it breaks down, but you're also giving an account of why it breaks down and why it has to in that way.

Seth: But I think there's a real discontinuity, because I did not understand the shift to *logos* from the appeal to sight. It therefore looked as if the problem of the image couldn't be solved, because the question isn't answered in terms of the visual paradigm. I hadn't seen that this was very much connected with the second sailing problem, that the move from the visual paradigm to *logos* meant that you could not go back to what you thought were the beings. You have to understand things in terms of the *eide,* which have a *logos* character to them that then breaks down.

Ronna: What happens to being?

Seth: Well, that's it. The whole thing is then moved up to the problem of linking being with *logos,* but it's no longer the being you thought you were talking about.

Ronna: What it means just to articulate a pattern, as you've been describing it, looks like a kind of structuralism.

Seth: Right. Literary criticism is very paradigmatic, or used to be, with absolutely no argument. The old-fashioned New Criticism was of this character. And that is in fact very much what I was originally doing in interpreting.

Ronna: There is a kind of intelligibility in bringing to light the organization of the work.

Seth: No, sure.

Ronna: So it wouldn't be surprising if there's a natural sequence you go through, where you have to read something first in terms of the structure, and only later come to see how the plot is responsible for that.

Seth: I've never been able to do them simultaneously. But I am amazed by the delay, the distance in time between getting the pattern and understanding the argument.

Ronna: Don't you think you've sped up in your understanding of things?

Seth: I don't know.

Ronna: You've sped up your production.

Seth: Although, thinking about how long ago it began, I'm not sure that's true. The *Philebus* goes back a long way, for instance, and the *Republic*, and the *Gorgias* does.

Michael: When you recently gave the talk on Euripides' *Helen*, it struck me that you weren't speaking simply on the level of paradigm, but you already had a notion of what it would mean to read it through paying attention to the plot.

Seth: But it was back when I wrote the Herodotus book that I knew about the paradigm Euripides had used for the *Helen*.

Ronna: Herodotus's account of Egypt?

Seth: Right. Euripides wrote two parallel plays, *Iphigeneia* and *Helen*, with exactly the same structure, because he was imitating books II and IV in Herodotus.

Ronna: So it isn't as if you now have a method, which would speed up the process of discovery?

Seth: No, it doesn't seem to work that way. All you know is that something like this should happen, but you don't know where or how it's going to happen. In fact, once you know that it should happen, maybe you can try too hard to make it happen.

Chapter 7

THE "INDETERMINATE DYAD"

THE LIMIT AND THE UNLIMITED IN THE *PHILEBUS*

Robert: The idea came up at one point that the key to seeing the dynamic of the argument is some kind of symmetry-breaking in a pattern. I was wondering whether there was a particular case in which that first became evident to you.

Seth: I would have thought that it began—but it certainly is little by little—with the *Philebus*.

Ronna: What was it about that dialogue?

Seth: The discovery of the importance *of* the *apeiron* [the unlimited]. I thought you could work out how Plato was dealing with the internal structure of *eidē*. There is an argument that shows it is not possible to move to the "ideas" because there is this intermediary level, on which it turns out that the *eidos* has a structure to it. There is an internal tension within an *eidos*, which I called the "indeterminate dyad."

Ronna: Plato never uses that formula, does he?

Seth: No, only Aristotle.[1]

Robert: So you think the *Philebus* was the beginning.

Seth: I recall writing to Strauss and saying that it looked as if that's what is implied by the definition of justice in the *Republic:* "minding one's own business" and "minding one's own business well" is an indeterminate dyad, and the whole *Republic* turns on that. And my guess was that Diotima's analysis of *eros* must be an indeterminate dyad along the same lines.

---

1. Aristotle discusses the indeterminate dyad in *Metaphysics* XIII.7.

Ronna: You mean the relation between poverty and plenty as the parents of Eros (*Symposium* 203a–4a)?

Seth: No, the parallel between *eros* and poetry, remember?

Ronna: *Poiēsis* as production in general, but poetry in particular (*Symposium* 205b–d)?

Seth: That's what I'm thinking of. Diotima asks, how come *poiēsis* has this general character, yet it's then limited to the poets? And how come, after *eros* is said to be desire for the good, everybody thinks it means just lovers, which seems to be a special class? She gives an analysis of *eros* parallel to the double meaning of "poet," so each has a comprehensive and a precise sense. The way her account of *eros* is split looked extraordinarily like the way that justice is defined in the *Republic*. So I proposed that this was a general principle.

Michael: Did Strauss respond to your letter about it?

Seth: I don't think so. Then years later I thought I discovered that *The City and Man* was based on the structure I am calling the indeterminate dyad, and it was central to the whole argument.

Ronna: How did you understand the indeterminate dyad at that point?

Seth: What's interesting is, I did it so backwards, because I didn't do the simplest case, which is the *Republic*, in which it's explicit that the definition of justice has a structure, in book IV. But I had come to see it first in the *Philebus*. If you analyze what is said about the limit and the unlimited [*peras* and *apeiron*], it turns out that this split cannot be maintained, but in fact they intrude on one another because each has another split in it, which shows that it has the other within itself. That's the example I used in writing to Strauss. I suggested that this was the model on the basis of which you could understand the *Republic*, and also the *Symposium*. But it's a very complicated model.

Ronna: Can you say anything more about the limit and the unlimited in the *Philebus*?

Seth: It has to do with the fact that the limit is split into two parts, namely the limit that is connected with the measured, which already has the more or less in it, and the other part, with no more or less in it, which turns out to be numbers, which have no connection with the real. So the account starts out with a false disjunction between the limit and the unlimited, but you're alerted to its falsehood by the fact that Socrates is not able to put together the *eidos* of the limit. He then turns to the mixture, because it turns out that only in the mixture could there be the limit that you wanted.

Ronna: Which already has some feature of the unlimited in it?

Seth: Right, whereas the limit that is not in the mixture only shows up in the form of numbers.

Michael: So is this the two measures of the *Statesman* (286c–d)?

Seth: Yes.

Robert: If you think of the *Philebus* as a model, would you say that the indeterminate dyad is this symmetry-breaking element that reveals the dynamic of the argument?

Seth: That's what I'm suggesting. Before I understood the argument of the dialogue I knew there was something paradoxical about the principles. But I had no idea of how destructive it turns out to be.

Ronna: What do you mean by destructive?

Seth: In fact the argument of the *Philebus* ends up showing that nothing is good. That is the consequence of eidetic analysis. You take each thing that belongs either to pleasure or thought, just as they are in themselves, and you can show that none of them is any good. So in fact Protarchus chooses something irrationally, that's the mixture, no component of which can be shown to be good.

THE VARIETY OF INDETERMINATE DYADIC STRUCTURES

Ronna: When I think of various cases in which you've used the term "indeterminate dyad," there seem to be several different uses. It's a formal structure, I realize. But are they all examples of the same thing?

Seth: What are you thinking of?

Ronna: Well, you thought your first discovery of it was in the *Philebus*, in the relation between the *peras* and the *apeiron*, each of which somehow has the other in it.

Robert: You said that what you found in the *Philebus* is the idea that there's nothing good: if you look at the life of pleasure and the life of mind, neither of them taken by itself is good, and Protarchus, without realizing it, is revealing something by choosing the mixture, where they're essentially together. Does that also exemplify this dyadic structure?

Ronna: Don't you want to say that's a product of eidetic analysis?

Seth: Yes, but that's the point. Eidetic analysis turns out necessarily to have this indeterminate dyadic structure.

Ronna: I see. You also referred to the definition of justice in the *Republic* as an indeterminate dyad. There's "minding one's own business" and "minding one's own business perfectly," a comprehensive and a precise sense. Then there's the *Symposium* case, which sounds very close to that. When you referred to the indeterminate dyad in the *Symposium* I thought you had in mind the relation between poverty and plenty, which are supposedly two parents of Eros but turn out to be one. And that seems to be a kind of indeterminate dyad too. But that was not, at least at that moment, what you had in mind. You were thinking of *poiēsis*, which has the broad meaning, "production," and the narrow meaning, "poetry."

Seth: And that becomes Diotima's model for her account of *eros*.

Ronna: So that account illustrates an indeterminate dyad of comprehensive and precise senses. Then at one point we were talking about the centrality of the sophist, because of the other, and you suggested that "the other" encapsulates an indeterminate dyadic structure.

Seth: Right.

Ronna: Okay, this is my last case!—the beautiful. We were talking about why the *kalon* is privileged. I think this came up when we were discussing why "The Being of the Beautiful" replaced "The Condemnation of Socrates" as the title for your study of the *Sophist* and *Statesman*. And you explained that this came from your insight into the *Hippias Major*, with its account of the beautiful in terms of the other, as an indeterminate dyad. So it sounds like the *kalon* is the "idea" which most obviously points to this structure.

Michael: I understood that to mean because of the way it simultaneously is self-contained and points beyond itself. But can I add something to the list of ways the indeterminate dyad comes in? I'm thinking, not so much of what the texts are about, but of the way they function. So in the *Phaedrus* you get Socrates' first speech in between Lysias's speech and the third speech, and it seems to work in such a way that, properly understood, the two extremes which it mediates between collapse into it. The same thing, as I understand it, happens in the *Gorgias*, where the Polus section is the mediating segment which, properly understood, the two extremes collapse into.

Ronna: Isn't this what happens with the three parts of the soul in *Republic* IV?

Michael: I think so. So this seems to be very common, just on the level of a hermeneutical principle.

Ronna: Would you call it an indeterminate dyad, then, when you have this kind of tripartite structure? There's a middle part that gets connected in some sense with one extreme, so that together they make up one over against the other extreme, but then it gets linked with that opposite and forms one with it over against the other. I thought Aristotle's *Physics* (I.7–9) might provide the most clear-cut case of this.

Michael: With *sterēsis* [privation]?

Ronna: Right, the way it collapses into *hule* [matter] in a sense over against *eidos*, but in another sense it is one with *eidos* over against *hule*.

Seth: Yes, I've understood it that way.

Ronna: So the question is how these various structures are related. Are there different species of the indeterminate dyad?

JUSTICE IN THE *REPUBLIC*

Seth: If you go back to the case of justice, it turns out that, if you take it in the strict sense, you get the well-ordered soul of the philosopher, where there is no justice.

Ronna: That's minding one's own business perfectly?

Seth: Right. But on the other hand, it turns out that this internal principle is supposed to entail minding one's own business in the sense of not overstepping certain boundaries, that is, the weak sense of justice.

Ronna: Just doing what he should do vis-à-vis others in the city?

Seth: Right. So the philosopher is to all other human beings as the city is to all in the city, characterized by this principle. There's a perfect match between the weak sense of minding one's own business and the "morality" of the philosopher, which from the philosopher's point of view is a direct consequence of justice in the strict sense, that is, his own ordered soul. That's the remarkable thing. It isn't as if one is contained inside the other as an eccentric part of it that could be isolated; but it turns out that it itself . . .

Ronna: The narrow sense?

Seth: Yes, the narrow sense contains, in this very peculiar way, the broad sense, which determines the justice of the class system.

Michael: You don't have to answer this now!, but is this the same as "The problem inherent in the surface of things, and only in the surface of things, is the heart of things"?[2]

Seth: I think it is.

Michael: The heart of things being the precise and the surface being the comprehensive?

Seth: You could put it that way.

Michael: So the indeterminate dyad then would also have to do with this dialogic mode of writing.

Seth: Right. Now if you look at the case of *eros*, it's more complicated.

Ronna: Can you clarify one thing about the first case? Do you want to say that the weak sense is aiming to be something it can never quite be and the precise sense realizes that aim or intention?

Robert: Then it would be like the highest exemplar.

2. On this statement by Leo Strauss, see chap. 6, n. 5

Seth: No, because if you think of it that way, in the case we're discussing, it looks as if there are four virtues, when in fact there are not four virtues but only one, namely wisdom.

Michael: And it's only by realizing that the perfect case is not the perfect case that it ends up being responsible for the ordinary case.

Seth: It turns out that the injustice of the weak sense is the justice of the weak sense and what makes it good.

Ronna: What is the injustice of it?

Seth: Well, that you only have class relations that are just, but no member of any class is justly placed by the class.

Ronna: Nobody is a carpenter by nature.

Seth: And so forth. But then it turns out, on the basis of the account of the degenerate regimes, that it's good that the city is unjust. When the city tries to be just on its own principle, you necessarily get tyranny, because you're not able to separate the individual from the principle of the city, whereas in every other regime, there's always a difference and that's what makes you free.

Robert: That's interesting.

Seth: So it's very much connected with the teleology of evil.

Ronna: A good consequence of a condition that didn't seem good.

Seth: And therefore the idealism of the *Republic* goes to show that modeling the structure of the city on this other structure—

Robert: The well-ordered individual?

Seth: —right, forces you to realize that in fact it cannot be modeled on it, and that it's radically different. Any attempt to make the city conform to that would in fact destroy the city—which is Aristotle's observation, as it turns out, I suppose, in book II of the *Politics*.

Ronna: Although it looks as if the only reason it's linked in the first place is that the well-ordered soul of the philosopher is the internalization of the class structure of the city.

Seth: That's true.

Ronna: Isn't that the explanation of why "minding one's own business" sounds almost like "minding one's own business perfectly"?

Seth: Yes.

Robert: It works in that one case.

Ronna: Or does that mean there's a distorted understanding of the soul of the philosopher?

Seth: Yes, that might be. Of course, in the presumably true understanding, the middle part of the soul vanishes, as an asymptotic case, where you only have the top and the bottom.

Ronna: That's what Socrates is meant to stand for?

Seth: Yes. And that's equivalent to making philosophy into a comprehensive science of all the arts; but it turns out, in the course of the argument, not to be right, that justice is a science.

Michael: Because impossible?

Seth: Yes.

Michael: So it looks like it's the same problem as in the *Metaphysics*. But it turns out, in this case, that the middle part of the soul, *thumos*, cannot be left out because in fact you can't do it this way.

Robert: You can't do what this way?

Michael: You can't have a comprehensive science of all the sciences. So if that's what not leaving out *thumos* means, then that's a sign of the impossibility.

Seth: In other words, to eliminate the central part of the soul is to eliminate opinion as the starting point, on the one hand, and on the other hand, to eliminate shame. And neither seems to be possible.

Robert: How did this point about getting rid of the middle part of the soul come up?

Ronna: We were asking, if the philosopher's soul is just an internalization of the class structure of the city, does that mean that it's skewed?

Seth: Right. But actually the account of the soul doesn't have to be true for the philosopher to be the representative of the fact that the ruling principle is identical with justice. And therefore there isn't any justice, there's just wisdom. And that's regardless of how many parts of the soul there may be or what in fact their true relation to one another is.

EROS AND POIĒSIS IN THE SYMPOSIUM

Seth: It looks like you can't have an indeterminate dyad unless there are three things, which can be shifted around. Therefore it's not accidental that the beautiful, the just, and the good constantly come up as a triad in Plato. In the *Symposium* you have a genealogy of *eros* where *eros* is identified with philosophy. Then you have an account of *eros* as the desire for happiness or the good. And then you have the problem of the lover. So you have three parts, and the question is how to put them together. The easiest way to reduce the three to two would be to say that the genealogy of *eros*, with the implication that *eros* is philosophy, is merely the inner truth of the lover.

Ronna: Every lover falls short of being the philosopher?

Seth: Right. And that seems to be the conclusion drawn from Diotima's ladder of love. So the beautiful is restored as being the highest theme, and pederasty is on the way up to this highest thing. But that looks as if it can't be true, because the good has been introduced in the meantime as being the true nature of *eros.*

Ronna: Or the true object of *eros?*

Seth: The true object of *eros,* which is universal. So it requires a reorientation to argue that the center of the comprehensive account of *eros* is in fact *eros* as philosophy. And the other part, which everybody thinks is *eros,* is in fact part of *poiēsis.*

Ronna: Oh. I don't know if I understood that properly before.

Robert: Can you elaborate on that?

Seth: What Diotima does is, having convinced Socrates that *eros* is *eros* of the good, she then asks him this question, If everybody wants the good, how come everybody is not called a lover? He doesn't know the answer to that. She then gives him this very elaborate account, which lasts to the end, that it's exactly parallel to the double meaning of "poet," which should mean "maker" but in fact means poet. But it turns out that what she is in fact doing in this analysis is combining Aristophanes' account of individuality with Agathon's account of *eros* in terms of poetry. The truth is that what is understood to be the lover is really the perpetuation of the self, which at the highest level is the perpetuation of the poet in the form of beautiful images of the other. So the poet preserves himself in the poem totally disguised in his praise of the beautiful, which is either reality or the law or heroes or whatever. It then turns out that the failure of self-perpetuation on the generative level is achieved in this phantom case by the poet, because it gives up *genesis* in favor of *poiēsis,* but it really is his; it's his product in a way that the child is not, and can never be, yours. Once you get that, it looks as if you have to take it and apply it to the *Phaedrus* account to see how the productive mode shows up in philosophy, in terms of the relation between dialectic and rhetoric. Then you get the indeterminate dyad within philosophy itself.

Ronna: The producing of speeches?

Seth: Yes, which looks on the surface to be very similar to what the poet is doing, but in fact contains within it this pointing to being, rather than to fiction.

Michael: So to get back to the *Symposium* for a minute, the three elements of the indeterminate dyad in Diotima's speech are what?

Seth: Eros as philosophy, *eros* as *eros* of the good,

Michael: And *poiēsis* comes in as . . . ?

Seth: Eros of the beautiful.

Robert: What happens to *eros* of the good then?

Seth: That's simply left as a problem for young Socrates. The question is whether he sees that what Diotima is implying is that you have to identify the good with philosophy. That's not said by her.

Ronna: And is it too for the preservation of the self?

Seth: That's where the move is made to the productive mode of *eros*. It looks as if, on the one hand, if you use the comprehensive/precise form, you get desire for the good, and then the lover in this productive mode. But that cannot be adequate, because the issue of happiness drops out from the precise sense; it's not preserved in the account of procreation. So that shows you that it has to be reargued. *Eros* as philosophy was put inside the nonproductive character of the desire for happiness, but you're not really shown why it's necessary. You are then forced to ask the question, what happens to the beautiful once this is done? And then it looks like the *Phaedrus*. So there is now within philosophy a productive mode, which, however, has been separated from the self. It's not a concealment within the productive mode of the end being the perpetuation of the self.

Ronna: Are we talking about the lover's construction of an image in speech by which to attract the beloved?

Seth: Yes, which is the same as what Diotima says in the *Symposium* about laws and learning and so forth.

Robert: Is there any difference?

Seth: The difference really turns on the fact that, in the *Symposium*, the poet is characterized as being the highest realization of the Aristophanic dream. It's as illusory as sexual reproduction, but it looks as if it compensates for that by the concentration of the self, if you are a maker. So what's missing is an account of the beautiful, which is supplied by the *Phaedrus*. That allows for a reorientation of the lover as maker, which brings the rhetoric of poetry back into dialectics.

Ronna: We should be alerted to this by the fact that Socrates drops the beautiful in the beginning of the conversation with Diotima and the good takes over. You seem to be saying that Diotima's account does not get back to it.

Seth: Well, it ends with a notion of the beautiful that is not erotic, which is in the form of the imagination. So this turns out to be a very complicated case.

Michael: Would it be fair to say that by the end of Diotima's speech, her account of the beautiful itself, which seems to be the utter de-eroticizing of the beautiful even though it's presented as an account of *eros*, is meant as an example of the kind of *poiēsis* the poets generate for ultimately selfish reasons, and that means the good? Doing what she's doing would somehow reflect her own good—which seems to be the rule throughout the *Symposium*. All the other speeches—you just don't think it's true in her case—without the speakers realizing it, are manifestations of their own good. So this is getting Agathon's speech right. It's really about poetry in that sense.

Seth: That would be the source of her antipederastic morality. Diotima is trying to make Socrates cease to be a pederast by getting rid of the self in the truly beautiful. There's no possibility of him believing that he himself can have a productive mode of preservation.

THE CONJUNCTIVE TWO AND DISJUNCTIVE TWO

Ronna: So far, I think we're reaching the conclusion that "indeterminate dyad" has to be understood formally enough to accommodate several structures that are certainly not identical.

Seth: No, not at all.

Robert: You did suggest that they all have a tripartite character. But I'm not sure that holds in the *Republic* example. If the definition of the just has a comprehensive and a precise sense—the perfectly ordered soul, on the one hand, and "mind your own business," on the other—there doesn't seem to be a third.

Ronna: Although each of them has an analysis that involves a triadic structure.

Robert: That's true. But it doesn't seem to be like the *Symposium* case, where you have *eros* as philosophy, *eros* of the good, and *eros* of the beautiful.

Seth: The remarkable thing is that the dyad of *eros* presented eidetically, if properly understood, is identical to the genealogy of *eros*, properly understood. Everything is contained in the correct understanding of the genealogy.

Ronna: The genealogy is the union of poverty and plenty?

Seth: Yes, which turns out to be a two that is really a one. It has its own indeterminate structure. So you have a genetic account, followed by an eidetic account, which prove to be the same.

Ronna: The conjunctive two—to use another of your formulas—of poverty and plenty as two entirely independent things, has to be turned into the disjunctive two, of poverty and awareness of poverty, if the genesis of *eros* is to be properly understood. But the only thing that exemplifies poverty aware of itself is philosophy.

Seth: And therefore the good.

Robert: You're saying that the entire genetic account is then followed by an eidetic one. Is that sequence, from the genetic to the eidetic account contingent? I'm thinking about the sequence, in *Natural Right and History*, from the *origin* of the idea of natural right to the idea, but I don't know if we want to go off onto that right now.

Seth: You could start with the *Phaedo* (60b–c), where the mythical model of pleasure and pain is set up to show that myth will necessarily have this split, which Diotima shows in the genealogy of *eros*. Or you could ask whether the mythical character of the *Republic*, which Socrates makes explicit, has again to do with the concealment of a disjunctive two behind a conjunctive two.

Michael: Is this an articulation of what it means to say that you have to start with the beautiful? You have to begin with a part separated off from everything else, which is the subject of a genetic account. It's as though you are always beginning in a myth, and therefore with something like a conjunctive two. But if it is to be properly understood, you have to show that what you thought was disconnected isn't really disconnected. That means you have to show the character of its connectedness, which has something to do with showing how it is really an indeterminate dyad.

Seth: That's right. Socrates starts with the being and nonbeing of the pre-Socratics. And this is precisely the conjunctive two, where you need both for genesis; but eidetically they don't allow that. So it looks as though you're forced to draw a Parmenidean split. And the Socratic move seems to have been to say that there was a faulty split between being and nonbeing. Once you see that this is the character of the being of the other, it is possible to put together genesis and *eidos* in a new way.

THE NEITHER-NOR IN THE *LYSIS*

Ronna: Do you take the move, then, from the conjunctive two to a disjunctive two to be identical with the move from a first to a second sailing? The conjunctive two is characteristic of myth because it is a structure of exaggerated separability that doesn't acknowledge intrinsic connections. Are you saying that what it means to enter on a second sailing is to correct this mythical understanding?

Seth: The mistaken understanding always seems to involve the overlooking of an in-between. That's explicit in the *Lysis*. Four accounts of friendship are given. There are two principles, same and other, which are explicitly pre-Socratic and poetic; and then a Socratic move is made by introducing the neither-nor. The neither-nor is an eidetic account of the genesis of *eros*; but no genetic analysis is given, and therefore desire is absent, as it is first presented.

Ronna: How exactly do you understand this neither-nor in the *Lysis*?
Seth: Remember the conversation comes at a certain point to the claim
that that which is neither good nor bad is that which could be the friend
(216d–e).
Ronna: And you're suggesting that the account of this claim in the *Lysis* is
the same as what is done genetically in the *Symposium* concerning *eros*?
Seth: But without desire. What happens is that you get a very complicated
account of knowledge of ignorance, or something like that, without desire.
Desire is introduced only later, but it turns out in fact to be the neither-nor
of the original account. In the meantime, the neither-nor has come to represent all beings.
Michael: So that could only happen because you began with the split between the good and the bad, as though they were perfectly clear. Then you
posit this mysterious thing, the neither-nor, which turns out to be everything.
Seth: And the neither-nor ends up having two meanings, one in terms of
all beings, and one in terms of desire. You have a comprehensive account of
beings characterized as neither-nor, which doesn't take into account desire.
It has to do with the resistance of beings to accepting the good. That's in the
discussion of the dying son, who is elevated to the status of the ultimate
friend precisely because he is dying, which is a crisis situation. But because
he is a neither-nor, there's a resistance to his shifting into this other category,
as good.
Ronna: And the principle behind the resistance to the good is the preservation of the self as it is? It's hard to understand why anyone or anything would
resist accepting the good, unless there is an attachment to the self and the
reception of the good would transform the self.
Seth: Into something good. So the son, when he's not in crisis, is desired
by the parents to be good. Whatever those goods are, they're being imposed
on a neutral being. Then all of a sudden, the son is in a crisis; he's going to
vanish as a being altogether, and consequently he becomes the *proton philon*
[first friend]. Existence itself becomes a good, which is against the very character of existence.
Robert: Because, qua existence, it's neither-nor.
Seth: Right. Then it turns out that this applies to philosophy. Philosophy
has the same split within it. On the one hand, you can characterize Socrates
as moved by the desire for his own understanding. So philosophy is subor-
dinate to his own good. Then he drinks the hemlock for the sake of philosophy. Philosophy at that point, because its very existence is at stake, becomes
the end for the sake of which Socrates is the means. It turns out that it is Soc-

rates who has put philosophy in continual crisis, by introducing political philosophy, which is always at risk. Consequently, only in the case of Socratic philosophy do these two accounts of the neither-nor, as the neutral and as desire, absolutely coincide. Therefore all philosophical understanding, as Socrates represents it, has to be in the category of crisis, because it always involves a problem that comes up as a crisis. In every other case, there is a split: the being is neutral until a crisis, then it shifts categories. Philosophy is the only case in which the being is to be in crisis. And it is in crisis in this double way—on the one hand, philosophical, on the other, political. So the *Lysis* seems to be the key dialogue for understanding the character of Socratic philosophy.

Ronna: You always say that about whatever you just finished working on!

Seth: That's true. Can I do it once more?

Ronna: Why not?!

Michael: Well, you always make a powerful case for it. Actually, that's an example of what you just said: that philosophy is always in crisis is confirmed by every dialogue you read, where everything seems to turn on it.

Seth: You can explain, in other words, why it necessarily has this accidental character to it.

Robert: The accidental character being?

Seth: The encounter with the question. The philosophical enterprise is totally contingent in its necessary structure, as opposed to pre-Socratic philosophy, which goes back before the Bible, and which will always be.

Robert: Just wonder as such?

Seth: Cosmological wonder is always present. It can take profound or not profound expression, but it's not in crisis.

Ronna: The funny thing about that is, we think of pre-Socratic philosophy as being solely for its own sake, and not for the good of the individual who pursues it; but you seem to be suggesting now that only when philosophy is perpetually in crisis, which began with Socratic political philosophy, does it become something for its own sake.

Robert: Precisely because it is already always concerned with itself, unlike the pre-Socratic.

Michael: Its own good is always in question. So it has to face the problem of whether its objectivity is sullied by the fact that it's for your good.

Ronna: I thought we lost that last step, that's what was bothering me. Can it be both simultaneously?

Robert: Which?

Ronna: I thought there was a split between Socrates' own understanding being the end for the sake of which philosophy exists and philosophy being the end for the sake of which Socrates is willing to sacrifice his life. Can those two be together?

Robert: They are together.

Michael: And the claim is that they have to be together, in philosophy.

Ronna: That's the indeterminate dyad of the *Lysis*?

Seth: Yes. And this is where you get three again. It sounds to me like a very plausible account of ordinary love, that it will take these two forms, which are usually distinct. The son could be despised by the father for being bad, as long as his life isn't at stake. That's perfectly understandable. But if he's in grave danger, he shifts categories. Some other good has come in concealed—maybe the father's own being is involved. But in the usual circumstances, parents want their child to be happy, not simply to be a perpetuation of themselves. There will be, therefore, a mixture of the two in any case of friendship or love. This could be seen as merely a reflection of Aristotle saying that what hatred means is, you desire the other not to exist. Then love shows up as the desire for the other thing to exist. You could make a proportion and say *philein* [to like] is to *eran* [to love] as existence is to the good.

Ronna: I didn't realize you were distinguishing friendship and love.

Seth: That's what it first looks like. But when you look at the Socratic case, it's not possible to make this distinction because, having put philosophy itself into crisis, by bringing it down into the city, Socrates has put himself into crisis at the same time. It's not accidental, therefore, that all his philosophical activity takes place during the Peloponnesian War or when he's on trial, so at any time he can be killed, inside or outside, and philosophy of his type will come to an end. Consequently pederasty is necessary.

Ronna: I don't follow that step.

Seth: You have to be concerned with the existence of philosophy, and so with the next generation. Hence it makes perfect sense that Lysis is the youngest interlocutor Socrates ever talks to. That's just on the political level.

Ronna: And how does pederasty fit in?

Seth: It's exactly like the son swallowing hemlock, so his survival is now in question. On the political level it has this structure to it, which looks as if you could still make a split between love and friendship, as long as there's no immediate danger. But then it turns out that the kinds of questions Socrates asks have a crisis character to them intrinsically, precisely because they all have to do with the good, showing up in the question, what should I do with the rest of my life? Since that is the character of the philosophical enterprise, there aren't any neutral questions, which would belong to the erotic part, as opposed to the *philein* part, but in fact the two are necessarily together.

Ronna: "What is?" questions would belong to the erotic part?

Seth: Yes, but in fact they're always crisis questions, and therefore can't be separated that way.

Ronna: Because they're never apart from the question of the good?

Seth: Right. They have to be decided. You're forced into them, not because of the "what is?" question, but because of the crisis situation. This questioning takes place ordinarily only in adolescence. So it comes around again to pederasty, in another form, in terms of the orphan.

Ronna: You mean the *Republic* passage, about the son who finds out that it's not his natural parents who have raised him (VII.537e–539a)? Isn't Socrates presenting that as an image for the experience of coming to question the opinions we've been brought up with?

Seth: That's right. So the "what is?" question is connected with the question of one's own legitimacy.

Michael: Does this mean that every philosophical question always arises as a result of a concealed urgency? That's one thing you seem to be suggesting. But now it sounds as if you want to say that it's precisely in adolescence that the two kinds of questions come together. But does every *ti esti?* [what is it?] question originate in a question of the good?

Ronna: It makes it sound as if you could never discover anything but what would satisfy your need.

Michael: I don't know. It's a queer kind of urgency in adolescence, because it doesn't have any real objective correlative—you can't get anything in the world that's going to satisfy it—it looks as though it's not a bad model.

Ronna: Another way to put the question would be this: is the good really the cause of being? Just a small question!

Seth: Well, I thought that was what you were asking. The generalization of this adolescent crisis is to see that the concealed connection between the being question and the intelligibility question has to do with the skewed way in which the question arises, through our interests.

Ronna: If you think about the *Phaedo* image, in Socrates' autobiography, if the sun in an eclipse meant that the good was always at work, but not recognized as such, yet for just that reason a cause of blinding, it's to avoid that, or at least to bypass it provisionally, that the second sailing is needed.

Robert: That would support this idea about the way the two kinds of question are always connected.

Ronna: But what you're trying to get away from, through the second sailing, is the distortion that comes about from the fact that when you thought you were looking at beings directly, you were really being blinded by the eclipsed sun, that is, by the unrecognized good.

Michael: Is it the same as asking this: when you discover, through a second sailing, a previous error or exaggeration, aren't you at the same time subject to exaggerating or erring as you work through it the second way? You have to figure out where you made the crucial mistaken assumption, but that doesn't mean that you're altogether immune now to the kind of erring that seems built into thinking. Of course, the second stage can't simply be subject to the same error, because then it looks as if you're not going anywhere. Is that the problem?

Seth: You could make it more specific. If you look at the structure of the *Lysis*, Socrates begins by asking, on what conditions should I enter the gymnasium? That is, what's in it for me? Then, curiously enough, after having criticized Hippothales' way of seducing Lysis, he comes forward as someone who is wise and erotic, who is completely at the disposal of Hippothales to arrange the softening up of Lysis to admit Hippothales as a lover. So what happens to his good? He just has this *techne,* which is at the disposal of anybody, and there's no self-interest, which was the source of his original hesitancy about stopping there, rather than going on to the Lyceum. So the question arises, what's in it for him? Ctesippus tells Socrates that Hippothales has been writing poetry about Lysis, but he says only what everybody says about Lysis, he has never been able to find anything peculiar in him. That seems to me why Socrates goes in. He wants to know what the connection is between his peculiarity and his erotic science. Socrates is asking the question, what is really my own? What can really be your own is what you don't know, because as soon as you know, it's universal. One's own seems to be the phantom images of the *proton philon,* that is, the means that you think will solve some particular problem, but won't solve that problem insofar as it belongs to the cosmos of the beings. The example Socrates gives is the son who has drunk hemlock, which means he'll be dead within twenty minutes, according to the *Phaedo.* The father doesn't call the doctor, but believes falsely that wine is the cure. And therefore the notion of the dear or the friend is spread from the son to the wine and to the cup.

Ronna: Why has Plato chosen this allusion?

Seth: When you think it through on the philosophical level, it looks as if the *proton philon* would be the answer to the *ti esti* question about something. The wine and the cup are the phantom images of the *proton philon.* But for the philosopher, who realizes that in fact he cannot know, those phantom images are the things he would be most affectionate for, because he doesn't know whether in fact they work.

Ronna: Are they hypotheses?

Seth: They must be things he takes seriously enough to know whether they are going to be useful for solving whatever question is the question for him at that moment, which has this phantom image character in relation to the true question. But he cannot know what the relation is between the wine and the cup and the true question. He has to solve the pseudo-question first, which is the way it came up, because that's the thing that is in crisis for him. He has this background of knowledge of ignorance, the knowledge that *sophia* is impossible.

Robert: It looks as if it could have the consequence of paralysis.

Seth: It does seem that it might stymie you from the beginning. But it turns out that there is another sort of problem that he can solve, which has this funny character: you believe that it's coming down from the ultimate order of things, but it's coming down in the form of a being in itself, not as a part. What makes it a crisis is simply the fact that it's now a question. It's something that one is concerned with, though without knowing what the grounds of the concern are. It might not be so obvious as in the case of the son.

Ronna: It sounds as if there would have to be one true question, and only when refracted through these urgencies do you get the hetereogeneity of questions.

Seth: No, I think the heterogeneity of these pseudo-questions indicates the heterogeneity of the true questions. The formula in the *Lysis,* which I didn't understand originally, is that the philosopher is someone who *believes* that he doesn't know what he doesn't know, that is, he doesn't *know* what he doesn't know. It looks as if philosophy is independent of the philosopher, because he knows that it has this structure but he is always falling short of that, insofar as he is guided by belief. That's the connection to the father, who believes that wine will be the cure; the philosopher is in the same position.

Michael: But that turns out to be good. Your own ignorance makes it possible for you to raise questions in a way that wouldn't be possible if things didn't throw themselves in front of you and demand that you try to cope with them in some way. So if you knew the principle according to which these accidental things were accidental, you would know what they represent, but you wouldn't know them; they wouldn't be occasions in the world for your thinking about them.

Seth: I think there's one word in the *Lysis*—*idion* [one's own], which Ctesippus utters accidentally, and Socrates says, "Well that's it. That must be me."

Michael: There's also the *"ti"* [something] in the first argument of the *Lysis,* that which is truly lovable beyond father and mother and so forth; you get pushed back to some unspecified something. Isn't this a teleology of evil process, in which yourself as *idion* gets in the way and simultaneously makes possible thinking about things?

Seth: That must have been the point in Parmenides' poem.

Ronna: What are you thinking of?

Seth: Parmenides' poem begins that way. The chariot, which is perception, is the guide to *noēsis*. So what leads Parmenides to the gate is what prevents him from going beyond the gate.

Ronna: It also sounds like a reproduction of the argument between Aristophanes and Diotima, about the relation between the *idion* and the good.

Seth: When Aristophanic *eros* comes into the *Lysis*, it's not in relation to the good, but simply as desire for one's own.

Ronna: So when desire is finally brought in, the good doesn't play any role?

Seth: Right. Then what happens is, in the last phase of the argument, when Socrates is summarizing all the possibilities, he omits the only one that remains, namely that the good is *oikeion* [akin] to everything. That's the only proposal that is not discussed. If that's inserted into the neither-nor, it turns out there is no neither-nor.

Robert: Because everything has this valence?

Ronna: But isn't it the neither-nor that is?

Seth: Yes, exactly. So you have to put this problem in a double fashion. On the one hand, everything has to be understood as neither-nor, and, on the other hand, everything has to be akin to the good.

Chapter 8

EROS AND THE CITY

HUMAN SHAPE

Ronna: You have referred at various times to human shape, and what it means for Plato, or for Homer. It's what the Olympian gods represent, isn't it?

Seth: Yes.

Ronna: Would the main source be Aristophanes' speech in the *Symposium?*

Seth: In that speech you could say it means law. Then in the *Phaedrus* it turns out to mean speech. And they're very closely linked. Within the notion of human shape the whole teleological problem is contained. The fact that men choose to be animals in the *Phaedrus* (249b)—they can choose whatever they want although they come back to man ultimately—means, of course, that they don't know there's a connection between their aspirations and their humanity. That's really an acknowledgment of Aristophanes' point.

Robert: How is that?

Seth: For Aristophanes originally man is not man. So Socrates in the *Phaedrus* myth says, it's true, most men will not choose to be human beings. They don't know that there's a connection between their being human and their having seen the hyperuranian beings.

Ronna: It looks arbitrary.

Seth: It's arbitrary because there doesn't seem to be any connection between the hyperuranian beings and the Olympian gods. There is no connection because the beautiful, when it's hyperuranian, is not in a shape that you can identify as either gods or men. The myth itself says it looks so arbitrary that in fact when men choose on their own, they don't choose the human shape because they don't see how it's connected.

Ronna: Is it the *Odyssey* that first made you think about this? Circe's turning human beings into pigs who still have their minds seems to be about this problem.

Seth: Right. It was particularly that sequence in the *Odyssey* that made this clear to me. Odysseus begins with a pun on *"outis"* and *"mētis,"* "no one" and "mind." He escapes because of this pun, which expresses his anonymity, the nonparticularization of mind.

Ronna: That's the starting point.

Seth: Right, then you have the Circe story followed by Hades. So the starting point is mind without body; the end of the sequence is body without mind, that's Hades. And in between you have the Circe story in which Odysseus is shown *physis,* and *physis* means that the two of them cannot be separated, and therefore it's the ultimate *pharmakon* against enchantment.

Michael: Internally in the Circe story we have this distinction between what happens to his men and what happens to Odysseus.

Robert: Becoming pig, becoming seduced.

Ronna: The threat of being unmanned.

Seth: Odysseus has to be warned separately about what it means to become naked—that he would lose his manhood—even after he had resisted the potion because of his understanding of the inseparability of body and soul. That means you need to go to a noetic understanding of *eidos* or *physis,* which is directly connected with mind, but mind very curiously loses its power below the noetic level. This is very Platonic, of course: all of a sudden when man is in his defective mode, of being male or female, and not pure human being, then he is open to transformation.

Ronna: Doesn't Odysseus have to make Circe swear an oath in order to have any protection?

Seth: The oath represents the law. It's standing in for the fact that, when man completes himself in his defectiveness, it's always under the form of the law. This is Platonizing Homer terribly, but it does look like this.

Michael: And Circe has to do this because she's afraid?

Seth: That he would kill her.

Michael: How does that fit?

Seth: I don't know. How can you kill a goddess?

Robert: His whole strategm is guided by Hermes?

Seth: Hermes came to him because for the first time Odysseus had acted justly, on behalf of his men. He had risked his life for his men. And the consequence is that the god comes down.

Ronna: The knowledge is a reward?

Seth: The reward is to reveal to him *physis.*

Ronna: So justice brings this cognitive consequence.

Michael: It must have to do with the fact that for the first time he understands them as *anthropoi* [human beings]. That's what justice means. So there's already a connection.

Seth: Yes, but Odysseus doesn't know that.

Ronna: What does it mean that he has to be warned separately about the danger of being naked?

Seth: The noetic form he has discovered is primary. Shame comes in on a second level and therefore looks as if it's pointing to the law. That's a Herodotean interpretation of nakedness. The sexual union is, after all, the union of a goddess with a man. So maybe the implication is, a goddess can become naked and not lose her shame.

Ronna: So he would be inferior.

Seth: But that's curious, because there's an entire story precisely about the goddesses being ashamed.

Ronna: Aphrodite and Ares (*Odyssey* VIII.300–332)?

Seth: Yes, whereas the gods are free of shame. Maybe it has to do with Circe being the daughter of the sun. That means anything can be looked at. So the fact that she's sexual is not for her a matter of shame; but it's impossible for that to be true for human beings.

Michael: Of course, as the story is presented, it's a tactic for her. The seduction is a means of avoiding this danger; it doesn't have anything to do with desire. So it's desire that's responsible for unmanning. You're not in control. But she is altogether in control of herself throughout.

Ronna: So how is this connected with the question of what human shape means? Maybe you could put the question this way: is there such a thing as noetic human shape? Or is human shape necessarily gendered, and therefore belonging on a different level?

Seth: That's the Genesis 1–2 problem. The Bible is saying there's a noetic human shape.

Ronna: It's not corporeal.

Seth: It can't be.

Ronna: And as soon as it becomes aesthetic it's male or female?

Seth: Right, and therefore defective.

Ronna: In Aristophanes' story, it sounds as if human shape does mean male or female only, because the splitting, which gives them the human shape, produces these gendered beings.

Seth: But notice that the gender is independent of human shape, because they're male and female and both in their cosmic form.

Ronna: That's true.

Seth: But they're not sexual.

Robert: If they weren't already male or female, there would be no identity to guide their search.

Michael: Although that's problematic too, because the search is, on the one hand, for a male or a female, but on the other hand, for someone unique.

Ronna: But it does show that there's a doubleness to human shape, and on one level it's something beyond gender.

Seth: So this is like night and day.

Ronna: Or heaven and earth.

Seth: Heaven and earth, right, or land and water.

Robert: How is it like them?

Seth: In other words, "day" has a double meaning. There's both day versus night and then day and night as one whole together, which we call "one day." One is aesthetic and one is noetic.

Ronna: And the aesthetic always splits?

Robert: Heaven and earth, does it work for them?

Seth: I think so. Together they become cosmos—that's the crucial move made by philosophy. So it looks as though philosophy becomes philosophy at the very moment this is laid down as an investigative principle. Everything has to be on the model of heaven and earth and cosmos. All the philosophers started this way. And they saw that all eidetic analysis ultimately is connected with causality. So the mistake of the mythographers was that they had split the eclipse of the sun from the shining of the sun. But once you recognize the cause of the shining of the sun, you should immediately see that it's the cause of the eclipse of the sun. It's not two separate problems. We know that goes back to Heraclitus. And Parmenides discovered that the evening star and the morning star are the same.

Michael: If we go back to the *Odyssey* for a second, it seems to me you can say, on the one hand, there is *anthropos* and that is a principle of recognition. I mean, you do recognize the person as a person on the street. Male and female emerge, it seems to me, on the level of desire.

Ronna: But it's interesting how disconcerting it is when you don't know. I had a very smart student once. I would talk to this person often, in the hallway after class, and I really couldn't tell for many weeks whether he was a boy or a girl.

Seth: This happened, according to Mrs. Trilling, to Lionel. When we met them in England, he had been staying at an Oxford College. And he looked down on the tennis courts from his room and said to Mrs. Trilling, "Oh look at that beautiful girl." She looked and said, "That's not a girl."

Ronna: So maybe the natural perception that's first for us is male or female, not human as such.

Michael: I'm not sure. What it might mean is that it's troubling to us whenever we encounter an object in the world that can't be understood simultaneously as an object of desire.

Ronna: If human shape means body, human body that's neither male nor female, though it might be grasped by scientific analysis, doesn't belong to our ordinary experience.

Michael: Well, you quickly look and count the people in a room.

Robert: That example is interesting, because the counting is already the noeticizing of the otherwise aesthetic distinction. All you need is the pure genus.

Michael: So when you're counting, you're already making aesthetic beings into monads.

Robert: Exactly.

Seth: Under certain laws, that wouldn't happen.

Ronna: You mean there wouldn't be a category of human beings?

Seth: Yes, in other words there would be slaves, women, and children. So that, in counting, some members of a tribe would say there are five people. And you'd say, "What do you mean, there are fifty people." And he would say, "No, I'm only counting. . . ."

Michael: But the question is whether they wouldn't in some way know, whether the *nomos* could ever really be that powerful.

Seth: Aren't there tribes in which what the Greeks would call barbarians are nonhuman?

Robert: Yes, the Nazis. I mean, that's the extreme case.

Seth: What happened when they counted? They were just counting something else?

Robert: Potential corpses. That is what they counted.

Michael: But it seems that there must always be some kind of recognition going on. So it looks as if there's something like aesthetic human being, or aesthetic *eidos* of human being.

Robert: In the Wahnsee conference, where Himmler gives this speech and says, you'll never be able to say these things, that must be connected with this. There's something you'll never be able to acknowledge. That must be a reflection, on a moral level, of this inescapability of the aesthetic *eidos*. On some level you can't help but recognize the human beings you see as human beings.

Seth: It is quite odd, isn't it, these criminals put on this Heideggerian level.

But maybe there's something to this funny connection between extreme politics and metaphysics.

Robert: You have to give an extraordinary rationale.

Seth: But I'm still not sure about this aesthetic *eidos*. Think of the funny mistake Socrates makes in the *Parmenides*.

Ronna: About man?

Seth: Yes, when he's asked whether there's an *eidos* of man. He says, maybe it's only what you see. Isn't that absurd?

Michael: You mean, you never see it?

Seth: Right. It looks as though the question is formulated in such a way that the answer has to be an idea.

Robert: Purely noetic.

Seth: It's an interesting passage in light of the *Odyssey,* where this has already been seen. Young Socrates, talking to Parmenides, hasn't caught up with it yet. He hasn't yet heard Diotima on *eros.*

EROS AND THE *KALON*: SOCRATES' MYTH IN THE *PHAEDRUS*

Ronna: We were talking before about human shape in Socrates' myth in the *Phaedrus* and being human defined by having had some vision of the beings. Can you say anything more about how you understand the relation between them?

Seth: Well, you have the nine types, which are determined by what one has seen of the beings (248d–e). And it looks as though, if you take that by itself, it means mind without body, with all the consequences that entails. But then you have the problem of putting that set together with another set.

Ronna: The erotic types, based on the Olympian gods (246e–47a, 252e–53b)?

Seth: Right. The problem is what the separation of these two sets means, and whether they can be put together.

Ronna: Do you think this has anything to do with the division of the dialogue in two halves?

Seth: Well, I think there is actually a simple connection between the first part and the second part of the *Phaedrus*. The first part, because it's about *eros*, is antinomian, and the second part, because it's against the law as written, is antinomian. So that's the thing holding the two parts together.

Ronna: Does that help explain how the connection should be understood in Socrates' myth between *eros*, which shows up in following one of the gods, and thinking, based on what one has seen of the beings?

Seth: I think the real difficulty is to understand *eros* in relation to the *kalon.*

It becomes an ontological problem about what the status of the *kalon* is in relation to all the other beings that philosophical thinking thinks.

Ronna: On the one hand, and in relation to the beloved and the gods, on the other?

Seth: Yes, right. If you break philosophical love away from the ontology, you're not looking at the *kalon* in its privileged position. It's not *eros* that has this privileged position; it's the *kalon*. Of course that raises the question of what is meant by the *kalon*. That certainly is *the* defect of modern interpretations of Plato.

Michael: What?

Seth: The problem of the *kalon*. It's conspicuous in certain things. One is the sliding of the beautiful together with the good, or with the just. Or simply mistranslating it, as Cornford does in the *Timaeus* of all places.

Robert: How does he translate it?

Seth: He translates it as "good." Then he has a note saying, in the *Septuagint* it means good.

Ronna: What is he referring to?

Seth: Genesis 1.

Ronna: "And God saw that it was good"?

Seth: Yes. By that time *"kalon"* had come to mean "good." So Cornford says, I'm going to use those standards of translation for the *Timaeus*.

THE TYRANT *EROS* IN THE *REPUBLIC*

Ronna: Could we talk about the relation between *eros* and *thumos*? I think you've suggested in various contexts that *eros* is tied to some natural object, in a way that *thumos* is not. In the *Republic*, though, it looks as if the culmination of the Thrasymachean principle is the *eros* of the tyrant, which leaves the tyrant with no real good. The dream-like character of the tyrant's *eros* means no reality and no good. But is the tyrant really *eros* incarnate? Because if he is, that would look as though *eros* doesn't have a real object.

Seth: I suppose the argument is, on the first level, that you have to differentiate the poetic *eros*, which is the tyrant

Ronna: The tyrant of tragedy, right?

Seth: Yes, and that has to be differentiated from philosophical *eros*. So you might say that one of the Platonic enterprises in terms of eidetic analysis is to make this cut. But it's very difficult to do, because the whole *Republic* shows that one infects the other to such an extraordinary degree. The philosophical *eros* turns out to be literally homeless and bedraggled, the way Diotima describes it. In other words, when you pull away from it everything that has been attributed to *eros* on the basis of a false interpretation of ordinary human experience, it turns out to be this very squalid thing, which is hard to recognize as *eros*. So the squalor and homelessness of *eros*, which is the truth about *eros*, has been overlaid by a thumoeidetic interpretation of it. The consequence is that when you analyze the degenerate regimes and the evolutions of the soul, it looks as though *eros* is gaining over against *thumos*, but in fact it must be *thumos* gaining over *eros*, because from the beginning *eros* has been suppressed.

Ronna: So love of honor, at the beginning of the decline, looks as if it's a peak of the thumoeidetic, but you're saying it's nothing compared to tyrannical *eros*.

Seth: Right. You might put it this way. *Eros* is to *thumos* as being is to individuality. And therefore *thumos* does have an object, this very funny object . . .

Ronna: The self?

Seth: The self, and other selves, which turn out to be totally politically constructed. If you go to the last sentence of Strauss's *Natural Right and History*, he says that this is perhaps *the* issue between ancients and moderns.[1]

Robert: Individuality?

Seth: Yes, the problem of individuality, which therefore looks as if it turns on this issue of *thumos*.

Ronna: You can't understand it starting from *eros*?

Seth: Right, but that seems crazy because it looks as though it's *eros* which is the individual.

Michael: But it's not the celebration of the individual; it's the individual manifesting himself in the celebration of something else. Whereas in *thumos*, in a way, that gets turned inside out; so in fact it's the celebration of the self, but that celebration turns into a universal and not an individual at all.

EROS AS PUNISHMENT: ARISTOPHANES' SPEECH IN THE *SYMPOSIUM*

Ronna: There seems to be a very different understanding of the individual if you contrast Aristophanes, Diotima, and the *Phaedrus*. If you oversimplify vastly, you could say Diotima drags love up to the beautiful as this universal in itself and loses the individual. The *Phaedrus* reduces the individual to the

---

1. "The quarrel between the ancients and the moderns concerns eventually, and perhaps even from the beginning, the status of 'individuality.'" This is the penultimate sentence of *Natural Right and History* (Chicago: University of Chicago Press, 1953).

instantiation of a type; so if you're a follower of Ares you love anybody who belongs in the train of Ares and there's nothing unique to the individual. It looks as if Aristophanes' speech is the only account of *eros* that really tries to capture the idea of the uniqueness and individuality of the beloved. But are we implying now that Aristophanes' speech, which in fact seems to capture everybody's imagination as the truest account of *eros*, is really about *thumos*?

Robert: You mean, because of what we were saying about *thumos* being linked up with this mutual recognition of selves?

Seth: I think there are two criticisms of his account: one is that it leaves out the beautiful, and the other is it leaves out the account itself.

Ronna: How do you understand the claim that the lovers would wish to be united forever?

Seth: In Hades, when they don't exist. There's something radically wrong, as Aristophanes must recognize, because the self of the original account involves a whole, but the account in Hades involves a one, without a whole. That, I think, is the crucial thing Aristophanes sees.

Ronna: What is the one in Hades?

Seth: The original account is the desire for the pursuit of a whole, of which you are a fragment. But when Hephaestus comes to the lovers and says, "Now I am going to tell you what you really want, which you're divining," it turns out that what you really want is to become one.

Robert: A monad.

Seth: A unitary self, no lover and no beloved, without the duality of the original spherical person, which is never really accounted for by Aristophanes. The desire for the self in the case of the lover requires that there also be an other, which somehow fits, and therefore that they be two even though they're one. But Aristophanes has to give that up because of the Olympian gods, so the whole is dropped. In the end you get the notion of a one that doesn't allow for the duality of a lover and a beloved, because all consciousness vanishes. There was consciousness at the beginning, in terms of proud thoughts, which they jointly held, presumably—although it's very obscure as to what the ground of that is—but it disappears in the present-day account, because you have no consciousness at all; you're just a ghost, or an image.

Michael: The speech is very powerful because at some level it clearly describes what the other speeches lack, the presence of the individual in *eros*. But the difficulty is that as soon as you take it self-consciously as the model for *eros*, then the individual ceases to be an individual and somehow becomes an abstract thing that you're pursuing. So it's that element of *eros* that you can't hold consciously, because as soon as you identify your love as the

love of this particular individual, somehow it ceases to be what it was. I wonder if that has something to do with the movement internal to the speech,
from the whole in which it is possible to have this duality to a one, in which
it is no longer possible to have self-consciousness.

Seth: I think it really turns on the status of *logos* and its relation to reason.
Aristophanes is talking about silent beings. The deepest thing he says is
about the divination of the soul: it cannot say what it really wants. But the
whole myth does not allow for mind, or even speech to be part of it. That is
very odd for a poet. There's no expression of erotic experience.

Ronna: What about Hephaestus?

Seth: Well, that's from the outside explaining it. But it turns out to be necessary because, once you allow the partners to talk, they would no longer be
able to preserve their individuality. Because in getting together—it's crucial,
in other words, that they're not able to say what they want—they would necessarily go to the *Phaedrus* model. But Aristophanes conceals that by giving
a psychic account in terms of the body. Although what he's really talking
about is the soul, by putting it corporeally, he conceals the fact that it necessarily has to involve *logos*.

Ronna: What do you mean by the *Phaedrus* model?

Seth: Aristophanes does not allow for unrequited love. He makes a model
of the rarest of all things, as represented in a funny way by Agathon and Pausanias, though he implies that it does not ordinarily happen.

Ronna: But he can't explain how it could ever happen.

Seth: Obviously the explanation is, you have to see something in the other,
which can then be linked with yourself through speech. That's how the connection is made.

Ronna: It all depends on whether *logos* is intrinsic or external to *eros*.

Seth: Right. But then it turns out that Aristophanes cannot separate the human experience from the level of bestiality. *Eros* started out as a totally human thing, a punishment put on man, not on other animals. So he had totally separated it from sexuality.

Ronna: That's just a product of the punishment.

Seth: Yes, it's not the essential thing.

Ronna: But the primary thing is not *eros*, it's the high thoughts, right?

Robert: It's *thumos*, isn't it?

Seth: I don't think it's *thumos*. What it really is—although Aristophanes
can't explain it because of his model—is the alienation of man from himself
through the city. The proud thoughts have to do with the fact that the soul is
not connected with the order given by the Olympian gods to man living in
the polis. That's concealed in Aristophanes' account. But it's clear that, since

these spherical men are under the control of the Olympian gods, their proud thoughts must be "we are superior to the *nomoi* of the city."

Robert: That sounds right.

Seth: But that requires an account of the mind. Once you say that the corporeal sphere really represents the soul, then the proud thoughts have to represent the relation of mind to the true cosmology; but that's not acknowledged by Aristophanes. So the account is all true in a way, if you were able to transpose it properly.

Ronna: If you said the spherical being is the philosopher?

Seth: If man as a spherical being had to do with the connection between the soul and the whole.

Ronna: That transcends the city?

Seth: Because it has to do with the mind and its understanding of everything. So if that's what he meant . . .

Robert: That would be the source of the pride.

Seth: Sure. But now the pride turns out to manifest itself in the pride of the politician.

Michael: The first sign of the pride, then, is the assault on heaven, when beings with a cosmic shape rebel against beings with a human shape. So it looks like an attempt to overthrow the gods, the very being of which is an announcement of the disproportion between the cosmic and the human.

Seth: Yes, so you could say the spherical beings are to the Olympian beings as the hyperuranian beings are to the Olympian gods in the *Phaedrus* account. And what Aristophanes is denying is the hyperuranian, keeping it within the visible universe. Therefore the rebellion is not as deep as in fact it ought to be.

Ronna: He's silent about that, isn't he?

Seth: He is silent about that.

Michael: You do have this one hint, that the same term—*megalaphronē-mata* [big thoughts]—is used in the Harmodius and Aristogeiton story in Pausanias's speech.

Seth: That's right.

Ronna: Could you say that the proud thoughts of the spherical beings versus the pride of the politician is a version of philosophic *eros* in contrast with the *thumoeides*?

Seth: Well, Aristophanes' speech is very complicated, because one wants to separate out the various implications of it as opposed to Aristophanes' intention, or what Plato hints that he did not understand of his own speech. But leaving that aside, you have this notion that the proud thoughts really reduce to antinomianism, without a ground, outside of the city. So it's floating free from any kind of permanent order. Aristophanes sees that as long as you have the city, you will have this. But he imagines a case in which, if in fact it were reversed, it would vanish; but you'd be left with proud thoughts that you could not account for.

Michael: So really the beginning of the speech is not the beginning, it's the beginning of the end.

Seth: It's the beginning of the end.

Ronna: Is there any satisfaction from political recognition in this secondary phase?

Seth: You could say, the proud thoughts really are a declaration by Aristophanes, "I have overcome the Olympian gods in my understanding." But he can't say that, because he doesn't allow for understanding to be a part of *eros*, which he's trying to give an account of. So it now has another source, but you don't know what the ground is anymore.

Michael: And that's clearly Plato's criticism.

Robert: We were talking before about the separating of mind from *eros*. Now it sounds as if you're saying that's exactly what happens in Aristophanes' speech.

Seth: Right. There's no account in the speech of the possibility of the speech—that's a rather funny criticism of the comic poet.

Robert: He gives a speech that leaves out poetry.

Michael: You could say that what Aristophanes is trying to do is to give an account of *eros* altogether without mind. The other pole is Diotima's speech, which begins as an attempt to keep mind and individuality, to use a modern term, together; but by the end, when it's just a matter of beholding, you have an account solely in terms of mind. I suppose the problem, then, is to keep these two problematically together.

Ronna: Does Hephaestus solve anything for Aristophanes?

Seth: It's only when Hephaestus comes in that the soul is introduced. That's quite odd, because the whole thing has been in terms of the body; so that is an admission that soul somehow comes through the Olympian gods. I think Aristophanes sees that this must be true. That's the Nietzschean theme. You can't have anything at all unless there are these constraints. The celebration of liberation from the city cannot be totally true.

Ronna: *Eros* can't be understood that way?

Seth: You can't get to *eros* without the polis; so in that sense Freud was right. It necessarily shows up as negative. But it would be a mistake, when that's recognized, to make the polis negative, because of morality.

Ronna: What do you mean by that?

Seth: I think Plato's criticism of Aristophanes, at least on one level, is that the hope he represents is dependent entirely on the existence of these constraints on *eros*. Aristophanes admits that if the constraints disappear, *eros* would disappear. But then he sort of takes that back and says that the constraints never do disappear, and consequently draws the conclusion that the only thing you can get is the spurious wholeness of the city, because the other whole is out of reach.

Ronna: How does Aristophanes understand that political wholeness?

Seth: For one thing, you have antinomianism within the law—the political man who rejects marriage. So it requires that the original cosmic pride be reduced to political recognition.

Ronna: The constraints that make *eros* possible are understood as a punishment, but the political dimension is already built into the starting point.

Michael: It's Jerusalem and Athens.

Seth: Yes, in a way. The demand for justice, on the one hand . . .

Michael: And the beautiful, on the other?

Seth: It is very remarkable. Plato was able to invent Jerusalem.

Michael: So it looks as if, without *eros*, you can't invent Jerusalem.

Seth: It makes the Song of Solomon rather interesting: what happens to *eros* within Jerusalem?

Ronna: It's supposed to be understood as a metaphor for the relation between God and Israel.

QUID SIT DEUS?

Ronna: I've been meaning to ask something about "Jerusalem and Athens" and what it means for Strauss. Does "Jerusalem" in that formula encompass Judaism and Christianity?

Seth: Yes, but Christianity, I think, is secondary precisely because it is taken care of by the philosophic tradition.

Ronna: It's already been incorporated?

Seth: In the West. I have a letter Strauss wrote to me, which in a way answers your question. That is, it shows how difficult it is to answer in a straightforward manner.

Ronna: Why don't you read it?

Seth: Okay.

> I believe that I should introduce an observation, which is apparently very trivial, by a broader reflection. Many years ago I was struck by the fact that

Glaucon, while wholly unprepared for the doctrine of ideas, accepted it almost immediately. The clue was offered by his reference to Momus. In brief he was prepared for the ideas by the gods, a certain kind of gods, gods who have no proper names. Everyone knows that Nike was present at Marathon and Salamis, etc., that she is the same whether sculptured by X or Y, worshipped in A or B, etc.; compare the reference in the *Republic* to the statue they are making of the just man. In other words, the ideas replace the gods. For in order to do that the gods must be a prefiguration of the ideas. But since the doctrine of ideas is not simply a myth, that doctrine must contain an answer to the question, What is god? From this I jumped to the conclusion that the primary and most important application of the question, What is?, is the question, What is god? Needless to say, this question is equipollent to the question, What is man? This conceit supplies the key to Aristophanes and to many more things. There is a very clear remark on this subject in Calvin's "Institutes," which I have summarized in full ignorance of the fact in the first two pages of the chapter on Calvin in my German book on Spinoza. I plan to use the key sentence from Calvin as a motto to my book on Aristophanes.[2]

So that in a way answers your question, right? Yes, it turns out that "Athens and Jerusalem" is central, but he didn't know initially how central it is.

Robert: That means there's an understanding that develops over time of what we refer to as the theological-political problem, what it really is about.

Seth: Yes, right. It goes back to the Spinoza book—otherwise he wouldn't have used the quotation from Calvin—but on the other hand it doesn't go back.

Ronna: So "theological-political problem" is another name for . . .

Seth: The problem of the ideas.

Ronna: But it seems as if it should belong to the Jerusalem side.

Robert: It doesn't sound that partial.

Seth: Right. In other words, he came to see that the Athens side comprehends the Jerusalem side.

Robert: It's already a dyadic structure in itself.

Seth: It's remarkable, isn't it?, how long it takes for this understanding to develop. It's another one of these funny things, a consistent path that is totally unclear. I was thinking of the wine and the hemlock in the *Lysis*. Strauss

---

2. This is from a letter Strauss wrote to Benardete, 17 May 1961, from Stanford. See Strauss's *Die Religionskritik Spinozas* (1930), in *Gesammelte Schriften*, Band I, edited by Heinrich Meier (Stuttgart: J.B. Metzler, 1996), 248–50; cf. Heinrich Meier, *Carl Schmitt, Leo Strauss und "Der Begriff des Politischen"* (Stuttgart: J.B. Metzler, 1998), 189.

starts with a crisis situation, which he describes in his autobiography, the German Jew, then it turns out to be this fundamental problem. I don't know how one could possibly have known that from the start.

Ronna: There must be something that directs you away from the urgency of addressing your immediate interests or you wouldn't go far enough.

Robert: I don't know. It might be another one of these "The surface is the heart of things."

Michael: If you think of what happens, you start with a question that's of immediate interest to you, then you have to divide it into parts, and the question takes over and begins to have a kind of logic that leads you. One question leads to another, and you can get very far afield from where you began, recognizing somehow the importance of the questions you were raising but knowing full well that you never would have seen it originally. That happens in ordinary situations, I don't know that anything more than that is needed.

Robert: But maybe you should add something to your description. That is, as you get further afield, you become aware of having drifted, and then you wonder, have you really drifted?; that requires that you wonder about the original interest and what this interest has become: is it the same? So you never really lose that.

Michael: So Strauss says, I quoted this many years ago, and now I understand why I quoted it, but I wouldn't have understood it if I hadn't been thinking about it. So in fact it does mean you're trying to put together what you were once interested in and what you've come to.

Seth: For Strauss the drift is always within political philosophy. That's what made him distinctive.

Ronna: But he was always thinking about mules.[3]

Robert: Well, that's what his letter means. When he said it's equipollent with the question about man, that means it's equipollent with the question about mules.

Seth: With what is. Did I tell you, by the way, about my influence on Rorty, about the mule?

Robert: I don't think I've heard this story.

Seth: I know this from Jose, I'm not vouching for it.

---

3. The mule, as the nonreproducing offspring of horse and donkey, is the analogy Socrates proposes for the *daimonia*, as offspring of gods and humans (*Apology* 27d–e). Benardete's 1974 memorial speech for Leo Strauss begins: "Leo Strauss was a philosopher." It ends this way: "The problem of wholes links the city through the soul with the beings. It might seem, however, from his published writings that the ideas were only of peripheral interest to Strauss; but Socrates has properly warned us against writing. In any case, in a letter to me, in reply to some objection of mine which I no longer can remember, Strauss wrote: 'I'm aware of the fact that the wholeness of a part does not preclude a plural: there is barely a moment in my waking life when I do not think of donkeys, dogs, and mules.'"

Ronna: You told Rorty about the significance of mules?

Seth: They had come up in my original *Statesman* paper.[4]

Robert: So this is after Chicago, and Rorty is already at Yale and reading your paper?

Seth: That's what Jose implied, but I don't know whether he really knows this.

Ronna: And he understood the nongenerating . . .

Seth: The nongenerating *eidos.*

Robert: You have a lot to answer for!

Ronna: Can we go back to the Jerusalem-Athens question? The gods that are replaceable by Platonic ideas look like Greek gods; so if it's all within Athens already, what does Jerusalem stand for?

Seth: It's rather interesting that in fact the quotation from Calvin has nothing to do with the Greek gods.

Ronna: Do you remember what the line is exactly?

Seth: It has to do with the question, *Quid sit deus?*

Ronna: But Strauss's example, Nike, seems so fitting. I don't know if the same point can be made about the god of Jerusalem.

Michael: Isn't the big difference that you could make the slide more easily between the Greek gods and the *eide,* so from Nike to an *eidos?* But the real puzzle turns out to be soul, and not simply something like justice. To the extent to which soul has a paradigm, and that somehow is the question, What is god?, which is really the flip side of the question, What is man?, you wouldn't get that in its pure form with the Greek gods, precisely because they do have this eidetic character to them, as well as being alive. So the unseen god isn't as unseen as it is in the other tradition.

Seth: In other words, that would mean that the triad is psychology, cosmology, and ontology. It somehow breaks the spell of Heidegger, when that is really seen.

Ronna: I'm not sure I understand that. What about political philosophy?

Robert: It's hard to understand it belonging to any one of that triad.

Seth: The crucial importance of political philosophy has to do with the realization of what it means not to know, because there is in fact something you can know, namely the polis, without knowing anything else. That seems to be the decisive move. A claim is made that this is a total interpretation of something that does not entail a cosmology of a direct kind from which it can be deduced, either by inference or deduction. Consequently, the whole

---

4. "*Eidos* and *Diaeresis* in Plato's *Statesman*," *Philologus* 107 nos. 3–4 (1963): 193–226; on the significance of the mule for an understanding of *eidos*, see especially pp. 198–199.

question of phantom image in terms of understanding comes up. You realize that the reason you can have this comprehensive understanding which is absolutely final is because of nonbeing.

Ronna: The nonbeing of the city, or just of the best city?

Seth: The city.

Robert: In what sense is nonbeing involved?

Seth: The understanding of the city requires the introduction of nonbeings into it. So it has tenuous links with soul, being, and cosmology. But, as the *Republic* shows, the city can be understood without all those questions being answered.

Michael: So it's somehow a reflection of knowledge of ignorance.

Seth: Yes, right. The extraordinary thing is, you can say you know that the city cannot solve the problem it claims to solve, but you do not know exactly where the difficulty will be in every form.

Ronna: What is the problem that the city sets out to solve but can't?

Seth: It's the claim that it can make man happy, that it can solve the relation between soul and body, as if there's a seamless whole, going right from satisfaction of body all the way up.

Robert: According to a single principle.

Seth: You know that this is false, and you know exactly why it is false, and that it bears on all these other questions, but also that it does not give you a direct access to these other questions.

Ronna: Including, What is the human? Isn't it perplexing that you could have knowledge of the city and not have knowledge of the human being?

Seth: That was the meaning of "The City and Man," why this dyadic title—you know one and do not know the other.

Chapter 9

PHILOSOPHY AND SCIENCE

CONCEPTS AND THE THINGS THEMSELVES

Michael: You made the remark on a couple of occasions that for a long time you thought of yourself as interpreting works without philosophizing yourself. I think it first came up when you were talking about studying with Strauss at Chicago. What about the other students? Young men of that age are not modest, not all of them anyway, so when they heard Strauss talking about philosophy, some of them must have thought of themselves as philosophizing.

Seth: I remember Strauss saying how important it was not to go beyond preparing the ground for the possibility of philosophy.

Ronna: Is this a kind of philosophic *sōphrosunē* [moderation]?

Seth: Oh yes. If Heidegger represented speculative philosophy in the twentieth century, it's clear that Strauss, on the one hand, was ostensibly in awe of it; on the other hand, he did not approve of it at all.

Robert: How did the admiration come out?

Seth: I remember Strauss pointing to some paragraphs and saying, "Nobody but Heidegger could have written anything like this."

Ronna: He didn't mean the idiosyncratic style?

Seth: No, no, he meant the insights into something. On the other hand, when he read what I had written on the *Antigone,* about the first stasimon, he wrote in a letter, "Well after reading you, reading Heidegger is like reading someone with hobnail boots." But I think the remarkable thing Strauss saw about Heidegger was that he could be overcome on the interpretative level and not on the philosophic level.

Ronna: Can you clarify that?

Seth: In other words, Heidegger's phrase *"grieschisch gedacht"* was so crucial to his interpretation of everything that a refutation could turn on that rather than a more direct approach, which would criticize his notion of *Dasein*, or *Zeit*, or something.

Ronna: I remember you mentioned the contrast with Nietzsche—his own thought was more independent of his interpretation of Plato than Heidegger's thought was.

Seth: Right. If one said Nietzsche misunderstood Plato, it didn't seem that it would have the same kind of consequences.

Robert: I'm still puzzled by this idea that one should understand oneself as preparing the ground for philosophy. If preparing the ground for philosophy is doing something other than philosophizing, what is philosophizing? It reminds me of Nietzsche's talk of the philosophers of the future. That's not us, we free spirits, but we're preparing. You know, Gadamer, after Heidegger and through Heidegger, tried to render hermeneutics identical with philosophy. He popularized this principle. But I don't think you mean something as general as he does.

Seth: I think Strauss would say that there's an enormous disparity between the way in which the questions now come to us, and the way in which they should be truly formulated. The way in which they come to us is so deeply infected by the tradition, and it's so all-pervasive, that you don't even know where the categories we use are coming from.

Ronna: Isn't that always true?

Robert: That may be the point. You're always in the position of needing to recover what's worth asking about.

Michael: If philosophy is asking the right questions, preparing the way to philosophize is asking the questions that will lead you to ask the right questions. But it looks as though any age is going to have roadblocks to asking the right questions. So maybe you're always just clearing the way.

Seth: It goes back to a point in the preface to Hegel's *Phenomenology*, about the distinction between the Greeks and the moderns—they begin with things and we begin with concepts. That's very beautifully analyzed by Klein at the beginning of the algebra book. So in general, it looks as if that's what they thought they were doing, Klein and Strauss. They were going back to the things from the concepts.[1]

---

1. In his essay, "Political Philosophy and History" (in *What Is Political Philosophy? and Other Studies* [Westwood, Conn.: Greenwood Press, 1959], 75), Strauss quotes Hegel on the difference between modern and premodern philosophy: "The manner of study in ancient times is distinct from that of modern times, in that the former consisted in the veritable training and perfecting of the natural con-

Ronna: They were carrying out the phenomenologists' slogan, "To the *Sachen selbst*"?

Michael: Do you think that Strauss really thought the Greeks began with things, in some way that we don't? And if he did, do you think he was right?

Seth: You could say this is a first-sailing formulation.

Michael: Which one?

Seth: From the concepts to the things. Then there's a second sailing, where the thing shows itself to be more problematic than you thought. I think Strauss was concerned with the difficulty in getting back to the right starting point for the first sailing.

Ronna: Is the substitute for the things, in this second sailing, opinions?

Seth: Yes, right, the whole Platonic shift, you know. So it makes a difference, as Strauss saw, whether you talk about state versus society or the polis.

Ronna: If you accept that everything is filtered through concepts, which go through revolutionary changes, talking about polis instead of state versus society is just imposing one grid of categories rather than another.

Robert: That's the history of *Sein*.

Seth: But the example of polis is interesting. It's a phenomenon that persists politically, regardless of the categories that have been imposed on it in different periods. It's striking that it's not in Heidegger, which would be precisely what you would think he would go back to, if he were trying to return to the *Sache* itself.

Robert: Or maybe he does go back to it, but without admitting that that's what it is.

Seth: Of course, if you do get back to the polis, it turns out to be subject to the theological-political problem and then you've gotten to the real issue.

Michael: It seems to me we've been suggesting two ways to understand what Strauss might have meant by preparing for philosophy, and I'm not sure how they fit together. One would be restoring something like what you could call "natural opinion," as opposed to the concepts we begin with. So presumably polis would be something like that. On the other hand, there's a danger to philosophy if people cease to think of themselves as trying to understand things and instead think of themselves as simply articulating con-

---

sciousness. Trying its powers at each part of its life severally, and philosophizing about everything it came across, the natural consciousness transformed itself into a universality of abstract understanding which was active in every matter and in every respect. In modern times, however, the individual finds the abstract form ready made" (*The Phenomenology of the Mind*, translated by J. B. Baillie [London, 1931], 94). Strauss refers the reader to Jacob Klein's "Die griechische Logistik und die Entstehung der modernen Algebra" for a more precise analysis. For Klein's algebra book, see chap. 3, n. 3.

cepts. And therefore what is absolutely essential is that you try, not just to articulate concepts, but to understand the way the world is.

Seth: Well, this might be too highfalutin, but couldn't you say that your second suggestion is a version of the problem of the good, but the first is a version as it were of the surface argument? They're represented simultaneously in Plato but they're very mysteriously related. It's easy to overlook the question of the good in focusing on the surface argument. So it's true that the argument of the *Republic* is much more "natural" than an argument in Rawls about justice. But what really makes it Platonic is the link with the question, Why are they doing what they're doing?, What is the good in it?

Ronna: If what philosophy is trying to do is figure out the nature of things, or the way the world is, isn't there something strange about saying that the right route to that is interpreting a text and trying to figure out what the author meant?

Seth: Could you make an analogy between the two-fold character of interpretation—

Ronna: And that is?

Seth: What does the author mean? and Is it true?

Ronna: Okay.

Seth: And philosophical thought? The philosopher would make a mistake if he thought that the question was, Is it true? before he came to the first issue, in regard to whatever he was talking about. So this two-fold character of interpretation—

Robert: Meaning and truth?

Seth: Right, would also apply to the world.

Michael: What does it mean to approach something and ask, what does it mean?, come to a conclusion about what it means, and then have what it means turn out not be true?

Ronna: You don't think there is an equivalent to asking, what does the author mean?, before asking if it's true?

Michael: Well, I can see how it's possible for an author to express something perfectly meaningful, yet it might not be true; but I'm not sure what the equivalent is outside a text.

Seth: I was thinking about error: you can't get at the truth about error unless you go through the experience of error.

Michael: So to understand the truth of *eros*, you have to understand how *eros* seems to those who fall in love, but that doesn't necessarily mean that what it seems to be to those who fall in love is what it really is. It has a level of meaning independent of the way it's experienced.

Ronna: You're examining some human experience, and you want to understand it as those who experience it understand themselves, or something like that, and that's like trying to understand the author as he understood himself. But that perspective is not what is simply true of these things.

Seth: Right, right. You can say the Platonic dialogues are imitations precisely because they imitate this two-fold structure. They present to you what it means for people to understand things as they do, but also show that there is another understanding that is not in agreement with that self-understanding at all, and then give an account of how the two are related to one another. Plato seems to have gone out of his way to represent this double character. You could do it apart from Plato, but you'd have to do exactly the same thing. And the amazing thing is when people try to do it, they in fact don't do it, but they analyze concepts and end up with self-satisfaction. That was Bloom's criticism of Rawls.[2] You have this elaborate structure, but it turns out to mean just the modern welfare state. You know, everybody who read Rawls and reviewed it said that this is very odd, that it should come out exactly that way. How could that happen?

Robert: I think Rawls ended up conceding this point.

Seth: Another example is Vlastos's criticism of Plato's interpretation of *eros*, based on his love for his wife.[3] It wasn't possible that he could misunderstand his own experience. That's absolutely rock-bottom.

Ronna: So there are two possible mistakes. One is that you're in touch with your own experience, but you can misunderstand it, and people don't recognize that possibility very easily.

Michael: You can argue that you will almost certainly misunderstand it even if you're aware of the possibility of misunderstanding.

Seth: You could say that education was originally designed to save you from your own experience.

Ronna: That makes sense. But then there's also the difficulty of getting to that level of experience in the first place, because everything is so derivative.

Robert: And I thought we wanted to say that the move from concepts to experience is just the first step in a second sailing structure. There's a second step in which the experience itself turns out to be problematic. You were suggesting that the polis is a good example of that: you have to move

2. Allan Bloom, "Justice: John Rawls v. the Tradition of Political Philosophy," *American Political Science Review* 69, no. 2 (1975): 648–62.

3. Gregory Vlastos, influential Plato scholar, taught at Cornell, Princeton, and Berkeley. He criticizes Plato's "theory of the love of persons" in "The Individual as Object of Love in Plato," *Platonic Studies* (Princeton: Princeton University Press, 1973), 3–34.

first to that natural starting point, but when you do, you then discover the theological-political problem.

Seth: Well, if we go back to what we were saying about the two-fold character of interpretation, there's a distinction between the thematization of something and the question of its truth, and the first is already rather difficult, I think.

Robert: Just making something a theme?

Seth: Right.

Robert: What would be an example to indicate the difficulty?

Seth: Let's say—this is too big—but you could say this is what the problem of the *Sophist* is in a nutshell: there's a thematization of hunting for the purpose of understanding the sophist, but there's no thematization of philosophy. That's what Socrates claims, as opposed to what the Stranger claims.

Ronna: Is Socrates implying that philosophy can never become thematic in itself?

Seth: It turns out it has to be done in a very indirect manner, so that the whole argument turns inside out. If that's to be understood generally, which is what it seems the *Sophist* is claiming, everything has to be sneaked up on, you can't do it directly. So the criticism of Parmenides is that he thought you could do it directly. In terms of this hunting metaphor, the beings are hidden and don't like to be caught. It's a very different thing for somebody to say, "How odd it is that we whisper," and to turn that into something we can really understand. It looks as if you'll always necessarily have this divergent structure. In the *Sophist* Socrates gives the key example, which is the philosopher: what the philosopher is, necessarily shows itself in a phantastic mode, and never directly. And that turns out to be the problem of being.

Michael: Are you suggesting this is the real meaning of Strauss's remark about preparing for philosophy rather than philosophizing?

Seth: Well, if there is a parallel between interpreting a Platonic dialogue and philosophizing it's because the structure of understanding is precisely what the dialogues show is the necessary structure of understanding. So if in fact you just abandoned interpretation and tried to proceed more directly yourself, it would turn out that you had to construct something like a Platonic dialogue.

Ronna: Is this what lies behind the first sentence in your essay on Strauss?[4]

---

4. "What philosophy is seems to be inseparable from the question of how to read Plato." "Strauss on Plato," in *The Argument of the Action: Essays on Greek Poetry and Philosophy* (Chicago: University of Chicago Press, 2000), 407.

Seth: Yes, right.

Michael: Strauss realized that interpreting a Platonic dialogue is philosophizing; but it doesn't follow that he thought that only by interpreting Plato
could one philosophize. Of course, it does look sometimes as if he wants to
make the claim that it's possible, in our age, only by turning to the old books,
or to Plato in particular.

Ronna: But after all, there was a Plato. Why couldn't there be another?

Seth: Right, you have to talk about the guy in Burma. That was Strauss's
example.[5]

Ronna: It's like the philosopher-king argument.

Robert: However unlikely, there's no logical impossibility.

Seth: It's curious how deceptive science is with regard to the problem we're
discussing, whether one can get behind the concepts and back to the things
themselves.

Robert: How so?

Seth: It looks to the scientist as if he's going to the things themselves, and
the philosopher can just think about other things.

Ronna: One can think about justice, while the other is thinking about molecules.

Seth: Right. But it turns out that the molecules are embedded in this theoretical construct, with all these terrible problems about causality and mathematics and so forth. So it's all been cut up for him as it would be in a text,
within the science itself.

Robert: I just saw a review of a book criticizing current scientific theory by
a man who worked at Fermi lab for many years. His big complaint is that all
these people have been totally lost in high theory. But nevertheless, the reviewer says, the book should not be titled "The End of Physics," because
physics is really about the experience of things, and that is not at all affected
by the various dead ends of all these theories.

Ronna: That's like saying there's always some opening out of the cave,
isn't it?

Seth: Maybe the reviewer is thinking of the distinction between cosmology

5. "We may think that the possible alternatives are exhausted by the great thinkers of the past. We
may try to classify their doctrines and make a kind of herbarium and think we look over them from a
vantage point. But we cannot exclude the possibility that other great thinkers might arise in the future—in 2200 in Burma—the possibility of whose thought has in no way been provided for in our
schemata. For who are we to believe that we have found out the limits of human possibilities?" "An
Introduction to Heideggerian Existentialism," *The Rebirth of Classical Political Rationalsim: Essays and
Lectures by Leo Strauss,* selected and introduced by Thomas Pangle (Chicago: University of Chicago
Press, 1989), 30.

and terrestrial physics, and the author of the book implied there is no distinction.

Ronna: Terrestrial physics being always open to our experience?

Seth: It's available, and therefore subject to experiment, whereas the cosmological problem is inevitably theory-laden.

Robert: You used the example a little while ago of state versus society as opposed to polis. Then the question was raised, what about the people who say that's just another concept? And the counter was, the polis in fact is something that does persist. That sounds like the analogue to someone saying the experimental physicist doesn't have to worry about the coming and going of theories because there's always this persisting world. Now you're saying, though, that there's a difference between the terrestrial and the cosmological spheres. But it does seem that experiment is the way to avoid these dead-ends. One of the recent Nobel laureates, [Samuel C. C.] Ting, told an anecdote about how he's never been able to learn anything from the theorists and if he were to follow them, he would never be able to get anywhere.

Michael: Of course, you can't ignore the theories.

Seth: It's the theory that is preparing what you're supposed to look for.

Michael: On the other hand, there's a world there, so there's something to confirm or deny. If you were simply stating it in the most radical form, you'd say, the theory may disappear, but the world to be described will continue regardless of theory.

Seth: But that ignores heat death. In other words, not just theory but the experimental physicist comes to an end. They're running out of time.

CLAIMING HISTORICAL ROOTS

Robert: We were talking about the difference between preparing for philosophy and philosophizing, and we contrasted Strauss and Heidegger in those terms; but the contrast doesn't look so sharp if you think about Heidegger's idea that you have to go back to find the historical roots in order to understand our present situation. Actually, there seems to be a very powerful contemporary desire to do that.

Ronna: It has to go back to Egypt.

Robert: Then you get these crazy conspiracy theories. Remember Lyndon Larouche, who had this reconstruction of all of history?

Ronna: The Persians and Macedonians . . .

Seth: Oh that's right. And in his journal there was a translation of the *Timaeus*, because Plato was the good guy, Aristotle was the bad guy—

Robert: And the Aristotelians had taken over.

Seth: Oh yes. In the fourth century, the Persian secret service was taken over by the Aristotelians, which then took over the British secret service and that was connected with the Zionists. It was all backwards. You started from the Zionists and worked backwards to Aristotle.

Robert: They had a whole theory about the Trilateral Commission and Nelson Rockefeller.

Michael: There are lots of these phenomena. Think of the Ayn Rand Objectivists. They divide the whole world between the Platonists and the Aristotelians; Aristotle is the good guy and Plato is the bad guy, and Rand is the perfection of the Aristotelians. Platonism has something to do with other-worldliness.

Robert: You want to show pedigree.

Michael: Also sprach Zarathustra—Nietzsche does it too, in his strange way. But imagine the following theory. The history of Western thought is a conflict between good and evil, the good being the very old, which somehow got displaced in modernity, beginning with Machiavelli. So there's a conflict between ancients and moderns. You can easily see how something like that has a kind of attractiveness, maybe partly because of the way it simplifies the massive number of ideas and texts you've got to try to get a handle on. Strauss's understanding is not the same as tracing everything back to the Persian secret service!, but there's still some connection between its attractiveness and the other.

Seth: Maybe it has to do with the self-alienation of the West, that one would ever be inclined to believe these things.

Ronna: It sounds as if you're trying to find one continuum, though.

Seth: Well, if you put it in terms of good and evil, you're in so much despair about the present that you see the source of evil as something that has spread everywhere, so you want to go back to understood those roots. It's interesting, though, how different science is in this regard.

Michael: In what way?

Seth: If you're on the cutting edge, you shouldn't need Port Royal or Descartes to back you up. That would be baggage. You could predict that at the very moment any established science begins to appeal to its origins, it's finished. Unless it's in this constant process of moving on and rejecting its past, then it's not science anymore. It shouldn't have a past. Even if there was a great figure, then it's somebody à la Descartes who has been totally absorbed, and we understand better than he did what he had grounded. But you don't go back.

Robert: It should be in this Modernist spirit. It all really does begin with us.

Seth: Or the next generation.

Ronna: We've talked about Chomsky before. Didn't he want to present his account in response to a prior model?

Seth: There wasn't any prior model really. He was the one who established this whole way of understanding things. But he did go out of his way to show that there was something in the history of philosophy that was connected with the problem he was tackling.

Ronna: Innate ideas?

Seth: Right. But it was not at all obvious in the way the theory was originally set up that it was a philosophic issue. If there was a transformational grammar for all languages, this could be true for the science of linguistics

Robert: It didn't have to go back to any philosophical precedents.

Seth: It looked as if it was supposed to be something like a computer program. You want to write a grammar that is as rational as possible: how do you get from very simple sentences to complex sentences? That's a machine translation problem: what program do you put in so you can change the declarative sentence into an interrogative by some kind of rule? But the moment Chomsky wanted to claim that this way of understanding things would give you a single algorithm and there couldn't be an alternative, then he had to say it must be based on the human mind.

Ronna: But he didn't originally understand it as an account of the nature of the mind?

Seth: I talked to him just when he began to think this way. I said he was moving toward Kant, he was going to have categories and so forth. Maybe I'm responsible for telling him he had predecessors.

Ronna: So we have a new conspiracy theory!

Seth: He was intrigued, and began to read all this stuff and then came out with linguistics. Chomsky at one time claimed there is a relation between his linguistics and his politics, didn't he?

Robert: Yes, right, freedom.

Seth: And the rationalists are to the empiricists as the good guys are to the bad guys.

Ronna: Why is rationalism free?

Robert: Because although it lays down formal constraints, there's no determining the infinite creativity.

Seth: That was his first point against Skinner. But in fact Chomsky was a behaviorist too.

Ronna: Why?

Seth: Because he believes there's a program in the brain which he is going to discover.

Michael: So this is Kant with a material thing in itself, a material transcendental ego.

Seth: It's like Freud.

Michael: Or like Wilfred Sellars, with his project of remaining somehow within the Kantian world but making the thing-in-itself material.

Robert: Neurophysiology.

Ronna: It's taken over, hasn't it?

Robert: It has.

Seth: Isn't Rorty connected with this?

Robert: He called himself a "physicalist" at one time and still touts Sellars, though perhaps for different reasons.

Seth: You know, Skinner's daughter was very famous at Harvard for having been brought up in a Skinner box.

Ronna: I liked his sleeping schedule.

Seth: What's that?

Ronna: It was completely deliberately determined: he would sleep for two hours at a time, then wake up for two hours, he had alarm clocks going all through the day and night.

Michael: The difficulty with this rational arrangement is, you can never talk to anybody.

Robert: Remember his first invention? When he was supposed to put his clothes away, a sign would come out and say, "Put your clothes away," and the moment he put them away, the sign would go back. As a consequence he never got dressed.

INCOHERENCE IN SCIENCE AND PHILOSOPHY

Michael: We've talked about the need for philosophy to be something more than the manipulation of ideas, to have some connection with the real. I wonder, if it fails in this, whether that can have political consequences.

Seth: Are you thinking of something in particular?

Michael: What about the Sicilian expedition? Maybe you could say there's a collapse of philosophy and politics, and the natural consequence is not that politics becomes more rational but that philosophy adapts itself to the politics of madness. So you get the justification for going on the Sicilian expedition and suddenly you have a theory generated to suit the circumstances.

Seth: Would this be too extravagant to say?—that this happens precisely within thinking when philosophy has disappeared. You still have thinking, but you don't have philosophy, and the sign is the way specialist thought gets infected with a kind of craziness.

Ronna: That would imply that philosophy is the moderating influence.

Michael: Somehow it puts a check on ideas by some sense of reality, which otherwise disappears.

Ronna: Of course, that's the opposite of what most people think philosophy means.

Seth: Absolutely.

Ronna: If philosophy does have a moderating influence, isn't it because of knowledge of ignorance?

Seth: Well, I was thinking about what happens if you have a theory of science and a set of institutions, but you don't have any grounding of the science itself, there's nothing guiding it.

Ronna: No theoretical ground?

Robert: Surely not from the inside, by nature not.

Seth: And after Hume, not from the outside. So, maybe the consequence is that it is not able to control itself. It might even be an advantage from the point of view of the sciences.

Robert: From within the perspective of the sciences, it's neither necessary nor possible that there be such a regulation. It's a denaturing if there's any kind of regulation.

Ronna: What do you mean by "inside" and "outside"?

Seth: On the one hand, within the science itself, on the other, the philosopher of science. But with Hume, the relation between them changes. His predecessors seem to have thought there was no distinction between philosophy and science.

Michael: I don't know. From the beginning, Bacon and Descartes know the activity they are engaged in is not the activity science is going to be engaged in. They seem to understand themselves as laying the groundwork for an activity which they had to prove possible. But it is still true that if you criticize Descartes' account of the movements of the heart you haven't criticized his philosophy.

Robert: It's interesting the way science understands itself as autonomous or self-sufficient and then everybody gets convinced that in fact it is that way, it needs no ground.

Ronna: And now those who consider themselves philosophers take their cue from natural science. They're metaphysical "physicalists" because that's what they think physics requires.

Robert: Of course. That's Quine, whatever physics ends up telling us. It's also Sellars, it will tell us at the end of the day. And it's Rorty too. The idea that philosophy provides a ground is a quaint idea. Everybody is talking about the end of philosophy, all in the light of science.

Michael: But the battle between the two gets refought within science itself. The people who say "just let us do our experiments" want nothing to do with cosmology, which seems to be responsible for the experiments that they're doing. Somehow there's a failure to acknowledge that what they are looking for is already influenced by some grandiose theoretical constructs.

Seth: What about the doomsday machine? Dr. Strangelove was right.

Robert: That was not just a film.

Seth: The Russians had it.

Ronna: What would it do?

Seth: It would set rockets off that would take radio signals to all the nuclear sites in Russia and everything would go off at once and destroy the world. It requires very few people to be killed for it to go off. Once the commander of the Moscow area gets killed, this whole thing goes.

Michael: If you take Heideggerian thinking as the model—thinking that has to be connected with the temporality of being—there's no point at which it's possible to make a claim about the real.

Seth: Is this connected with the universal acceptance of cosmological theory about the beginning of the universe?

Ronna: The big bang?

Seth: Right. In other words, if you accept that the universe comes out of nothing, you're already in a temporal frame, at either end. Heidegger's thinking looks as if it's inevitable as a reflection on that.

Robert: An absolute beginning that you could account for would be something like a pure *Vorhandenheit,* a pure presence, which is exactly what Heidegger denies. You're always in an *epochē.*

Seth: It's interesting that science on its own comes to this radical metaphysical conclusion. Curiously, it's not bothered by the difficulties.

Robert: It's just responding to the data and its own theories that it's generated.

Ronna: Are there any steady-state theorists left?

Seth: Not anymore, because the evidence didn't back them up.

Robert: The uniformity of background radiation, that's what really did it.

Seth: The interesting thing is that the incoherence of the theory is not a bar to its exploitation. What would be impossible within philosophy seems to be absolutely characteristic of science. So Einstein develops a general theory of relativity which, if it's true, shows that the theory is wrong.

Ronna: Can you explain that?

Seth: The theory says that Newton made a terrible mistake in not realizing that once he'd introduced gravitation the universe must either be expanding or collapsing; it cannot possibly be steady.

Ronna: And why is that?

Seth: Because bodies attract one another.

Ronna: So they're either getting pulled apart or together?

Seth: It's impossible for it to be in a steady state. If you accept that, it necessarily means that the universe came from an origin, which was a single point. Then Einstein's theory about gravitation cannot be true, because it gets to a point, that is, when it collapses, when the theory does not hold. So you have a universal theory which says that it is not the universal theory. It has to be part of another theory.

Ronna: But no one was ever bothered?

Seth: No. First of all, it took a long time until people realized it. And then, the effects were so beautiful and the theory is so beautiful, that no one would give it up.

Michael: This is true of science partly because science builds on previous science. Insofar as a theory works as a correction of the previous theory, it's acceptable. But isn't that also the way that the history of philosophy works? That's why it turns out that many thinkers are not going to the *Sachen selbst;* they're going to the previous thinker, and therefore certain things that might strike you as rather incoherent in a theory are brushed aside because they expose difficulties in a previous account. You could say the obvious difficulty of Heideggerian relativism is of that order, like the Einstein problem. At face value, it's a theory which is in a way incoherent because it's got a claim that it can't back up. So it doesn't look as though the history of philosophy is different from the history of science.

Robert: But I thought the point was that, if it's philosophy, then you have a sufficient reason to . . .

Ronna: Demand coherence?

Robert: And reject the theory if it doesn't live up to that.

Michael: But I'm suggesting that in fact that's not what happens. There are certain problems in the Heideggerian account which at first glance . . .

Seth: Look insoluble.

Michael: But you don't worry about that for a while because it has such enormous power in other ways that you bracket those problems, or you somehow claim that it's not really a question. And that seems to have to do with the fact that it's a response to a previous theory.

Robert: In what way does the power of Heidegger's thinking persist despite the awareness that there's something incoherent about it?

Michael: Take Strauss's criticism. He never names Heidegger, but his criticism of simple relativism is that it involves a logical contradiction: if it is speaking the truth about the world, that should make its own claim false. This criticism is brushed aside repeatedly because it's so simple-minded, but it's not answered really. It has something to do with the fact that what Heidegger is doing has a kind of power that makes one want to say, either that's not really a problem, or it's a problem but you can bracket it.

Robert: If you first acknowledge the incoherence and then acknowledge that there's a continuing power, is that taking up Heidegger as if it were something like a scientific theory, so you don't care about the incoherence? Or are you trying to pick and choose? You think his idea of *Geworfenheit* makes sense, and *Geworfenheit* can be pulled apart from relativism, so you don't need to worry. I'm just trying to compare this with the Einstein case. Or take the incoherence in Newton; yet people say the Newtonian theory has an application within certain limits.

Ronna: Can you remind us what the incoherence in Newton is?

Seth: The fact that it has gravity and a nondynamical cause of motion. If there's gravity, then the laws of motion can't be true.

Ronna: All of them?

Seth: The crucial law, that something at rest stays at rest and something in motion stays in motion. The theory of gravity says that won't be true: everything at rest will be in motion, everything in motion will be at rest.

Ronna: Was Newton aware of the problem?

Seth: No, because he developed his theory, which is a dynamical theory, based on gravitation, and then imposed it on a space that is nondynamical. There's something unintelligible about that. Only with Einstein did people see that the two were incompatible. So it operated for three hundred years. It's absolutely amazing.

Robert: But you think the case of Einstein is not like Newton, that it's going to take years before it becomes clear to people working with the theory that there's a fundamental incoherence in it? People are aware that it has a limited scope of application. So if it's true that there's some commonality between philosophy and science in this respect, is it like, say in the case of Heidegger, that you think you can still apply some of the fundamental categories without running into all the consequences of the basic incoherence?

Ronna: Could you just say every theory is generated by some problem, and in applying itself to that problem it may be fine; but ultimately it reaches a point where it ceases to be coherent? Is it fair, then, to hold it responsible beyond that point? Why not say every theory is partial?

Robert: Because Einstein's theory understands itself as absolutely comprehensive. But it turns out that, in its comprehensiveness, it points to a moment that undermines its very universality, and yet that moment is generated out of itself.

Ronna: What is that moment?

Seth: Down to Planck time, which is ten to the minus thirty-second seconds, it's perfectly true. But you can't go beyond that.

Ronna: That's pretty good, isn't it?

Robert: That's what everybody says from the relativistic point of view about Newtonian physics: "within these confines." All they mean is that it's applicable with results so minutely divergent that for all practical purposes it's acceptable. It's almost as though the good is indifferent at that point to truth or lack of truth.

Michael: I'm still not sure the history of philosophy is so different. Take Kant and Hegel. There's an understanding that the whole apparatus Kant develops is in some way right, but there's something crucial left out, so there needs to be a fundamental revision, and with Hegel you get something like that. He's not going back to Kant's grounds for developing the transcendental ego, but going back, discovering a flaw in the theory, and trying to amend it; he is not trying to rethink whether the beginning for Kant might be the reason for the relative flaw. At some level the problems get generated out of previous thinkers.

Seth: Let's ask this question. Is it always true in philosophy that when this happens there's a "therapeutic pay-off"?

Ronna: From the problematic theory?

Seth: Yes. Freud would be the key example. You have a psychoanalytic theory which is not quite coherent. But there is a pay-off. And that's comparable to science. The question is, are there things that happen like that, say with Heidegger, and maybe even with Kant and Hegel?

Michael: It looks as if there may be two notions of truth operating, one in terms of theory and one in terms of . . .

Ronna: Practical success?

Michael: Well, that would be the modern way of talking about it. But somehow it's what makes knowledge of ignorance possible. You can become aware of the fact that a theoretical account is inadequate without knowing what the ground is. It turns out there are certain positive things that are made possible by a particular understanding of the world that you don't want to just throw out because the theory that gave rise to them proves to be incoherent in the end.

Seth: You could say, it's like a set of *nomoi* that allow a tribe to live, but the grounds of the *nomoi* are as nutty as you can imagine.

Robert: Life goes on in the light of these *nomoi*, yet not only is there no clarity about it, but they may be utterly crazy. Yet in a way it doesn't matter.

Seth: Not only does it not matter, but you can push it farther. Just because it's incoherent, certain human possibilities emerge that look very impressive.

Ronna: Can you give us an example?

Seth: I was thinking about Antigone. What she believes is totally incoherent, if you try to formulate it.

Ronna: About the relation between body and soul and how that fits with the practice of burial?

Seth: Yes.

Ronna: We've somehow ended up with a teleology-of-evil principle at work, where something flowers from an incoherent ground that you would have precluded if you had more rational control.

Seth: Of course, we began by talking about something accepted despite incoherence because of the horizon of comfort in it; but in the case of Antigone it's just the opposite—it's absolutely terrifying.

EDUCATION, EXPERTISE, AND THE SOUL

A MATHEMATICIAN AND A PHYSICIST AT HARVARD

Seth: You know I recently went to Cambridge for the sixtieth anniversary of the Harvard Society of Fellows. At dinner, sitting on my right was a mathematician, and on my left was a physicist. Each of them talked to me independently, and both wanted to talk about wisdom. The mathematician said, "There are no wise mathematicians, but there may be wise physicists." And the physicist said, "There are very few wise physicists. But one of them was Fermi."

Michael: But these two are not hearing each other?

Seth: Right. I talked to one for the first part of the meal, and the other for the second part. The physicist told me a little about his background in Europe. His family owned a huge printing establishment. The day after Hitler became chancellor they came in with a gun and said, "This is now ours. Get out." So they just left, in '33. Partly because of this, and maybe partly because he was a physicist, he seemed very solid. He was about twenty-five years older than the other man, and it seemed as though he had been formed in a way that you could understand.

Michael: Unlike the mathematician?

Seth: The mathematician was trying to invent himself. He had written a book, a summary of algebraic geometry, for which he was well known. Then he had taken up ancient Japanese music, in which he was now an expert: he knew archaic Japanese, and had been studying for many years, with the instruments. This was to make himself into a being.

Robert: He didn't identify himself with his mathematical work?

Seth: No, he thought that's only what he was as a professional, whereas the other was the real thing.

Ronna: Which was artificial.

Seth: It was so completely artificial.

Ronna: The profession isn't enough. People feel they're incomplete and have to fill something in, but the filling in is not connected to the person in any natural way.

Seth: I was thinking about Blanckenhagen, or Grene. It looks as if you could say, if you're an Anglo-Irishman living at this time, there's an influence that makes a kind of sense. And that seems to be gone.

Robert: So now you have to find some content or other to give yourself an identity.

Seth: This is connected, I think, with the whole issue of experience and teaching.

Michael: How do you mean?

Seth: The character of teaching, à la Descartes, is to speed up the process of understanding, or to give the impression that you can speed it up.

Robert: You can leapfrog.

Seth: Somebody forms himself on the basis of the life he has lived, then he transmits it. But the life is not transmitted, only the rubrics, not grounded—

Robert: —in the experience that gave way to them to begin with.

Seth: Right.

Ronna: Hasn't that always been true? Or is it that now there's something lacking in the experience that the student brings?

Michael: As a teacher you always try to transmit the question to which your answer is an answer so the student gets both, though it never works really. But maybe in the past you could assume that the student would come with his own reason, it wouldn't be your reason—so Aristotle looks different from Plato even though the questions somehow remain constant. But now it looks like a more radical problem. You're a mathematician and write a book, but it's not in any way really connected to you; so now you're going to go study Japanese music.

Ronna: Could the real issue be mathematics—the split between the art and fulfillment of the soul?

Seth: That's what I thought at first, that it was the difference between physics and mathematics. But then I started thinking about Strauss, or

Klein, or Kojève in contrast with their students in the next generation, or the next two generations.

Ronna: And the difference turns on the role of experience?

Seth: I would think so. One time I was with Strauss when a woman from Poland, who was there on a grant, came to visit him. She stayed about half an hour. When she left, Strauss commented on how different she was from American women. There was a stamp on her that went deeper, or appeared to go deeper, than somebody the same age who had grown up in America. It was noticeable in just that short time.

Michael: So does this help explain the mathematician, and his felt need to invent himself? In a way it makes him a more interesting type, at least the type of character you'd want to find in a Platonic dialogue, to break open.

Seth: That's true.

Ronna: More likely to be the unhappy consciousness.

Seth: So one goes to the analyst and the other doesn't, you could make that prediction.

Michael: You admire the one who doesn't go to the analyst because he's solid in some way. On the other hand, the one who does go to the analyst knows there's something wrong, so in a way there's a kind of superiority.

Seth: You could say there's an inverse proportion, maybe not inverse, but there's a relation between the degree of longing, represented by the mathematician, and the absence of the possibility of its being filled. But it turns out, I would think, that this longing in the past was extraordinarily structured by things . . .

Robert: From early on.

Seth: In a way that is consistent, but for that very reason, restrictive. That kind of structuring, though, seems to be a thing of the past.

Robert: Without that, you have someone who does mathematics, but he can't fall back on "I am a mathematician," and the "am" has to get some being, so you look for something to try to be.

Seth: If you put it that way, it turns out to be the *Republic* problem—on the one hand, *technē*, on the other hand, the soul, and education has to put a stop to this kind of factionalization. That makes it look as if the problem belongs to the nature of political society as such.

Ronna: So the jack-of-all-trades is the mathematician who does Japanese music.

Seth: Right, but you can put it in terms of the *Republic* and say that the difference is that the mathematician is not an educated man, while the physicist is.

Robert: When you think of the construction in the *Republic*, you've got the city of arts, then you have the education, and the whole problem is how they go together. It looks as if everything is keeping them apart.

Seth: One could say the education is a version of the problem of the will.

Ronna: Why do you put it that way?

Robert: You want to be somebody?

Seth: Yes, as opposed to one's functional role in the city. The paradox of the *Republic* is that the fulfillment of the will gets identified with the fulfillment of the *technē*, through the claim that justice is knowledge.

Robert: When it shouldn't have anything to do with that.

Ronna: Although with Thrasymachus, *technē* was willful to begin with.

Seth: That begins even prior to Thrasymachus. The two are identified already with Polemarchus, then Thrasymachus just fits into that. But it starts out in a very arbitrary way, without any proof at all that this could possibly be the case.

EDUCATION AND CLASS STRUCTURE

Seth: These issues, about the way the *nomoi* and education mold people, come up in something I've been reading by Thomas Arnold. He was the father of Matthew Arnold. This is from the preface to his edition of Thucydides.[6] He's talking about the ancient city.

> Citizenship was derived from race; but distinctions of race were not of that odious and fantastic character which they have borne in modern times; they implied real differences often of the most important kind, religious and moral. Particular races worshipped particular gods, and in a particular manner. . . . And therefore the mixture of persons of different race in the same commonwealth, unless one race had a complete ascendancy, tended to confuse all the relations of life, and all men's notions of right and wrong, or by compelling men to tolerate in so near a relation as that of fellow citizens differences upon the main points of human life, led to a general carelessness and skepticism, and encouraged the notion that right and wrong have no real existence but are the mere creatures of human opinion.
>
> Now to those who think that political society was ordained for higher purposes than those of mere police or of traffick the principle of the ancient commonwealths in making agreement in religion and morals the test of citizenship cannot but appear wise and good. And yet the mixture of races

6. Thucydides, *The History of the Peloponnesian War,* with notes by Thomas Arnold (Oxford, 1835), vol. 3, xvii–xviii. Thomas Arnold (1795–1842) was the head master of Rugby School and Regius Professor of Modern History at Oxford.

is essential to the improvement of mankind, and an exclusive attachment to national customs is incompatible with true liberality. How then was the problem to be solved; how could civilization be attained without moral degeneracy; how could a narrow minded bigotry be escaped without falling into the worse evil of Epicurean indifference? Christianity has answered these questions most satisfactorily, by making religious and moral agreement independent of race or national customs. That bond and test of citizenship then which the ancient legislators were compelled to seek in sameness of race, because thus only could they avoid the worst of evils, a confusion and consequent indifference in men's notions of right and wrong, is now furnished to us in the profession of Christianity.

Ronna: So you have races or tribes, on the one hand, which furnish distinctive customs and ways of life, but in the form of restraints; then you have Christianity, which opens things up and has a kind of universality, but it's still not free.

Seth: From what I've read of Arnold, it looks as if there are really two important elements, the Hellenic and the Hebraic, which have to be preserved, and the difficulty is that they cannot be put together.

Ronna: Which Arnold knew?

Seth: He definitely knew. But he seems to have thought that by taking the religion out of the Hebraic and taking the rationality out of the Hellenic spirit, you get something that could be combined in terms of the noble or beautiful. And that turns out to be England, or a possible England. It becomes a perfect *eidos* for education—"the best that was ever thought and said," something like that. If you read his letters, you get the sense that the thing combining the Hebraic and the Hellenic is the historical sense, which is superior to both of them.

Robert: Is the historical sense supposed to be in both, or it doesn't come from either?

Seth: It doesn't come from either, but from the Germans. He was very involved with German Biblical research.

Robert: He wants to say that Christianity represents the transcending of these different *nomoi*, which give people a particular character. But it isn't simply the solution.

Seth: Well, don't forget, the thing Arnold leaves out, or just hints at, is imperialism. You have capitalistic imperialism, taking on the same kind of universality that Christianity has explicitly. He later remarks that the basis for Aristotle's understanding of things is one hundred and fifty-three constitutions; this implies that imperialism and Christianity make it impossible for us ever to have that kind of experience.

Ronna: The world is too homogeneous?

Seth: Right, and that was 1842.

Robert: If we go back to the mathematician, who represents job without any self—the self he would have had if some *nomos* had taken care of it in that way—it looks as if there's something like Arnold's Christian principle operating.

Michael: But no longer as overcoming the variety of *nomoi*.

Robert: In principle there are none left to overcome.

Michael: But then it turns out you have a kind of democratization without an overcoming—

Robert: Which is the *telos* for Christianity. If you give it two thousand years to work, to the extent that it succeeds, you have precisely the difficulty you just mentioned—it has nothing now to feed on, to continue to be this overcoming.

Ronna: The end of history.

Seth: So the thing that saved Christianity was paganism.

Robert: Well, it couldn't be simply Judaism; if anything, it would have to be Judaism as symbolized in all the *nomoi*.

Michael: So the Jewish question?

Robert: Right. How does the theological-political problem fit in here?

Seth: I think it has to be understood in terms of divine providence.

Ronna: Can you explain that?

Seth: The Jews are an unassimilable element that reveals that the city cannot possibly fulfill what it claims it can fulfill. So the Galut is this mark on history of what cannot be solved. You see societies believing they could solve the problem, attempting to get rid of it in a brutal manner.

Robert: So this is the real meaning of "final solution."

Michael: You have two possibilities, total assimilation or Hitler.

Ronna: Assimilation or annihilation.

Seth: That's it.

Ronna: But what is it that the city aims to fulfill that is beyond its capacity?

Seth: You might say that what the city aims at is the incarnation.

Ronna: What do you mean by that?

Seth: That the body and the soul, and the demands of both, can be perfectly satisfied within itself.

Michael: And in the same way.

Seth: You could say that what Marx saw was, you simply strip off the higher claim, make it entirely body; and when that condition is satisfied, lo and behold, the other one will also immediately be satisfied.

Ronna: Doesn't the beautiful come in, with an appeal to the sacrifice of self-interest by the individual?

Seth: A sacrifice of the self because you become just a cog.

Ronna: No nobility?

Seth: Not at all. But with the division of labor, and ten million percent productivity, you only work at your job for a few seconds and then you have the rest of your time.

Robert: For Japanese music.

Ronna: You fish in the morning . . . But isn't there a certain idealism in the attraction to communism, say for people like Blunt. What is that?

Michael: That's Marxism pre-revolution. You can explain that idealism in the traditional way as the longing for a common good and the willingness for sacrifice. But that's not supposed to be what makes the average man after the revolution content with his lot.

Ronna: What about a longing for justice?

Seth: But it's a longing for getting rid of the conditions which made themselves possible.

Ronna: In the British case, you mean?

Seth: Yes, like Blunt.

Michael: Was he an aristocrat by birth?

Seth: I don't think so. He was trained that way.

Ronna: It's paradoxical, isn't it? Once you reduce everything to the satisfaction of needs of the body, if there is an idealistic moment, it has to motivate devotion to something much lower.

Seth: It's certainly paradoxical.

Michael: There are two idealistic attractions. On the one hand, communism is the riddle of history solved, and it knows itself to be the solution; so there's the alleviating of age-old injustice. But presumably after that, you get the new man, who's never been subject to injustice, who's somehow just free, whereas all human beings up to this point have been alienated.

Seth: The experience of alienation in a class structure would come across as being due to the arbitrariness of your position.

Robert: Geworfen.

Michael: But once you do away with class structure, it comes back in different forms, like the anger of modern feminism. There's a sense of being *geworfen* into a world you didn't make, which is quite correct. And the conclusion drawn is that there's something unjust about it, which is also correct.

But then there's a sense that where there's suffering, there must be somebody responsible for it, without the idea that it might be the necessary condition, that it's fundamentally irrational.

Michael: Did you ever talk to Bloom about what happened in '69?

Seth: Yes, we talked about it. His experience of it always seemed to me, at the time at least, to be exaggerated. But then it turned out, if you think of the first book, that he was in fact correct.

Michael: *The Closing of the American Mind?*

Seth: Yes. He had understood that the events had in fact this very deep effect, which was proved by the violent reaction to the book. It would have been a description of a past historical episode, and people would have said, "Oh, that's what it was like then, and this was really what was going on," like the meeting of left and right that he described. But then it turned out, by a strange historical coincidence, that this new leftism, of political correctness and feminism and anti-phallocentrism and anti-Western attitudes, all came together at exactly the moment in which the book was published, so he rode a wave. This is the first time, he said, he had gone to the top. It turned out that he had in fact seen correctly what had been going on under the surface of the universities in all this time.

Michael: That was very funny, because it almost looked as though the book had been a cause of this reaction. But if you think about it for a minute, you realize there had to be, as you say, something beneath the surface.

Seth: So in fact he had got the thing right from the beginning. And they found an enemy in the book which they would have had to invent otherwise. That would also go along with the fact that he said that many college presidents, with whom he talked for the first time because of the book, responded to it, because they were under enormous pressure.

Ronna: They said he captured their experience?

Seth: Oh yes. It turned out to be all true, in a very strange way. If you read the book before knowing of the reaction to it, you'd say the reason it might become popular is that anybody of a certain age would find an account of their own experience in it. But then it had this built-in argument for the classics, because Bloom said that his account was only intelligible ultimately in light of Plato. And if you didn't go back through Rousseau and Nietzsche and so forth to Plato, you could not possibly understand it. So it had an implicit argument for reading these books. Then there was a fantastic reaction attacking the books, through him, maybe because people wanted to think they were a unique phenomenon, which could not have been predicted. If Bloom was right, they were not riding the wave of the future but in fact everything had all been spelled out before they were born. Certain things belong to the nature of democracy and so forth.

Robert: It's not their own. It's all being done through them. They're puppets. This has been scripted already. Think of *One Dimensional Man.*[7]

Seth: The claim that you can combine *eros* with the political is, of course, the *Republic.* But it's supposed to be a post-Marxist, post-Freudian discovery.

Michael: The reaction comes from people in the universities now, but many of them were students in the times Bloom was describing. You don't want either what you're doing now to be scripted, or what you were doing then. It was an attack on the present situation, and on the founding moment, the sixties. So it was absolutely predictable that this should have happened.

Seth: With this very odd thing though: it has, on the one hand, a Platonic paradigm behind it, and on the other hand, a contemporary union of Nietzsche and Marx, of right and left.

Ronna: That seems to be connected with the strange way Nietzsche is being read now, without the ranking of human types, which looks so central to Nietzsche.

Seth: So this is just perspectivity taking over.

Robert: And will.

Michael: A thousand goals without one goal. It's not a thousand and one. But it turns out there's a fundamental tension—this has a history too in existentialism—on the one hand, the notion that everybody is free, on the other hand, that everybody should be free. And it looks as though there's a retreat to the descriptive account, away from the normative. The will is whatever benefits oneself. So there's a democratic principle too.

Ronna: The psyche is just a thousand aims with no ordering principles, just anarchy of drives as the ultimate expression of human potential.

Michael: This is Hobbes with no monarch. It's the state of nature internalized.

Seth: It also sounds like Freud, doesn't it, like libido?

Robert: Many people, including Freud himself, saw this tie to Nietzsche.

Michael: But even in Freud there's still a structure to the libido. There are certain drives that are more powerful and, even if it's for that reason, in some way more important.

Robert: Whereas structure for Nietzsche only arises through the contestation of certain anarchic wills; there's no internal articulation. If you think about the pale criminal in *Zarathustra,* that's the way it gets described.

7. Herbert Marcuse, *One Dimensional Man* (Boston: Beacon Press, 1964).

Michael: Although it does look in *Zarathustra* and elsewhere as though the comprehensive is more important. Christianity emerges as the great enemy, not just because it's a powerful sect, but because it has the capacity to organize all the other goals. Not every value can perform this function of unification. Not all of them can be tyrants. And it looks as though there's some respect on Nietzsche's part for those that have this capacity.

Robert: Especially if you think of the *Genealogy*. But even in the case of Christianity, you need the contestant. The organizing of the new valuation can only take place through the contrast.

Chapter 10

CHRISTIANITY AND ROMAN WRITERS

"CIRCUMCISION OF THE HEART"

Michael: I've been thinking about this funny connection we've talked about, between radical politics and metaphysics. It seems to be necessary when something flies in the face of what's so obviously real that you have to have a very powerful theory to undermine the reality.

Seth: You could say that's the characteristic of religion.

Michael: But you'd want to make distinctions among the religions we know, because it doesn't seem to be as true of Judaism.

Seth: Nor of Hellenism.

Ronna: Is it really the principle of Christianity then, paradigmatically?

Seth: It may be, because of the double move with regard to carnality—on the one hand, the incarnation, on the other, the total spiritualization of everything. It contains within itself its own enemy.

Ronna: But in containing it, I suppose it transforms it.

Seth: Paul has a remark about the "circumcision of the heart," based on Jeremiah (Romans 2:25–30, Jeremiah 4:4; cf. Deuteronomy 30:6). It looks as though what it means is something like self-contempt. What was originally a mark of distinction, to separate out the tribe, and therefore providence, comes to be understood as a stain, or a defect. And the pride that came with the mark of distinction then requires a circumcision of the heart to abase it, self-abasement.

Ronna: This is in Jeremiah?

Michael: Or in Paul?

Seth: It's in Paul, working out what's already in Jeremiah. One way of talking about Christianity is to say that it took the prophets and used them to replace the law. This mantic interpretation of the law became the law. So repentance, which is really dependent on the return to the law, gets an independent status.

Ronna: It freed an element that was a second sailing within Judaism and made it the whole.

Seth: Right, made it the whole and therefore could claim that it was the fulfillment.

Ronna: And "circumcision of the heart" means an experience of humiliation?

Seth: Yes, which suggests that, on this new level, you're looking to Hellenism as a standard. Herodotus understands the Egyptian practice of circumcision as an attack on beauty. They give higher rank to purity than to beauty. What's important is being clean, that is, the elimination of the body. Circumcision, then, is part of a general practice of denying the body, leading to the tension that you have a totally carnal religion but decarnalized, the decarnalization of the body.

Ronna: It goes with death being so central.

Seth: Yes, right.

CHRISTIAN WRITERS AND ANCIENT POETRY

Seth: In reading the Christian writers, one thing that's striking is how seriously they take ancient poetry. They understand it absolutely literally and attack it on the grounds that it is totally absurd.

Robert: Absurd, meaning?

Seth: Obscene, or just improbable. But it's not taken as being in any way a matter of indications.

Robert: Metaphor?

Seth: Right, or just poetic, more generally.

Ronna: No *huponoia* [underlying meaning; cf. *Republic* 378d].

Seth: Right. The poetry is always understood as a literal account.

Ronna: It's like Euthyphro, who takes absolutely literally the poet's stories about the gods.

Seth: Exactly. They take it as Euthyphro would. It looks as if it's connected with the fear that their own writings will be understood as poetry, when they think of what they're saying as literally true.

Robert: So it took Bultmann—I don't know if he knew this—to go back and try to poeticize the entire teaching in order to save it, against the threat of the literalizing through science.[1]

Michael: You can understand why they were afraid. If the whole project of Christianity is to decarnalize the body, and get to a level where it's no longer understood as body, then you're taking all the interesting things away from body that you could use to make good images. On the level of imagery, it loses hands down.

Seth: This might be connected with Klein,[2] it just occurred to me. If decarnalization, which means depoeticization, necessarily leads to symbolization . . .

Robert: In Klein's sense?

Seth: That's what made me think of it. You preserve, as it were, the possibility of talking poetically, but with this funny price you pay, that it has to be immediately symbolized.

Ronna: The meaning?

Seth: Yes. Then it turns out that symbolization leads to an extraordinary amount of deduction. So "three days" or "on the third day," in Matthew or in John, is pointing to the resurrection. Curiously enough, it's very hard to know why it's mentioned that three days later he did something. Of course in the end you know it has this meaning, but in itself it doesn't have any meaning at all.

Michael: Which is very different from ancient poetry, where you'd say, it has to be long enough so he'd really be dead. You have to figure out why it had to be three days, in the plot. But here it works in a different way, foreshadowing the importance of the number three, or something like that.

Ronna: Isn't the crucial thing the unique way in which faith is central to Christianity? The test of faith requires taking these things literally. As soon as you start to symbolize, you're just understanding the nature of things through symbols. But if you're really going to experience faith, you have to believe that God really became a man and the virgin gave birth, you have to believe these literal events.

Seth: But the difficulty is that the events themselves have no meaning, because they're just events.

Ronna: But imbuing them with any meaning would already put this faith into question.

---

1. Rudolf Karl Bultmann (1884–1976) was a New Testament scholar.

2. This is an allusion to Jacob Klein's account of the sources of modern symbolic mathematics in *Greek Mathematical Thought and the Origin of Algebra* (see chap. 3, n. 3 and the discussion above in chap. 9, pp. 181–82).

Seth: That's true. So it looks as if it can't become coherent, in the sense that no event is connected to any other.

Robert: Everything is contingent.

Michael: But it becomes crucial to the meaning of the event that it actually happened. So you're not just analyzing what something means. There is a difference between trying to figure out what it might mean that God became a man, or a virgin gave birth, and believing that the event actually happened. It looks as though that preserves a certain realm of faith that doesn't have to do simply with interpretation.

Seth: But then the curious thing is that the faith has to do with the event being a sign of your own immortality. It doesn't really have to do with the actual event.

Robert: It's a sign and not a symbol, because the event narrated is a pointer, but it doesn't have any meaning in itself.

Seth: What's interesting is, it looks as though the story of Jesus has to be taken as a paradigm case. He has to represent a human possibility. The meaning of the incarnation is that there is a chance of eternal life . . .

Robert: For you too.

Seth: Right, for you too. So Lazarus is the last event, prior to the passion of John, standing for a sign on this side of the permanent resurrection. Then you have at the end of the passion the second sign of the permanent resurrection. The crucial event really is that he comes back and meets with them. You have the body after he is dead. So, this could be you.

Robert: And in fact will be, if only you have faith.

Ronna: Of course, the rituals, at least, reinterpret everything symbolically: the wafer and the wine are the flesh and the blood.

Robert: But the events which the rituals reenact on the level of symbol, these events themselves are not poetic, not to be interpreted anew. Bread and wine are to be interpreted, but flesh is not to be interpreted and blood is not to be interpreted. That's the real thing.

Seth: Well, not exactly. In John, there's bread and true bread; but true bread is a sign, or a symbol, of eternal life. It turns out there's this funny Platonism.

Robert: Does that mean now that poetry sneaks back in?

Seth: I'm not sure. It looks as though, by the transfer from true bread to eternal life, you're actually getting rid of the poetry that you've introduced.

Michael: So bread is to body as true bread is to true body, and therefore potentially immortal body?

Seth: That's right. Phenomenal bread is the manna that the Israelites get, and then there's the true bread, which has this other meaning.

Robert: And the true body is the decarnalized body, the body of the resurrected self.

Ronna: This phenomenal bread that John identifies with the manna of the Israelites, does that mean he's identifying Judaism with body?

Seth: Yes, I think so. You know this question Jesus is asked, about the woman who marries seven times, seven brothers? The question which is put to him is, with whom is she married in heaven? And Jesus has to say that there is no marriage in heaven. There is no body. It looks as if this goes back to Aristophanes. Christianity takes the Aristophanic image and adds immortality from Plato and says, that's what you'll get. But in order to do that, it requires the same move that Aristophanes makes. That is, it's not your body; it's another body, of a different order, spherical or Uranian body or whatever.

Ronna: It doesn't involve parents, it's an autonomous individual.

Seth: It's the individual, but it's not sexual.

Robert: It's noetic individuation, which sounds like an *Unding*.

Seth: If you go back to the *Odyssey* passage we were discussing about human shape,[3] it looks as if two different things are getting mixed up here.

Ronna: The appeal is to your own immortality, as an individual. But doesn't the whole idea of being "in Christ" put that into question?

Seth: It's a question about what "in" means. Individuality, which on the one hand looks extraordinarily democratic, has on the other hand an element of the vindication of lowness, that you're triumphing over everybody else. And individuality means, in the language of the New Testament, "nonbeing." To be a nobody is to be one of *ta mē onta* [the nonbeings]. *Ta mē onta* are the ones who are going to become somebody, and those who are somebody are the beings.

Robert: It's Nietzschean revaluation.

Michael: That's where Nietzsche got it from, in the *Genealogy*.

Ronna: This concern with the redemption of the individual seems to belong to Christianity's rebellion against Judaism. The dead in the Hebrew bible just sleep with their fathers. There's an absorption into the ancestral.

Seth: But in Christianity there's a curious tension between the married couple and the individual that I don't fully understand.

Ronna: What are you thinking of exactly?

Seth: The most obvious thing in moving from Judaism to Christianity is that you go from the family to husband and wife. There's an enormous emphasis on adultery in Christianity. You could say, incest prohibition is to

3. See chap. 8, pp. 164–65.

adultery as Judaism is to Christianity. So the spiritualization of the notion of the individual is based on "one flesh" of husband and wife, not just yourself.

Ronna: How do you reconcile that with what you said before, that there's no marriage in heaven? That sounded like the eternal is the individual.

Seth: But there's a part of the law the New Testament writers are not willing to give up.

Ronna: Marriage?

Seth: Yes. Perhaps because in fact it's so powerful as an image for individuality. You choose your mate, you're not born into it.

Michael: But the emphasis on the married couple does seem to be at odds with the importance of the individual.

Seth: This has to do with the problem of Genesis 1 and 2 again. They haven't made up their minds as to what man really means.

Robert: Noetic versus aesthetic?

Seth: Yes, right. According to Daube, the Rabbis interpreted Genesis 1 in Aristophanic terms, man as androgynous.[4] It's striking, from the point of view of our discussion of poetry, that here is in fact a case in which a poet's image is taken up in the interpretation of the sacred text and it's understood absolutely literally: this is what "one flesh" means. Christianity is obviously an unrolling of the history of Israel, in other words, trying to go behind Genesis 2 and everything that follows and get back to Genesis 1.

Ronna: That's a good way to put it. And it's antinomian.

Seth: Yes, yes, yes.

Robert: And it gets rid of the fundamental division between god and man. You could say this is the real meaning of incarnation, of God becoming man: you don't allow for the noetic-aesthetic distinction.

Michael: Which would mean that poetry is real.

Ronna: We've tied everything up rather neatly!

PAUL'S LETTER TO THE ROMANS

Seth: This brings me to my interpretation of Paul and the history of the world! In Romans—which is the only one of the letters that doesn't have an occasion attached to it or a specific issue involved, so it looks as though it's significant that it's addressed to the Romans—he gives this account of why present-day man has no grounds for defense. It is because the invisible things of God, which are seen by the mind in the creation, have been denied, and men worship the creation rather than the creator. So it's this funny Pla-

---

4. See David Daube, *The New Testament and Rabbinic Judaism* (Salem, NH: Ayer, 1984), 71–79.

tonic language again, this collapse of poetry and nonpoetry. Then follows the consequence of this failure to worship the creator, for which they have no excuse, which is lesbianism and homosexuality. That's the sign of the misuse of nature. God darkened their heart in this manner. And lesbianism is put first. That's very striking. It is the particular case Paul gives to illustrate the denial of the creator on the basis of looking at creation. This one case is then followed by a generalization that includes all sins whatsoever.

Robert: Why do you think lesbianism or homosexuality is the sign of this darkening of the heart and forgetting the creator over against the creation?

Michael: Does it have to do with the fact that homosexuality or lesbianism is really behaving as though you're a noetic *anthropos* and not a man or a woman, and as though this world were already the noetic world? It would point to the worshipping of this world as if it's already got all the characteristics that are supposed to come in the next world in Christianity.

Robert: So it's a short-circuiting.

Seth: Right. And that would fit with Augustus.

Michael: What about Augustus?

Seth: Well, if you go back to Paul's account of the history of the world, it begins with the introduction of sin and death through Adam and Eve. They usher in a long historical period in which there is sin and death but no consciousness of sin and therefore of its relation to death. That period is followed by Moses and the law, which means the Pentateuch and the revelation of sin, the consciousness of sin coming with the law. Paul describes his own early life as a state without knowledge of sin, because he doesn't have knowledge of the law. So there's this sort of libidinal child. The problem is, how come the redemption occurs now, since there has been this consciousness of sin for so long? Why is this the appropriate moment? As Paul explains the turning away from the creator to creation, it took the form of the worship of corruptible man, on the one hand, and of birds, four-footed creatures, and reptiles, on the other. This looks at first as if it means Hellenism and Egyptian religion. But I think it means the death of Augustus and his divinization, where everybody knows that he's dead and a corpse but he's made a god anyway. There is an acceptance of Egyptian religion into Rome, without being justified anymore as a native tradition, so that everyone knows it's totally spurious. You reach the point of complete false consciousness, which is the ultimate consequence of sin. But at the other end of the Mediterranean, there is the true God, who in fact became a corpse and then a god.

Michael: So it turns out that, since in a certain strange way the beliefs are identical, the time is ripe for a takeover.

Seth: Yes, right.

Ronna: They look alike from the outside.

Michael: So one can slip into the other.

Seth: And therefore faith is crucial, because it's really the consciousness of something you know is untrue.

Michael: If there's only *nomizein* [to hold or practice as a custom], if religion is just doing things publicly, the laws of the Roman religion such as they are could be in a way identical with the laws of this new religion; so if there's going to be any real difference, it has to be an internal one.

Seth: And therefore there is this revaluation. The man who is killed is a slave, as opposed to the head of the state, and he becomes a god. Everything is inverted.

Robert: You get Nietzschean revaluation again.

Ronna: So that's why Paul wrote the letter to the Romans?

Seth: That's what I think. No one knows what the occasion was. It looks as though it's his way of addressing—

Robert: The grand historical moment.

Ronna: And you think that Rome made this possible?

Seth: It does look that way.

CHRISTIANITY AND THE ROMAN EMPIRE

Michael: You have looked at several Latin authors—Virgil, Tacitus, Apuleius—with the question of their understanding of Christianity in mind, isn't that right?

Ronna: Premonitions?

Seth: Premonitions or a vague awareness that something radical has happened.

Ronna: When did Apuleius live, again?

Seth: Second century.

Ronna: So he knew.

Seth: He knew about Christianity.

TACITUS

Robert: What is it in Tacitus that you've referred to in this regard?

Seth: The two religions, you mean, in Tacitus's *Annals*, in book I?

Robert: Can you remind us of that?

Seth: Well, it has to do with this odd thing. You first become aware of it if you read Syme's two-volume work on Tacitus.[5] There's almost nothing in it about three quarters of the first book of the *Annals,* which is mostly about the suppression of two rebellions by the troops at the time of Augustus's death and the consequences that followed. These events don't seem to be very important historically, yet Tacitus devotes an entire book to them. So you're very curious. It turns on his two sons. One is Drusus, his real son, and the other is his adopted son, Germanicus. Drusus, he says later in the book, was thought to take too great a delight in the gladitorial games, although blood was cheap. But before that Drusus was sent to quash a rebellion of the Panuthian forces. The rebellion was initiated by a man who is part of the theatrical claque. He makes up a speech about a brother, whom he doesn't have, whom he says the commandant killed, and he asks, "Where can I bury my brother?" There's an eclipse of the moon that night and the soldiers immediately think that, as the moon fades or grows brighter, their rebellion will succeed or not. Drusus and his advisors take advantage of this superstition, execute the rebellious leaders, and it's solved. Meanwhile, Germanicus goes to the Rhine troops, which are much larger and divided into two groups. The rebellion is widespread. He goes there with his wife and child, Caligula, who is called "Little Boot" after his army boot. So Germanicus arrives and makes an appeal to them. While he's speaking, some of the soldiers say, "Why don't you become *princeps.*" He immediately jumps down from the tribunal, draws out his sword and puts it to his chest and says, "I would rather die on the spot than show bad faith to my father and the *princeps.*" As he's doing this, a soldier in the crowd says, "Take mine, it's sharper." This completely shocked everybody. Germanicus fails to control the troops and the rebellion spreads. His way of solving it is to tell the commanders, on the captain level, to kill everybody in the camp whom they think is guilty. Many people, innocent and not innocent, are killed by the captains. Then Germanicus comes the next day and says, "This is not what I meant. We're all guilty. We have to expiate this blood by exterminating the Germans." So he leads them on a fruitless campaign through Germany, ostensibly to punish the Germans for a defeat that the Romans had suffered years before. Now it's the family of Germanicus that leads directly to Nero. First there's Caligula and then Nero, through his daughter, Agrippina. So he is responsible for the character of the whole line, not Drusus, who was killed, or dies, in the second book. When he is speaking about the death of Germanicus, Tacitus uses this very strange expression, *persuasio,* of his having been poisoned by a voodoo ceremony, or Germanicus was convinced that that's what happened, which has-

5. Ronald Syme, *Tacitus* (Oxford: Oxford University Press, 1958).

tened his death. It looks to me as if Tacitus is setting up the old religion, understood in Lucretius's way, as opposed to the new religion.

Ronna: The old religion being?

Seth: That of Drusus, cosmic gods who show their favor. Whereas this new religion is one in which everyone is found guilty.

Michael: With rather dire consequences.

Seth: A totally incompetent commander, but you don't admit it and you blame others, or you blame yourself by blaming everybody else at the same time.

Ronna: Unjust.

Seth: Unjust, but also totally pointless. Because, given the difficulty of having triumphant generals on the borders of the empire, the empire had in fact become limited. The empire became moderate with Augustus, not because they were moderate in character, but because they were compelled to be, since otherwise anybody who became a popular general with his troops could control Rome. So naturally no expansion. What Germanicus was doing was absolutely crazy. He was doing precisely what would lead to his usurping the empire from Tiberius, despite the fact he was so moral he would never do that. So it's a pointless enterprise, with thousands of soldiers lost; storms come up and they don't know what they're doing. He's the only one who has dreams, by the way.

Ronna: Germanicus? In all of Tacitus?

Seth: Yes, until you get to Nero, when other people have dreams.

Michael: This must have to do with turning inward, which is somehow predictable, given that you have Rome founded on principles of conquest, which it has either gotten too big to continue, and has become a danger to itself, or looked at from another point of view, it has already conquered everything. It looks like the problem of a universal empire coupled with this kind of religion somehow forces a turning inward. And you want to say that Tacitus had actually seen this?

Robert: The end of the expansion?

Seth: The end of the expansion, which meant that the true nature of Rome was to be an infinite imperial power.

Ronna: Which in a way Christianity fulfilled.

Seth: That's right. Curiously enough, in Lucan this is almost spelled out. When he's writing about the civil war, between Pompey and Caesar, he begins by saying, if there had not been a civil war, the Roman empire would have expanded all over the world and there would have been rule by law. Then he turns to Nero, who's ruling, and says, I don't need a muse if I have you. And then he says, "*Verweile doch,* on earth before you go to heaven, because when you get to heaven, all the gods will allow you to sit wherever you want. And wherever you sit, I hope the place will be over Rome, and then the world will be united by love."

Ronna: Nero as precursor of Christ.

THE MEANING OF AUGUSTUS

Michael: Caligula and Nero are somehow what's to follow, and Tacitus is already aware of this. How do you understand that?

Seth: Well, what they all see—and this has something to do with the problem of depoeticization—is that Greek poetry has become real.

Michael: With Augustus?

Seth: With Augustus, the whole notion of the transcendentality of the *kalon*, which is the character of poetic religion, has been cut off, because now it's been fully realized by a man on earth becoming a god.

Robert: So the Greek gods get replaced.

Ronna: Concretized.

Seth: Concretized, right, in an individual. There's no longer either imperial expansion or aspiration, along with the collapse of the political entirely. So everyone has become a slave. At the same time that there's no longer any *eros*, there's no *kalon*. And immediately after this, that is, as soon as the Julio-Claudian dynasty gets set up, everybody in the family begins to reenact Greek tragedy, ending with Nero killing his mother and reciting tragic poetry on the stage. Claudius marries the daughter of his brother, in accordance with the fact that barbarians have always allowed this. That was the argument given to the Senate.

Robert: Everything's being acted out.

Michael: It's not simply done on the stage for spectators, which shows something about the character of Rome. The things that were once poetic stories now somehow come into being. But it must be significant that it's Greek tragedy in particular that gets realized.

Ronna: It's all these criminal things, right?

Seth: Necessarily, sure. You can put it this way. If Greek poetry in this mode is the reassumption of the barbarian within the poetic, then you have now the total realization of the barbarian in reality.

Michael: I don't quite understand why this has to happen once Augustus becomes god.

Robert: I thought you were saying there were two things, the end of imperial expansion and the loss of the *kalon*.

Ronna: Why can't the emperor embody the *kalon*?

Seth: He does embody it, no longer as a statue, though, but as a human being. As a statue of course, it points beyond itself; but if it's a human being, there's nothing beyond. And that's crucial for the *kalon*.

Robert: There's a detranscendentalizing.

Seth: Right. You can see Christianity fits with this in an extraordinary way. It is carrying this out on a massive scale.

Robert: So it's connected with what we said before about Christianity's denial of the ultimate difference between god and man. There is no transcendence.

Seth: Yes.

Ronna: And it's doing this in a depoliticized way.

Seth: Yes, and just because it's doing it in a depoliticized way, it's offering true freedom.

Ronna: You don't have to be a Roman?

Seth: Well, two funny things happen. Christianity gets set up before the destruction of the second temple, that is, before, within the empire, the last vestige of what it means to be alien on earth disappears, represented by the Jews. So Christianity looks like it should have a confirmation of itself in the destruction of the second temple and therefore the abeyance of the ceremonial law. At the same time it seems to be acknowledging what everybody knows in their hearts but not as a fact, because on some level there are still slaves and free—that everybody is now really a slave. And therefore the only way out of this absolutely all-embracing empire, now that Judaism is gone, is—

Robert: Spiritualization.

Ronna: The other-worldly.

Seth: Right. There seems to be some awareness by everybody that this is the new situation.

VIRGIL

Michael: How do you see this understanding already present in Virgil?

Seth: Virgil writes a nihilistic poem, where the triumph of history turns out to be the end of history, with no hope in the future and a total rejection of the past.

Ronna: What does this triumph consist in then?

Seth: The account Virgil is giving assumes that the republic is over. That means that everything from the end of the kings to Augustus is finished. Yet Augustus is at the beginning, presumably, of the future. But in book VI of the *Aeneid,* it is said of his successor, who is supposed to be Marcellus, that he is going to die young. So there is no future.

Ronna: It's hopeless.

Seth: It's really hopeless. There is a golden age, for ten seconds. That's one thing. The other thing is, you see that the whole poem is based on the proportion: as Homer was to the Greeks, so Virgil is to the Romans. That's more or less the translation. The difficulty—which the poem is really about—is that Homer was before the Greeks and made the Greeks.

Robert: While Virgil is the owl of Minerva.

Seth: That means that the poem is a counterfactual: if I, Virgil, had been before Rome, then Rome would be the worthy successor of Greece.

Ronna: But Rome isn't founded by a poet; a poet isn't the legislator of Rome.

Robert: But I am not before, therefore . . .

Seth: This comes out in the twelfth book. Throughout the poem, Virgil has been referring to the followers of Aeneas as the Aeneadae, then Juno says, they have to be called Italians. So Virgil writes a poem in which he admits that this is just a poetic name for another people. That explains why Aeneas comes out of the gate of dreams that are not realized, in book VI.

Ronna: Why do you say that?

Seth: After Aeneas has gone to Hades, he says there are two gates,

Ronna: You mean, from the *Odyssey* (XIX.560–67)?

Seth: Yes, right. Dreams that are true come out of the gate of horn, and dreams that are false come out of ivory. Aeneas comes out of ivory. And then you have six books of falsehood.

Michael: It's clear textually that there's something to what you're saying. But what does Virgil think it means? Why does he think that there are only ten seconds of perfection? What is it about Augustus? Why is the creation of empire really the end? Can you see that in the poem?

Seth: I suppose the most obvious way is that in book VI, Anchises tells Aeneas that the Romans are not the equal of the Greeks in terms of either philosophy or art, but they are their superiors in terms of rule. And this is their true task. The way it's put, though, is in terms of empire, that is, continual empire. What he says makes no sense—to spare the weak and put down the proud—unless you're expanding. The remark holds for everything prior in this idealized history of Rome, for Rome up to Augustus, but cannot hold for Augustus.

Michael: So it's really an account of Roman principles that will reach their fruition and leave Rome bankrupt with nothing left to do.

Seth: Right.

Ronna: And make Christianity necessary?

Seth: Yes, something like that. So the interesting thing is, Aeneas desires to be the founder of a city. He does found a city in Thrace. He calls it after himself, and therefore the people after himself, the Aeneadae, not the Romans. The name of this city would have to have been *Ainos*, "terrible," you know, *deinos*. That's the name of the city, "terror."

Ronna: It's a pun?

Seth: Yes, that is made clear. But that city is destroyed. They cannot stay there. Then Aeneas is given this future, in which he is told that he will not be a founder. The founding will begin three hundred and thirty years later. So it is going to take three and a half centuries before Rome is established. He has no hope. But he continues anyway.

Ronna: In what way?

Seth: He takes on his shoulders at the end of book VII the armor and the shield, which describes Augustus meeting Cleopatra. He doesn't know what it means, but he accepts it anyway.

Michael: He can't possibly know the meaning, because it's all in the future.

Seth: It's meant to be contrasted with the shield of Achilles, which is perfectly intelligible. You just look at it and you know what it means.

Ronna: But this is historical.

Robert: So this shows the discrepancy again between the Greek and the Roman, the fact that it doesn't function the way the shield of Achilles does.

Seth: I was thinking of Lessing's criticism. Remember he says there's no motion, no life.

Robert: Well, that's the point.

Ronna: Do you think Lessing knew that?

Seth: I don't think so. I think he was taking it straight. No poetry then, that's what he was saying.

Ronna: You need this temporal dimension.

Seth: Yes, it goes back to our old point. Lessing put his finger on the character of poetry, that it has to have this dynamic in it. It can't just be a pattern. That's confirmed by this passage in the *Aeneid* of pure prose.[6]

Robert: What is that?

Seth: In one of the later books, Aeneas goes to Rome, without knowing that it's Rome. He asks for help against the Latins. And the king—who is a Greek king, by the way—can't give it to him. So the implication is that if he had in fact founded Rome with this Greek king, then Rome would be Greece and Virgil would be Homer.

Ronna: But it can't be done.

Seth: It can't be done. There is an entire book describing the scene between Aeneas and the king in Rome, who advises him to get help from the Etrus-

---

6. See chap. 6, pp. 123–24.

cans. And then, Virgil says, he sent a messenger to the king of the Etruscans and he sent the troops. So the whole story, which is needed to account for the triumph, is treated in pure narrative.

Ronna: Like the historian.

Seth: Right. And you see you could reduce the whole *Aeneid* in the same way. Virgil shows how his own poem could be wiped out.

APULEIUS

Ronna: What is the version of the Roman-Christian relationship that you find in Apuleius?

Seth: It's directly connected with the issue of sex. He tells a story in which he postpones telling you that the author of the story is the character in the book. That is revealed along with the fact that he converts to the religion of Isis and Osiris only in the eleventh book.

Ronna: Out of eleven?

Seth: Yes. The book has a preface saying it is written by someone brought up knowing Greek who has learned Latin, so the Latin is not up to the Greek. It begins with the narrator, who is named Lucius, but you don't know that until later. Lucius is, of course, the Latin translation of Phaedrus. He's going to a town, Hypata, in Thessaly, and he meets two people on the road. One of them is saying to the other, "Oh I don't believe that." And Lucius, who has great *curiositas*, which turns out to mean the will to believe, wants to hear the story. The story is told by this man Aristomenes, about his old friend Socrates, whom he met as a beggar in a town, and who told him this story. Socrates had had an affair with a witch. As soon as he says that, Aristomenes says, "Oh you deserve the worst possible punishment in the world." Socrates tells the story, how he got involved with this witch and lost all his property and so forth. Eventually Socrates and Aristomenes come to a tavern. While they're sleeping there at night, a witch comes in and urinates on the narrator, Aristomenes, who also sees the witch cut off a man's head. He's in absolute terror and says to himself, "Oh, they'll think that I did it. I'll never be able to explain how I wasn't brave enough to defeat a woman. So I will be punished." He wants to leave, so he goes to the door. But the innkeeper says, "How can you go out in the middle of night? It's filled with robbers and highwaymen. If you go out, everybody will think that I'm responsible for your death." So he goes back into his room. When dawn comes, Socrates gets up from his bed and they continue their journey. At one point Socrates says, "I feel awfully thirsty. I had this strange dream last night, in which my head was cut off. I feel so thirsty. I see a stream, going by a plane tree." So they go over to the stream, Socrates goes to take a sip of water, and his head falls off. He's dead.

Ronna: Explain that one!

Seth: That's the way the story begins. The person who is with Aristomenes doesn't believe this; he thinks it's absurd. Then Lucius justifies the story and says, "To all of us happen experiences that no one else believes. For instance, you swallow a crumb which is about to choke you to death. It seems quite impossible for this to happen, unless you've had this experience." Finally Lucius comes to a town, where he has letters of introduction to Milo, who is very stingy apparently and won't give him any supper, but keeps him up all night telling him stories. In the morning he goes to the marketplace to buy some food. He buys a fish, at a rather high price. After he buys it, he meets a friend of his, who's now a magistrate governing the markets. When he finds out what the price is, he takes it out of his hands, goes back to the market, and has his lictor trample on all the fish, including Lucius's. So he doesn't have any food. Then he meets an aunt in town who invites him to a dinner party. His aunt tells him that the wife of the man he's staying with is a witch. He immediately decides to seduce the servant girl, named Photis, because it would be against the law and morality to seduce the wife. So he seduces her, or Photis the servant girl seduces him. When he goes to the dinner party at his aunt's house, he's told that the next day is going to be the feast day to the god Laughter, an old established god in this town. His aunt says to him, "I wish you could think of something for entertainment tomorrow." On his way home, he sees three huge men, armed with swords. Photis had told him that noble highwaymen terrorize the town at night.

Ronna: Noble?

Seth: Yes, a gang of noble ruffians. Lucius takes out his sword and kills all three of them. He goes into the house and immediately thinks, "How am I going to defend myself when the magistrate comes in the morning? They will think that I'm guilty." So the magistrate comes and they take him into the theater where the trial is to be held. In the middle of the arena are the three corpses, covered with a sheet. Lucius tells a story which is totally false. While he's telling the story, everybody is laughing in the entire theater, including his host Milo. When he's finished, the magistrate says, "Pull off the sheet." So he does and there are three wineskins, which have been perforated exactly at the points where he had stabbed the men. So it's apparently this elaborate joke. He feels terribly humiliated. He goes back home and Photis comes to him carrying a whip, saying "I want you to beat me, until you draw blood. I am responsible for the fact that this happened to you. My mistress is in love with a young man. And she told me to gather up his hair from the barber. But as I was doing it, the barber noticed me and I had to desist. Then as I was going home, I noticed that someone was shaving the hair off wine-skins. So I gathered that hair. That was the hair my mistress put into her con-coction and those were the three young men whom you stabbed." Now the two stories cannot be consistent with one another. The story that Photis tells is not consistent with the whole episode being an elaborate joke planned by the city. One involves magic and the other doesn't. Lucius, however, takes ad-vantage of Photis by forcing her to steal the ointments of her mistress. We learn at this point that in fact he had never had sex with a woman, but was a homosexual. Photis now allows him to commit sodomy. Then he sees the mistress change into a bird, and he wants to be a bird. But instead he be-comes an ass.

Ronna: Something goes wrong with the magic?

Seth: Photis gives him the wrong jar. So he becomes an ass.

Ronna: No wings.

Seth: No wings. So it's the *Phaedrus,* only the horse is replaced by an ass. Now it turns out that the ass is the enemy of Isis, that is, of Set. And Set is the Egyptian equivalent of Typhon. Remember Socrates said in the *Phaedrus* that he wanted to know if his soul was as complicated as Typhon. So you have a man whose one lapse, which transforms him into an ass, is heterosexual-ity. In the course of the story he becomes more and more pure.

Ronna: Is there a key to this?

Seth: I think the crucial thing is the story of Cupid and Psyche, which is told in books IV through VI. Two key things happen. Up to the Cupid and Psyche story there is no word of punishment; then there are seventeen oc-currences of "punishment," beginning with that story. So it's the turning point. The Cupid and Psyche story is in fact an account of what happens af-ter the *Phaedrus,* with the metamorphoses being told by Phaedrus, some-body who doesn't think there's any difference between truth and opinion. Hence horses can be asses. Phaedrus is giving his own account, and it turns out to be an account of the history of the world. The pre-Olympian gods, who were originally Egyptian gods, became transformed into Olympian gods by the poets; they are then replaced by the Platonic gods, who spiritualize the Egyptian gods, and finally combine with Roman law to become the new gods of the future.

Ronna: Pretty comprehensive!

Seth: It's going back to the Egyptian religion, of Isis and Osiris, but linking that up with Roman law, as you'll see in a minute, plus the elimination of *eros.*

Ronna: How does that happen?

Seth: The way it happens is this. The Cupid and Psyche story is in three parts. Psyche is the youngest of three sisters. She is so beautiful that the worship of Venus stops and everybody begins to worship her as the true Venus. Venus of course gets very angry. So the first stage, you have soul without *eros*. Then Cupid is supposed to punish Psyche, but instead falls in love with her. At that point you have soul and *eros* together, but soul doesn't know it. Finally Psyche, instigated by her sisters, looks at Cupid, and now knows that it's *eros*, and therefore loses him. That's the third stage, the soul knowing *eros*. Then the last stage is soul and *eros* getting together—in a Roman marriage ceremony. And every soul is now immortal. So the meaning of the name "Psyche" is that every soul is now a proper name. This is the last stage after Plato.

Ronna: Through the Roman law?

Seth: Yes. So when it begins, we're told about Cupid that he is totally lawless. But at the end of the story, Jupiter says, "We must make him stop being lawless and marry him permanently to Psyche." In order to do that, Psyche has to be immortal. So the whole thing turns on the fact that Psyche as a proper name stands for soul as individual soul, and therefore there's no *eros* anymore. The consequence for everyone who hears this story—the girl and the woman who tells it and the girl's fiancé—is that they're all killed immediately afterwards. And Lucius, as a man, becomes the punisher of adulterers. He now has a use for his long ears. Remember that in the *Phaedrus?*— the mistake about the ass and the horse was that the ass is the domestic animal with the longest ears and there is no use for them. It now turns out that they do have a use. He's able to overhear.

Ronna: A spy?

Seth: Yes. He can overhear conversations between lovers and therefore punish adulterers. He crushes their fingers and reveals them.

Michael: Isn't this going back to the question of human form again? How does that fit?

Seth: One of the interesting things is, when Photis comes to him for the first time, he gives an elaborate praise of her hair, with the argument that a woman's hair is a sign of her natural modesty; although women try to display their charms by being totally naked, their hair shows that this is in fact not the case, but that something has to be concealed. At the end of the story, Lucius has shaven his head completely. And he has become a lawyer in Rome.

Ronna: A shameless rhetorician?

Seth: In other words, he becomes Lysias. Lysias triumphs, under the law.

Ronna: The nonlover (see *Phaedrus* 227c)?

Seth: Right, the nonlover.

Michael: Were you suggesting that this whole apparatus is somehow an account of Christianity?

Seth: Well, there is actually a Christian in the story, a woman.

Robert: You mean someone who is said to be a Christian?

Seth: The word is not used, but it's clear that that's what she is. So Apuleius knows about it. It's connected with the enormous emphasis in the story on adultery and punishment, plus the immortality of the individual soul, all within the context of the law. It looks as though he sees that that's what's coming.

Robert: Roman law and Christianity are operating together?

Seth: The way I understand it, he sees that Socrates has revealed the truth of the Homeric gods, that they're simply versions of human *eros*. Consequently, they're destroyed by this interpretation. Then, rather than being replaced by higher deities, they're replaced by the past.

Robert: The reason that they're destroyed by this interpretation is?

Seth: Well, now you know what it is, you see.

Ronna: You can't worship them?

Seth: You can't worship what you know is simply a human phenomenon.

Michael: Is this just an announcement of what's coming, but not, say, like Tacitus, a critique of the situation? Tacitus seems to be indicating that there's something awful about this coincidence of Roman imperialism and Christianity. Is that true in this case?

Seth: I think so. The very striking thing is, it's all set up in terms of these three parts. A story is told after the Cupid and Psyche story, which is the only funny story after it, and the only one said to be a digression and not put in time. It's a funny story about adultery. But the actual stories that involve adultery are really terrifying.

Ronna: Terrible things happen to the adulterers?

Seth: Oh yes. In one, a servant, or maybe a slave, falls in love with a free woman, even though his master has allowed him to marry another slave. The wife commits suicide and kills the child. The master finds out about it. He binds the slave, pours honey over his entire body, and he's eaten alive by the ants. So the way I would put it is, it's a story about how Socrates was defeated by magical forces that he had in fact released but couldn't control.

Michael: And that's Christianity?

Seth: Or something like it.

Ronna: But if you say there's this strange combination in Christianity of the religion of love and eternal punishment, here it sounds as if love is abandoned and replaced by punishment. I thought you were saying that in the

Cupid and Psyche story, love is conventionalized, *eros* brought into the fold of the law, and that's the destruction of *eros*.

Seth: Yes, I think so. But it's a little more complicated. Psyche has been tempted to look at Cupid while he's sleeping because of her sisters. When he flies away, she completely forgets about the fact that it's her own curiosity that made her do it. She goes back to the two sisters and says, "My husband is divorcing me and he's planning to marry you two." She tells the two sisters separately. "All you have to do is go to this mountain and jump off and Zephyr will take you away, and bring you to him."

Ronna: So that's a reworking of the Boreas and Oreithyia story from the *Phaedrus*.

Seth: Right. And of course they both are killed. So the very first thing she does is to punish her sisters for her own crime. The next thing she does is to climb up a big mountain at noon, looking for Cupid. She sees some farm tools abandoned haphazardly around the temple, and she starts collecting them in groups and dividing them. Psyche, in other words, begins to philosophize when she is away from Cupid, and after she has acquired *thumos*, as shown by her killing of her sisters. So before she becomes immortal she becomes fully human.

Index

Albritton, Rogers, 92
Alfarabi, 38–39, 42
Apuleius, 220–25
Arce, José Maria, 9
Arendt, Hannah, 105, 107
Aristotle: *Physics*, 148; *Politics*, 150
Arnold, Thomas, 199–201
Augustus, 212, 216–17

Bacon, Helen, 59
Baldwin, James, 56–57
Bard College, 36–37
Barker, Ernest, 35
Barr, Stringfellow, 76
Bart, Robert, 74
beautiful, the *(to kalon)*, 99, 105, 139, 142,
    148, 153, 168–69, 216–17; and the just
    and the good, 134–35, 151
Beazley, John Davidson, 53–54, 58–59; and
    Lady Beazley, 54, 63–65
Benardete, Diego, 88
Benardete, Doris, 7
Benardete, Jane, 94
Benardete, Jose, 6, 17–18
Benardete, Mair Jose, 7
Berlin, Isaiah, 34, 80
Berns, Laurence, 23n.22
Binder, Judith Perlzweig, 59
Blanckenhagen, Peter Heinrich von, vii,
    11, 16–17, 27–34, 37, 43, 46–47, 48,
    54, 85

Bloom, Allan, vii, 8, 15, 21–23, 25, 26–27,
    44–45, 48, 50, 184, 203–4
Boeckh, Philipp August, 61
Bowra, C. M., 58–59, 68
Brann, Eva, 59–60, 88
Brooklyn College, 7
Brooklyn Tech, 5–6
Brown, Norman O., 71
Bruère, Richard, 25
Buber, Martin, vii, 48
Buchanan, Scott, 76
Bultmann, Rudolf Karl, 208
Burnyeat, Myles, 77, 113
Buttrick, George Arthur, 87–88

Cairns, Dorion, 19
Cambitoglou, Alexander, 63
Caplan, Simon and Fannie, 79–80
Carter, Elliott, 65–67; and Mrs. Carter, 66–
    67, 107
Casson, Lionel, 103
Cherniss, Harold, 31, 108–9
Chomsky, Noam, 91–92, 189
Christianity, 175, 200–201, 205; and ancient
    poetry, 207–11; and circumcision of the
    heart, 206–7; and Roman Law, 224
city *(polis)*, 121–22, 132, 150, 172–74, 178–
    79, 182, 201
Clausen, Wendell, 90
Clay, Jenny Strauss, 38
Colorado, Count, 31–32

227